The
Murder
of Moses

"Talk about a cold-case murder getting hot new attention! Rand and Rose Flem-Ath bring some first-class detective work to bear on one of the most important, albeit lost, stories of Western civilization, and they come to some shattering conclusions. Long ignored by mainstream academic scholarship, the extraordinary views of the father of psychoanalysis, Sigmund Freud, on the identity and fate of the Hebrew lawgiver Moses finally get some richly deserved attention. In a dramatic tale of wartime danger and personal hardship suffered by Freud and his family, the Flem-Aths offer a rare glimpse into his little-known quest to track down the details of a sensational and controversial hypothesis that he knew might get him cast out of his own community, if not killed. The result is riveting and the book is a true page-turner."

J. Douglas Kenyon, editor and publisher of
Atlantis Rising magazine
and editor of *Forbidden History,*
Forbidden Religion, and *Forbidden Science*

"Scouring the highways and byways of our ancient past, seeking clues to the true story of the biblical Moses, Rand and Rose Flem-Ath have come to some radical conclusions that are bound to cause controversy. If their conclusions are right, then a significant piece of what we thought we knew of our religious heritage will almost certainly have to be revisited. A tour de force of original thinking."

Scott Creighton, author of *The Great Pyramid Hoax*
and *The Secret Chamber of Osiris* and
coauthor of *The Giza Prophecy*

"This culmination of many years of exhaustive, in-depth research reaches fascinating conclusions that are far more than mere speculation. The Flem-Aths survey perennial Jewish folklore as well as a myriad of previous investigators' findings in order to demonstrate how Old Testament scribes altered those biblical texts to favor the biases of the priesthood. I learned much more sensible history from this intriguing work than any Sunday school class would ever be permitted to teach."

ALAN GLASSMAN, AUTHOR AND BOOK REVIEWER
FOR *NEW DAWN* MAGAZINE

The Murder *of* Moses

How an Egyptian Magician
Assassinated Moses,
Stole His Identity, and
Hijacked the Exodus

Rand and Rose Flem-Ath

Bear & Company
Rochester, Vermont

Bear & Company
One Park Street
Rochester, Vermont 05767
www.BearandCompanyBooks.com

Bear & Company is a division of Inner Traditions International

Originally published in 2014 by oncetherewasawayPress under the title *Killing Moses: Solving History's Oldest Cold Case Mystery*
Revised edition published by Bear & Company in 2019

Cataloging-in-Publication Data for this title is available from the Library of Congress

ISBN 978-1-59143-336-1 (print)
ISBN 978-1-59143-337-8 (ebook)

Printed and bound in the United States by McNaughton & Gunn

10 9 8 7 6 5 4 3 2 1

Text design and layout by Priscilla Baker
This book was typeset in Garamond Premier Pro with Roxborough, Legacy Sans, and Gotham Narrow used as display typefaces

To send correspondence to the author of this book, mail a first-class letter to the author c/o Inner Traditions • Bear & Company, One Park Street, Rochester, VT 05767, and we will forward the communication, or contact the authors directly at **themurderofmoses@gmail.com**.

For August, Cole, Hayley, Heidi, and Zo.
For all the wonderful memories
of miles wandered together.

For the great enemy of truth is very often not the lie—deliberate, contrived, and dishonest—but the myth—persistent, persuasive, and unrealistic. Too often we hold fast to the clichés of our forebears. We subject all facts to a prefabricated set of interpretations. We enjoy the comfort of opinion without the discomfort of thought.

JOHN F. KENNEDY

Contents

Acknowledgments

A heartfelt thank you to Jon Graham for championing our book so that we can bring our fascination with this ancient mystery to a wide audience. The stellar cast at Bear & Company: Jeanie Levitan, Manzanita Carpenter, Kelly Bowen, Patricia Rydle, and Jennie Marx, with her eagle-eyed editing, have made it a pleasure to move the manuscript through its many stages to publication.

This book would not have been possible without the forty years of research (undertaken in secret) by Sigmund Freud (1856–1939). Freud, in turn, relied upon the insight of the German Egyptologist Ernst Sellin (1867–1946) that there were two men who took the name Moses: one legitimately by birth, the other by impersonation. In unraveling the various sources of the documentary hypothesis, we relied upon the works by Richard Elliott Friedman (1946–), Martin Noth (1902–1968), Joseph Estlin Carpenter (1844–1927), and Robert Henry Pfeiffer (1892–1958).

Authors' Note

This book is the result of a decade-long investigation into the mystifying life and death of Moses. His story contains many puzzling contradictions that defy the usual widespread myths about his character. These inconsistencies offer clues pointing to a history-changing crime and its cover-up. This subterranean story is buried within the pages of the first five books of the Bible.

We have adopted a strictly secular point of view. No religious agenda guided the research. Like hard-nosed detectives we made every attempt to separate the dogma from the facts as far as they could be deciphered. (See appendix 2 for our research methodology.) As we unpeeled layer after layer of mystery and secrecy surrounding our prime suspect, we found evidence of an ancient crime compelled by motives as old as humanity itself.

1

An Unlaid Ghost

I have occupied my whole life with standing up for what I considered to be the scientific truth, even when it was uncomfortable and disagreeable to my fellow men. I cannot close it with an act of disavowal.[1]

SIGMUND FREUD

It was the worst day of his life. All the loving father's prestige could not help his daughter now. The entry in his diary was typically curt: "22 March 1938: Anna at Gestapo."

In view of the desperate circumstances, the family doctor had slipped Anna a supply of the barbiturate Veronal. If there was no rescue from the Nazis, the drug would provide the girl with the ultimate escape of suicide. Puffing constantly at a cigar, the father waited, pacing the floor like a caged animal. But Anna Freud had inherited a cool intelligence and a stoic self-discipline that would save her life. Inside a cold corridor at Gestapo Headquarters she gambled everything by pushing forward to the head of the line of detainees waiting to be interrogated. The method behind her madness was driven by the terrifying certainty that if she hesitated until the day's end the Nazi bureaucrats would sweep up those remaining in the queue like litter and dispatch them to a concentration camp. There would be no returning the next day to take care of unfinished business.

Anna's bold strategy worked and to the relief of her anguished father she found her way back through the streets of Vienna to the home where her family had lived for forty-seven years.

The reality that the bullying, terrorizing, and murdering of Jews had become a psychopathic sport had hit home. "During the spring, some five hundred Austrian Jews choose to kill themselves to elude humiliation, unbearable anxiety, or deportation to concentration camps."[2]

SS Reichsführer Heinrich Himmler had been constantly braying for Sigmund Freud's imprisonment. The American consul general, John Cooper Wiley, intervened to buy the famous analyst some time but Freud feared he was too old and weak to make the transition to a new life and he doubted that he would be granted the precious permit needed to settle in another country. But his daughter's chilling experience accomplished what the burning of his books in Berlin and even the brutal German occupation of Austria could not; it changed Freud's mind about the wisdom of remaining in his homeland.

During these dangerous times, his intellectual pursuits had demanded a self-censorship that was alien to him. The father of psychoanalysis had been fascinated by the dominating figure of Moses for decades and began writing his version of the prophet's story in 1934. But he'd soon recognized that his controversial pursuit of this historical mystery might cause serious trouble, not only for himself but for the Jewish people. He wrote to his friend Lou Andrea-Salome about the lure of the Moses enigma and the blasphemous theory he'd formulated: "And now you see, Lou, this formula, which holds so great a fascination for me, cannot be publicly expressed in Austria today, without bringing down upon us a state prohibition of analysis on the part of the ruling Catholic authority. And it is only this Catholicism that protects us from the Nazi."[3] He goes on: "And so I remain silent. It suffices me that I myself can believe in the solution of the problem. It has pursued me throughout my whole life."[4]

He managed to publish two articles about Moses in obscure journals. But his fear of a possible backlash from the Catholic Church prevented him from finishing the book that had obsessed him for so long. He decided to let it "lie hid until the time comes when it may safely venture into the light of day, or, until someone else who reaches the same opinions and conclusions can be told: 'In darker days there lived a man who thought as you did.'"[5]

It wasn't long before Freud's trepidation was proven justified. Austrian priests became spin doctors for the Nazis. It was not unknown for a swastika flag to be hoisted above a Catholic church. But by now the psychiatrist who had introduced the most radical and controversial theories about the nuances of the human mind had finally understood that he must flee the barbarians. Freud was forced to acknowledge that no allies, Catholic or otherwise, would be rushing to defend the Jews. The near loss of Anna had muted his defiance and forced his rage to surrender to pragmatism. At the age of eighty-one Sigmund Freud had to find a way to leave his home and save his family. He wrote to his son, "Two prospects survive in these trying times, to see you all together, and to die in freedom."[6]

The Nazis did nothing to ease his transition. Their perverse "certificate of innocuousness" was designed to rob any potential emigrant of their entire financial means. It was enacted with excruciating precision and guaranteed that the target would only escape the regime with little more than the clothes on their back.

While Freud endured the wait for his exit visa, he revisited his collection of books and a lifetime's worth of papers. Despite overwhelming stress and the pain of a terminal illness (Freud had been diagnosed with cancer of the palate) he could not give up his obsession and worked at least an hour a day on *Moses and Monotheism*.

After three months of anxiety he was finally granted permission to leave Austria. But not before his signature was demanded on a statement testifying that he had suffered no ill treatment from the Nazis. Freud declared, "I can most highly recommend the Gestapo to everyone."[7]

Fortunately, the SS officers who read this gem of sarcasm did not possess the sensibility to detect it. Sigmund Freud left Vienna accompanied by his wife, Martha, Anna, their housekeeper, and a young physician, and his chow dog. "Safety came," he wrote, "at 2:45 a.m. on June 5, when the Orient Express crossed into France at Kehl. Free!"[8]

London welcomed the Freud family with open arms and he settled into a home in Hampstead. A constant stream of visitors made their way to his door. One call delighted him. A delegation from the Royal Society arrived carrying their Charter Book for him to sign. The Charter had never been removed from the offices of the Royal Society on behalf of a commoner. Such efforts were reserved for kings.

It had been the psychoanalyst's habit to simply sign "Freud" but the Society gentlemen explained that only lords were permitted to use their surname as a signature. Bowing to convention he signed as "Sigm. Freud." Later, he boasted that he'd joined the company of Sir Isaac Newton and Charles Darwin in the Charter Book. For the first time in his life he experienced fame. Rather than seducing him, it reinvigorated his studies.

Despite the advancing cancer and constant disruptions Freud relentlessly persisted with his work. Less than two weeks after arriving in England he returned to his desk and the mystery of Moses: the project that haunted him like "an unlaid ghost."[9] He had found new purpose and the prospect of publication. But the juggernaut that was the Nazi machine proved to be just one of the obstacles facing the publication of *Moses and Monotheism*.

The first inkling that Freud's last book held secrets that could upset time-honored beliefs had come in 1937 with the publication of his short article in the obscure psychoanalytical journal, *Imago*. Entitled "Moses an Egyptian" it put forward the radical notion that the greatest Jewish prophet was not Jewish at all, but in fact, an Egyptian.[10] When the subject of his book leaked out, Freud was pressed from all sides by well-intentioned and/or self-serving objectors. In questioning the prophet's nationality, he was accused of ripping from the Jewish people what little comfort remained to them in a time fraught with tragedy. Even an eminent historian of science, Charles Singer, urged Freud to repress wider publication. Singer feared that the English churches might read the book as antireligious and in retaliation abandon their condemnation of anti-Semitism—with disastrous results.

Freud replied, "I have occupied my whole life with standing up for what I considered to be the scientific truth, even when it was uncomfortable and disagreeable to my fellow men. I cannot close it with an act of disavowal."[11]

Moses and Monotheism was released on May 19, 1939. The scent of war was in the air. Freud died in September, the same month that World War II was unleashed. Catastrophe swept away any serious consideration of his last book and he was robbed of the chance to defend his thesis. Of those who did address it, many were eager to put the great psychoanalyst "on the couch," arguing that Freud was fixated on Moses because of a profound discomfort with his own Judaism. Nobody took up the further exploration of his revolutionary idea and Freud never saw the fruition of his long obsession.

MICHELANGELO'S MOSES

It was 1901 and Freud was in his mid-forties when his fascination with Moses began. During a visit to Rome he stood mesmerized before Michelangelo's marvelous sculpture of the prophet that stands in the church of San Pietro.

The commanding image of that powerful figure never left him. Despite regular returns to the site, his curiosity remained keen. In 1913 he wrote to Ernest Jones, "through three lonely September weeks I stood daily in the church in front of the statue, studied it, measured it, drew it, until that understanding came to me that I only dared to express anonymously in the paper."[12]

"Anonymously" because Sigmund Freud was aware of the explosive territory into which his obsession was leading him. *Moses and Monotheism* begins almost apologetically, "To deny a people the man whom it praises as the greatest of its sons is not a deed to be undertaken light heartedly—especially by one belonging to that people."[13]

The name *Moses* is so familiar that we've forgotten that the word held an unfamiliar and foreign ring to the ancient Hebrews. In the Egyptian language *Moses* meant "son of." It was always, without exception, added to another name—usually that of a god such as Thoth or Ra. Although easily understanding a name like *Ra-Moses,* which would translate as "son of the god Ra," the single name *Moses* would have been puzzling and would naturally elicit the question, son of whom? To Freud the name strongly indicated that Moses's parents were Egyptian and not Hebrew. "It might have been expected that one of the many authors who recognized Moses to be an Egyptian name would have drawn the conclusion, or at least considered the possibility, that the bearer of an Egyptian name was himself an Egyptian. In modern times we have no misgivings in drawing such conclusions. What hindered them from doing so can only be guessed at. Perhaps the awe of Biblical tradition was insuperable. Perhaps it seemed monstrous to imagine that the man Moses could have been anything other than a Hebrew."[14]

The second chapter of Exodus reveals that Moses was born in Egypt during the reign of a tyrannical pharaoh who planned to kill all first-born Hebrew sons. Moses's frantic mother managed to hide him for three months. Later versions of the tale tell of a devious trick used by Egyptian authorities to find the marked children. The forces charged with carrying out the brutal ruling carried a sobbing baby with them. The baby's cry caused nearby infants to join in a sympathetic and deadly chorus of wails, exposing their cover. Moses's mother knew that "she could no longer hide him" and resorted to a famous and desperate measure to save her son. Constructing a basket from reeds, she water-proofed it with pitch, placed Moses in this temporary "ark" and pushed him into the arms of the river.

While his older sister, Miriam, watched anxiously from the water's edge the prophet-to-be precariously floated along the Nile. Miriam saw the pharaoh's daughter accompanied by her maids as she arrived at the river's edge to bathe and watched as the young women quickly retrieved the helpless infant from the water. The pharaoh's daughter realized that Moses must be one of the hunted Hebrew children, but overcome by compassion, took him as her own. Pretending to be a maid, Miriam apprehensively approached the royal entourage and pointed out that the infant would need a wet nurse. "And the pharaoh's daughter said unto her. Go. And the maid went and called the child's mother."[15] By this clever trick Miriam reunited Moses with his birth mother.

Freud doubted the veracity of this colorful story. He argued, as others had before him, that the evocative tale was fabricated and was based upon a much older story, the Legend of Sargon, about an Akkadian monarch who reigned in the third millennium BCE—long before the time of Moses:

> Sargon, the mighty king, king of Agade, am I.
> My mother was a high priestess, my father I knew not.
> . . .
>
> My mother, the high priestess, conceived me, in secret she bore me.
> She set me in a basket of rushes, with bitumen she sealed my lid.
> She cast me into the river which rose not (over) me.
> The river bore me up and carried me to Akki, the drawer of water.
> Akki, the drawer of water lifted me out as he dipped his e[w]er.
> Akki, the drawer of water, [took me] as his son (and) reared me.
> Akki, the drawer of water, appointed me as his gardener.[16]

Eventually, Sargon becomes king. There are, of course, differences between this story and the one told in Exodus. Sargon's was a rags-to-riches tale. The boy of noble birth is raised by adoptive parents of lowly station and reclaims his titled birthright as a man. In contrast, the story of Moses is of a boy of lowly birth raised within the royal court of Egypt only to discover that he is not really an Egyptian prince but the son of a slave. The fact that the Moses story reverses the normal rags-to-riches storyline, so common in world mythology, convinced Freud that the details of the fable had been changed to depict Moses's origins as those of a humble Hebrew slave rather than a highborn Egyptian.

Freud claimed that Moses's true heritage had been deliberately suppressed by Jewish editors of the Bible who couldn't stomach the idea of such an authoritative prophet not being born to a Jewish mother.

He believed that exiled Jewish scholars had invented a more palatable legend during their captivity in Babylon where they had most certainly read the legend of Sargon and were inspired to adopt it for their own propaganda purposes. By a simple cut-and-paste job they conferred upon their hero a fully Hebrew birthright more fitting of the great prophet.

In a second article for *Imago,* Freud took his idea much further, arguing not only that Moses was a full-blooded Egyptian but also, shockingly, that he was a follower of the Eighteenth Dynasty pharaoh Akhenaten (1375–1358 BCE), who introduced the world's first religion based upon the idea of a single god.

Freud wrote that the core of this radical view was "the dependence of Jewish monotheism on [this] monotheistic episode in Egyptian history."[17] Monotheism was, in his view, an Egyptian invention, not Hebrew. Ultimately, Akhenaten failed to convert the ancient Egyptians, who promptly reverted to their traditional beliefs after he died. But his radical ideas were kept alive by the priesthood of On (or Heliopolis— meaning "city of the sun") because Akhenaten equated the sun with the one, all-knowing, single God. As we will see, the priests of On were of special importance to Moses.

IMPOSTOR

In 1922, the noted German Egyptologist Ernst Sellin dared to argue that there had been two individuals who went by the name of Moses. A key line from the book of Hosea provided a vital clue, "And by a prophet the LORD brought Israel out of Egypt, and by a prophet was he preserved."[18] Sellin took this passage to mean that Moses was replaced by a second and hidden prophet. His esteem as one of Germany's foremost Egyptologists inspired Sigmund Freud in his own theory that incorporated the idea of a *second* Moses into what he regarded as his most revolutionary, if not his most important, work.

Freud's theory was colored by his interest in promoting another archetype central to psychoanalysis. His famous Oedipus complex, or mother complex, was already a well-established theory but he needed a father complex to complement it. He speculated that the origins of this phenomenon could be found during the mythological past when the father ruled as an unbridled tyrant. Because only this "primordial father" was permitted to have sex, the young men rebelled and killed him. Freud believed that an unconscious hatred and jealousy of their leader governed the young men of Israel and in an unconscious mimicry of our primordial ancestors, they murdered Moses.

MOSES AND AMERICA

Christopher Columbus was seven weeks into his fateful journey of discovery when an unexpected swell in the ocean shifted the *Santa Maria* westward. That night, September 23, 1492, he wrote in his journal, "The rising of the sea was very favourable to me as it happened to Moses when he led the Jews from Egypt."[19] His words were the first of many to anoint the New World with the revered prophet's name.

Regardless of the facts of the original exodus, the enduring myth has come to possess a life of its own that frames much of our understanding of history. Moses has, without exaggeration, been a motivating factor in the story of America from Columbus to Obama. "One man is America's true founding father" writes Bruce Feiler. "His name is Moses."[20]

American history is permeated with the Moses myth. The classic story follows the trials of a tribe of slaves freed by a charismatic leader who guides them across a life-threatening sea, through a punishing desert, and finally, to a mountaintop overlooking the Promised Land. After having reached safety, a sacred covenant is created with God that seals their freedom and releases them forever from the cruel oppression of the brutal masters who ruled the land they had fled.

The words seared into the Liberty Bell—Proclaim Liberty thro' all the land to all the Inhabitants Thereof—are taken from a passage in Leviticus that refers to that desperate flight from Egypt led by the prophet.[21] When the French gifted the new nation with the Statue of Liberty they sculpted into her hand a tablet reminiscent of the one

Moses received at the Mountain of God. On her head they placed a radiant crown that the historian Marvin Trachtenberg says, "may allude to the 'rays of light' about his [Moses's] face after revelation."[22]

The risky journey of the *Mayflower* was inspired by the story of the exodus. The despised European kings replaced the oppressive Egyptian pharaoh; the Atlantic Ocean was transformed into the Red Sea, and America became the dreamed-of Promised Land. The Constitution became the new covenant that promised the people freedom to worship the God of their choice. When the 1776 War of Independence was declared, Thomas Paine christened his revolution by comparing England's King George III to the pharaoh who had oppressed Moses and his people.

Bruce Feiler tells us that, "on . . . July 4, after passing the Declaration of Independence the Continental Congress asked John Adams, Thomas Jefferson, and Benjamin Franklin to come up with a public face of the new United States. They chose Moses."[23]

Moses holds an esteemed place in the hearts of many Black Americans. He led his people from a life of bondage into a Promised Land. During the Civil War, the underground railway provided escape from slavery to the free states. "For millions of Africans enslaved in the South," writes Feiler, "Ohio was the Promised Land. And the Ohio River was the Jordan."[24] When Abraham Lincoln signed the Emancipation Proclamation the freed slaves revered the president as a new Moses. The last words he spoke to his wife, Mary, expressed his longing to see Jerusalem.[25] Half the eulogies in his honor compared him to Moses.[26]

A century later, on the night before he was assassinated, Martin Luther King Jr. held on to the power of the myth in his unforgettable, prophetic speech:

> We've got some difficult days ahead. But it really doesn't matter with me now, because I've been to the mountaintop. And I don't mind. Like anybody, I would like to live a long life. Longevity has its place. But I'm not concerned about that now. I just want to do

God's will. And He's allowed me to go up to the mountain. And I've looked over. And I've seen the Promised Land. I may not get there with you. But I want you to know tonight, that we, as a people, will get to the Promised Land![27]

Shortly after President Barack Obama was inaugurated, Andrew Young, Rev. King's friend and colleague in the struggle for civil rights, told author Bruce Feiler, "We are living in a biblical time. The amount of time that passed between Martin's assassination and Obama's election—forty years—is the same amount of time the Israelites spent in the desert."[28]

The Moses myth still holds America in a strong grip.

MARLOWE'S BLASPHEMY

Freud's obsession over the veracity of the Moses story was anticipated long before either he or Sellin explored the possibility that there was a second Moses who had played an equal role in the legendary drama. Suspicions about the biblical icon had intrigued both the Elizabethan playwright Christopher Marlowe and the nineteenth-century German writer and genius, Johann von Goethe.

When the English Privy Council was convened on May 29, 1593, a government informer, Richard Baines, formally charged the playwright Christopher Marlowe with blasphemy. The complaint that was sent to Queen Elizabeth I read:

Containing the opinion of Christopher Marlowe concerning his damnable opinions and judgment of religion and scorn of God's word. . . . He affirmeth that Moses was but a Jugler and that one Harriot, being Sir Walter Raleigh's man, can do more than he. That Moses made the Jews to travel 11 years in the wilderness, ere they came to the promised land to the intent that those who were privy to most of his subtleties might perish and so an everlasting superstition remain in the hearts of the people. That it was an easy matter for Moses, being brought up in the all the arts of the Egyptians, to abuse the Jews.[29]

The sensational charges accused Marlowe of stating that the sacred figure of Moses was no more than a second-rate illusionist. He had made the sacrilegious statement that the only reason that Moses had succeeded with such tricks was because the Israelites were remarkably gullible. "Marlowe's Blasphemies" also charged that the famous tale of the forty years of wandering in the wilderness was an exaggeration. Marlowe claimed that the purpose of the supposed exile was not to build up the strength of the Israelites by toughening them up, as rationalized in Exodus, but instead was a ruse designed to cover up a deep secret. Before Marlowe could expound upon his charges he was murdered by a secret agent of Queen Elizabeth I. His shocking conviction that Moses was a mere illusionist died with him and was forgotten—until now.

GOETHE AND THE ASSASSINATION OF MOSES

In 1819, Johann Goethe wrote "Israel in the Desert" partly as an attempt to show how later editors of the Bible had tampered with the story of Moses. At the time, many biblical scholars were busy trying to disentangle the various strands that composed the first five books of the Old Testament attributed to Moses and named the Torah (the Law) by the Jews. Goethe was disturbed by what he saw as the deliberate insertion of artificial laws into the text that only impeded the progress of the stories. He believed that the narrative of the heroic adventure had been bogged down by unnecessary, and unwelcome, depictions of religious ritual.[30]

Goethe's aesthetic convinced him that misleading words had been added to the scriptures. Like an art historian peeling away the layers of paint covering a lost masterpiece he revealed hidden seams and overlapping pigments that implied that there were different authors, some of whom were obsessed with religious ceremony. According to Goethe these late, bogus, and unwelcome additions spoiled the natural flow of the stories.

The same meddlesome writers had exaggerated critical time scales. Goethe considered the idea that a great prophet had wandered the desert for forty years with thousands of people in tow to be absurd. It called into question Moses's fitness as a commander and painted him in a ridiculous light. Goethe concluded that the only explanation must be that the forty years was symbolic, noting other instances in the Bible where the number forty was used symbolically.* Remove the corruption of the text, especially the illegitimate time scale, Goethe reasoned, and Moses's dignity would be restored, revealing the prophet of God as more of a hero and less of a buffoon.

Strangely, Goethe never asked the question, why? Why did these interfering editors feel so compelled to distort the time frame of the texts? What was their motive? Goethe was the first to propose that Moses had been murdered but he failed to consider the possibility that the editors of the Torah were the descendants of the very conspirators who had carried out the murder. Their motive in distorting the text was to whitewash the shameful actions of their ancestors.

To Goethe, Moses's piousness didn't compensate for the prophet's faults as a leader. His princely education counts for nothing. He describes Moses as "curt and introvert, and barely able to communicate." He was especially unimpressed with Moses's dismal military leadership, remarking that during the Israelites' first battle the prophetic leader "retreated to a mountain to pray" leaving others to face the enemy. Goethe saw Moses as an honest, strong-willed man consumed by the mission of leading his people to the Promised Land whose tragic flaw was a weak personality inadequate to the task. Moses was, at best, incompetent; at worst, ridiculous.

Goethe paints him as a pathetic character forced to press through the unforgiving desert leading an unruly tribe who had left behind slavery but at the same time had been wrenched from the great Egyptian culture and dragged into a primitive life. For Goethe, such a fate was

---

*Noah and his family, for instance, were tossed about by the waters of the Great Flood for forty days. Jesus spent forty days in the desert resisting Satan's temptations.

"the saddest condition in which an excellent man can find himself." He goes so far as to conjecture why the exiled Moses didn't have the courage to end his own miserable life. Baffled as to why this "hotheaded man of deeds, could needlessly stumble about the desert" Goethe set about "rectifying the schedule in time and space" so that the prophet could be restored to his rightful place in history.

In contrast, he has nothing but praise for Jethro. (*Jethro* is the Christian name for Moses's father-in-law. In Judaic literature he is more frequently known as Reuel.) Reuel was the high priest of Midian when Moses arrived there as a fugitive wanted for murder in Egypt. Goethe regarded Reuel as a wise, shrewd, and natural leader. The Midianites were, in Goethe's telling, much "better educated" than the former slaves of Egypt, and Reuel possessed the prerequisite cultural background, and more importantly, the temperament to assume the leadership of a nation.

Appalled that Moses couldn't create the necessary structure to keep order among the disgruntled Israelites, Goethe concluded that God's prophet was hopeless in meeting the increasing demands of his people. He was only saved from the consequences of his inadequacies because Reuel intervened and persuaded his son-in-law to adopt a paramilitary organization to control the mob.

Goethe speculated that Moses was finally brought down when two young men, Joshua and Caleb, tired and angered by their foolish, arbitrary leader, assassinated him to spare the people from any more of his dangerous bungling. They were justified, Goethe wrote, because without strong leadership the Israelites could never conquer the Promised Land. The murder of Moses was a political necessity.

COLD CASE FILE

When there are no witnesses to a murder, detectives are trained to discover the guilty party by asking who had the "motive, means, and opportunity" to commit the crime.[31] There is only one character in the Moses story who fits this bill. The insights of Marlowe, Goethe, and Freud all provide clues to his identity and point to evidence of his ruthlessness.

Marlowe gave us the means by which the murder was accomplished. He believed that Moses was an illusionist whose acts thrilled and baffled the children of Israel because they were naive in the ways of an Egyptian-trained magician. These acts of illusion concealed the murder of the prophet and allowed an impostor to step into his place. Goethe believed that the story of Moses had been tampered with by scribes with a powerful agenda. Their late editing of the original spoken stories distorted the truth by inserting artificially long periods of time into the text. Removing these exaggerated periods of time reveals what was concealed. We take Goethe's argument further. Once we remove the artificial time scales that were shoehorned into the text by the manipulative editors it becomes apparent that our prime suspect had the perfect opportunity to murder Moses.

Freud insisted that Moses was an Egyptian. Denying the Jews a genetic link to the greatest of their prophets was something he did with great reluctance, especially since his people were facing the Nazis in 1939, the year his book was released. The idea that there was a second Moses was something many of the faithful found deeply disturbing.

Unlike Freud we don't believe that the death of the "first" Moses resulted from a spontaneous murder. One man was powerfully motivated, possessed the skills of a magician, and had the opportunity to murder Moses.

Our suspect is Moses's father-in-law Reuel, the man Goethe held in such esteem.

THE MASKED MOSES

Strangely, Freud never referred to the veil that Moses wore during the final years of his reign even though its existence supported his theory of a second Moses—an impostor.

Why did Moses conceal his face?

The American scholar Thomas B. Dozeman was the first to suggest that Moses was, in effect, double masked. The original mask was seen by the tribe as a terrifying glow. The second mask was a veil.[32]

We suggest that having trained as a magician in Egypt, Reuel wore two masks when he hijacked the Exodus. We learn that "the origins of the word *mask* are unclear, but it probably comes from the Arabic *maskhara* (*mashara*), which meant 'to falsify' or 'transform' into animal, monster, or freak. In the Middle Kingdom, Egyptians used the word *msk* to refer to leather or 'second skin.' This word most likely entered the Arabic language as *msr*, which for Muslims meant 'to be Egyptianized,' or to wear a mask as did the ancient Egyptians."[33]

In Arabic, the word *mask* has two meanings, "to falsify" and "to transform." Both were critical to Reuel's murder plot.

Today, we generally regard masks as a means of concealment, often harmlessly, such as for Halloween, masquerades, or plays. But in the ancient world a mask carried a much more potent connotation linked to the notion of transformation. When a person covered their features with a mask they did so with some trepidation since they believed that they were in danger of being possessed by the demon, god, or spirit it represented. This was forcefully portrayed in the movie *The Mask,* in which Jim Carrey's character is possessed by the ancient spirit of a mask. His body becomes the agent of a charming and charismatic fellow possessing the powers and immunities of a cartoon character. This was all in fun, but in the ancient world the possession of a person by a supernatural agent was deadly serious. The depiction of such a phenomenon always struck fear into an audience.

At his first encounter with his Maker, "Moses hid his face; for he was afraid to look upon God."[34] It was a natural reaction because the people of Israel lived in terror of direct contact with God, believing that the mere sight of him would bring immediate death. They'd been warned, "man shall not see Me and live."[35]

Moses became the exception. He alone was permitted to face the Almighty. The consequences of such encounters were surprising and shocking for the children of Israel. The prophet's face was transformed by his encounter:

And when Aaron and all the children of Israel saw Moses, behold, the skin of his face shone; and they were afraid to come nigh him. And Moses called unto them; and Aaron and all the rulers of the congregation returned unto him: and Moses talked with them. And afterward all the children of Israel came nigh: and he gave them in commandment all that the LORD had spoken with him in mount Sinai. And till Moses had done speaking with them, he put a veil on his face.[36]

Reuel's *shining face* represented a mask of possession. When Moses's face shone, the Israelites believed he was not himself. He had been "transformed" into an agent of Yahweh and was prone to fits of rage. When "the children of Israel saw Moses, behold, the skin of his face shone; and they were afraid to come nigh him."[37] To calm their fears the prophet placed a veil over his shining face. The veil was in effect a second mask, a further concealment. The Israelites welcomed the new covering believing it protected them from Yahweh's glowing reflection, which could kill them.

When he was veiled, Moses walked freely around the camp without inciting fear and it became a potent symbol of his authority, much as British judges once wore wigs. In contrast, when he appeared without it and revealed his shining face it meant that he had stepped into his sacred role as prophet.

Both masks served the magician Reuel well after he usurped Moses's role. The tribe, fearing his shining face, turned away but listened with rapt attention to his every word. When his face was veiled they accepted his orders as those of their legitimate leader. None but a select few ever saw Moses's face again. These few would pay for that knowledge with their lives.

The most perplexing thing about the leader with the concealed features was his total transformation. Moses underwent a dramatic personality change. The first Moses was shy, a shepherd who rarely spoke publicly—possibly due to an embarrassing stutter or perhaps, as Freud suggested, because his first language was Egyptian rather than Hebrew.

But the "new" Moses was a dynamic and unpredictable extrovert in possession of a powerful speaking voice. The debilitating stutter had vanished.

Before the arrival of the masked Moses there were no accounts of Israelites turning against each other. But the first act of the new Moses was to order the death of three thousand of the tribe. Why this brutal edict? Did the anonymity of the mask inspire a more dynamic, eloquent personality who hid behind its cover to enforce his power with an act of unprecedented violence?

Or had the real Moses vanished? Replaced by another man hiding behind the mask?

2

———•———

Prime Suspect

All the old knives that have rusted in my back, I drive in yours.
PHAEDRUS (C. 15 BCE–50 CE)

All detectives know that people are nothing if not predictable in their
motives for murder. Every police archive testifies to the power of
greed, revenge, jealousy, and lust to create havoc. Cases of violence committed in the name of eradicating an enemy, enforcing blind dogma, or
satiating the psychopath's compulsion to kill, choke the justice system.

Revenge was the fire that consumed our prime suspect. Reuel, whose
name meant "god's friend,"[1] a title he wore with increasingly devious
intent, would never be satisfied until he'd eradicated Moses and fulfilled the biblical mandate of "an eye for an eye."[2] But what diabolical
wrong had this man suffered that drove him to commit such a brutal,
history-changing crime?

THE VENDETTA

The Godfather movie seared the image of the Sicilian vendetta into modern consciousness. In just one of many iconic scenes from the movie,
Michael Corleone strolls through a quiet village and wonders aloud

about the scarcity of men in the dusty streets. "They're all dead from vendettas," says his bodyguard. But the history of blood feuds reaches much further back in time than the vicious tempers and tantrums of the Cosa Nostra. A lethal mixture of dishonor and vengeance has fueled violence throughout many cultures and across thousands of years.

The ancient Greeks routinely destroyed enemies in the name of dishonor, and during the Middle Ages revenge was touted as a sacred duty. The rival clans of Ireland and Scotland never missed an opportunity for a good fight to the death, preferably over someone's insulted honor. Citizens of the Byzantine Empire lived in fear of gang warfare and street violence precipitated by vengeance-seeking mobs. And Japan's legendary Samurai were charged with upholding at any cost the honor of an individual, an entire tribe, and of course, their leader. Countless societies have been compelled to practice their own finely tuned or crude traditions of retaliation over real or imagined wrongs.

In the biblical age, an impressionable youth named Reuel had been weaned on the often-repeated tale of his villainous uncle's theft of his family's birthright—an uncle who had not only gotten away with his crime but had added salt to the wound by assuming a position of great power and prestige. The seed of this vindictive blood feud was planted on the day that twin boys Esau and Jacob, fathered by Isaac, the founder of the Jews, were born.

The reason behind one of the most significant of all vendettas was bizarre in its simplicity. One twin had to be anointed as the firstborn. That older twin, Esau, was to become Reuel's father. Esau was later betrayed by his younger twin, Jacob (later known as Israel), when he stole Esau's identity at a critical moment, ensuring that neither Esau nor his son Reuel would ever inherit their rightful role as leader of the Hebrew people.

Reuel grew to adulthood obsessed with avenging this far-reaching wrong. It didn't help that the torment was constantly exacerbated by jealousy of Israel's children, his cousins. Because of Jacob's dramatic deception they now enjoyed great privilege in their unwarranted positions as leaders of the dominant tribe. Reuel plotted day and night to seize back the control his father had lost. Thus, a biblical vendetta was born.

HUNGER

Esau and his twin were at odds from the beginning. Esau was a hunter and warrior and the apple of his father's eye. As the firstborn son he was automatically granted a birthright, a tangible inheritance. The second born, Jacob, was something of a mommy's boy: a dreamer who preferred the solitude of camp to the dangers of hunting, but a young man realistic enough to know that he held distant second place in his father's esteem. He also knew only too well that the priceless birthright was his older brother's by tradition. Nevertheless, the toxic seed of resentment was sown early. After all, Jacob was only the younger by a minute or two.

That resentment erupted one day after Esau returned to camp from a long, futile hunt. Exhausted and ravenous, he found Jacob cooking a savory meal of red lentils. Esau was "faint" with hunger and begged his brother to fill a bowl for him. Never one to miss an opportunity, Jacob refused and instead offered a sly bargain, "Sell me this day thy birthright," he demanded.

His mouth watering, Esau responded, "Behold, I am at the point to die."[3]

Jacob tantalized Esau with the pot of steaming food. It had the desired effect.

Esau asked himself—if he was going to die from hunger anyway—"What profit shall this birthright do to me?" Probably not taking the contract seriously in that moment, Reuel's father impulsively traded his precious birthright for a pot of red lentils.

Extortion won the day for Jacob. From this point on the brothers already tenuous relationship quickly deteriorated into enmity, reaching its nadir when their father decided that he would ignore the shabby agreement between the twins and bestow his final blessing on Esau despite his foolish loss of the precious birthright. But Isaac was naive about the degree of his second son's disappointment and the strength of his will. He also underestimated the sheer determination of his wife, Rebekah, on behalf of her favorite twin. As a result, when the decisive moment came . . . something went terribly wrong.

> And it came to pass, that when Isaac was old, and his eyes were dim, so that he could not see, he called Esau his eldest son, and said unto him, My son: and he said unto him, Behold, here am I. And he said, Behold now, I am old, I know not the day of my death: Now therefore take, I pray thee, thy weapons, thy quiver and thy bow, and go out to the field, and take me some venison; And make me savoury meat, such as I love, and bring it to me, that I may eat; that my soul may bless thee before I die. And Rebekah heard when Isaac spake to Esau his son.[4]

Isaac's weak eyesight made him vulnerable to Rebekah's manipulations. When Esau left the camp to go hunting his mother laid a trap on behalf of Jacob.

> And Rebekah spake unto Jacob her son, saying, Behold, I heard thy father speak unto Esau thy brother, saying, Bring me venison, and make me savoury meat, that I may eat, and bless thee before the LORD before my death. Now therefore, my son, obey my voice according to that which I command thee. Go now to the flock, and fetch me from thence two good kids of the goats; and I will make them savoury meat for thy father, such as he loveth: And thou shalt bring it to thy father, that he may eat, and that he may bless thee before his death. And Jacob said to Rebekah his mother, Behold, Esau my brother is a hairy man, and I am a smooth man: My father peradventure will feel me, and I shall seem to him as a deceiver; and I shall bring a curse upon me, and not a blessing. And his mother said unto him, Upon me be thy curse, my son: only obey my voice, and go fetch me them.[5]

Rebekah's resolve would not be stymied by Jacob's practical fears. She covered his hands with gloves made from goat's hair to delude her failing husband that Jacob was hairy like Esau. Relying on Isaac's deteriorating state and the power of suggestion she was confident that she could pull off her bold coup. Jacob still feared that the disguise would fail. But urged on by his mother he forced himself to go through with the dangerous gamble. There was no doubt that the ultimate prize of leadership was worth the risk.

> And Jacob said unto his father, I am Esau thy firstborn; I have done according as thou badest me: arise, I pray thee, sit and eat of my venison, that thy soul may bless me. And Isaac said unto his son, How is it that thou hast found it so quickly, my son? And he said, Because the LORD thy God brought it to me. And Isaac said unto Jacob, Come near, I pray thee, that I may feel thee, my son, whether thou be my very son Esau or not. And Jacob went near unto Isaac his father; and he felt him, and said, The voice is Jacob's voice, but the hands are the hands of Esau. And he discerned him not, because his hands were hairy.[6]

Jacob had succeeded! He'd stolen the final blessing literally from under Esau's nose through a cold, calculated act of *impersonation*. "And Esau hated Jacob because of the blessing wherewith his father blessed him: and Esau said in his heart, The days of mourning for my father are at hand; then will I slay my brother Jacob."[7] Aware of Esau's rage, Rebekah, the mastermind of the scheme, beseeched Jacob to flee to her brother's land.

Esau's anger burned unabated, but he resolved to take his fate into his own hands. Eventually, he conquered the mountainous desert country of Seir where he installed himself as king. By coincidence, the names *Esau* and *Seir* both mean "hairy,"[8] an unfortunate reminder to Esau of the betrayal of both his mother and his twin. He renamed the subjugated land *Edom,* the Hebrew word for red, possibly to mark the infamous red lentils incident* when he first tasted the extent of his brother's ruthless ambition.

In the meantime, Jacob had made his way safely to his uncle's home.

---

*We can't know for sure if it was the red lentils that inspired Esau to name the land Edom. We know his original birthright was lost for red lentils, but there are other explanations for the name he gave to his kingdom. Edom may refer to the great walls of red sandstone at Petra, in the very heart of the land. Or perhaps Esau had red hair. We favor the "red lentils" explanation because it fits the context of establishing a new birthright, one Esau could pass on to his eldest son.

Laban had two daughters, Rachel and Leah. Jacob met Rachel beside a well where he helped her haul heavy loads of water for the family's thirsty flock. Smitten, he asked Laban for her hand in marriage. Laban drove a hard bargain—imposing the condition that Jacob work for him without pay for seven years. The seven years seemed to Jacob "but a few days, for the love he had to her."[9] But Laban had set in motion a monumental plot of greed and deceit; its true nature to surface much later.

After Jacob fulfilled his obligation of service, Laban arranged a wedding party and celebration for his son-in-law. But when it came time for the marriage to be consummated Laban slipped his older daughter, Leah, into Jacob's tent. No doubt a generous flow of alcohol helped complete the cruel deception. In his drugged state Jacob fell for the ruse, bedded Leah, and sealed his fate. He was now trapped in a marriage with his beloved Rachel's older sister. Jacob would never fully forgive Leah, but the real sting of his bitterness was saved for his uncle. Oblivious to the many guests still lingering at the celebration he shouted at Laban, "What is this thou hast done unto me? Did not I serve with thee for Rachel? Wherefore then hast thou beguiled me?"[10]

Laban calmly reiterated the custom of the times, "It must not be so done in our country, to give the younger before the firstborn."[11] Jacob was forced to bite his tongue. The great deceiver had been deceived by the same ploy he had used against his own father—impersonation.

Jacob agreed to serve another grueling seven years so that he could take Rachel as his second wife. Leah was a loving and loyal partner who bore him seven children. But it was clear that her husband's heart belonged to her sister. His happiness when they finally married was tempered by Rachel's long years of infertility, which were finally broken when they rejoiced in the arrival of a son, Joseph.

THE TALISMAN

After twenty years of servitude to Laban, Jacob finally rebelled against his father-in-law. Fleeing with Leah and Rachel, their eleven sons* and

---

*Rachel's second son, Benjamin, was born after Jacob and his family deserted Laban.

their daughter, Dinah, he hastily decamped without telling Laban. Laban was furious when he realized that they had slipped away from his authority. Especially when he discovered that a precious teraphim, an ancient family relic used in ritualistic magic and described by the Torah as "images," was missing. The teraphim was so precious to Laban that he worshipped it as a god. His daughter, Rachel, aware of its value and perhaps seeking some form of compensation for her husband's long years of slavery, had stolen the talisman.

Jacob, unaware of his wife's daring theft, was oblivious to the danger charging the air when Laban, accompanied by a small army, caught up with the small, rebellious troop. Laban lashed out, accusing Jacob of being a thief.

Scoffing at the charge, Jacob taunted his father-in-law, "With whomsoever thou findest thy gods, let him not live."[12]

The family was held hostage while Laban turned over every tent in a frantic search for his prized idol. But the wily Rachel had hidden the teraphim under the saddle of her camel. She refused to dismount, protesting, "Let it not displease my lord that I cannot rise up before thee; for the custom of women is upon me."[13] It was a clever ploy. Spinning the prejudice that menstruating women were unclean and not to be touched, she concealed her theft and foiled Laban. Eventually, he reluctantly accepted the loss of the teraphim and blessed his daughters before leaving.

Why was Laban so disturbed about losing this mysterious item?

The scholar Elias Auerbach (1882–1972) presents a convincing case that Laban's teraphim was in fact a mask. It is implied in 1 Samuel 19 that the object resembles a human head. When Saul sends bailiffs to seize David, his wife places a teraphim on his pillow as a ruse to trick the authorities into thinking he is sick in bed. Auerbach concludes that the mystery object is "a face mask" because it gives "the appearance of a man and can also be placed beneath the saddle of a camel."[14]

If Laban's talisman was a mask it makes sense of one of the strangest episodes in Genesis—an incident that occurred shortly after this heated confrontation in the desert over a missing teraphim.

WRESTLING WITH GOD

Why Jacob would take his family to Edom where his estranged brother, Esau, who hated him, now ruled, is one of the unexplained mysteries of the Torah. Perhaps he had deluded himself that the passage of time had cooled his brother's fury and that he would be forgiven for stealing the final blessing. But doubt plagued him and as soon as his feet touched Edom's soil he fell to his knees praying fervently, "Deliver me, I pray thee, from the hand of my brother, from the hand of Esau: for I fear him, lest he will come and smite me, and the mother with the children."[15]

Jacob knew that, accompanied by his sons and four hundred armed men, Esau was riding to confront him. To mollify his brother, Jacob sent servants to intercept him bearing the valuable gift of five hundred domestic animals. They also brought the appeasing message that Jacob was offering himself as Esau's loyal servant.

While enduring the excruciating wait for a response Jacob took his small tribe across the Jabbok River to set up camp. That night, he wandered away from his family into the wild where he was ensnared in a violent encounter that is considered one of the most puzzling stories of the Bible and still baffles biblical scholars:

And Jacob was left alone; and there wrestled a man with him until the breaking of the day. And when he saw that he prevailed not against him, he touched the hollow of his thigh; and the hollow of Jacob's thigh was out of joint, as he wrestled with him. And he said, Let me go, for the day breaketh. And he said, I will not let thee go, except thou bless me. And he said unto him, What is thy name? And he said, Jacob. And he said, Thy name shall be called no more Jacob, but Israel: for as a prince hast thou power with God and with men, and hast prevailed. And Jacob asked him, and said, Tell me, I pray thee, thy name. And he said, Wherefore is it that thou dost ask after my name? And he blessed him there.[16]

So, what is going on during this strange encounter? The text is unclear about who is blessing whom. And who is the antagonistic stranger? A man? Or are we supposed to believe that God has lowered himself to grapple with Jacob? The prophet Hosea offered a compromise: "And he fought with an angel and prevailed."[17]

It's odd that the text is so vague considering that this was the notorious exchange that led Jacob to change his name to *Israel,* meaning "one who struggles with God."[18] Richard Elliott Friedman notes, "The curious thing is that several of the biblical stories involving angels contain confusions such as this, that is, confusions between when it is the deity and when it is the angel who is speaking or doing something."[19] He adds, "We are never told why they are struggling."[20]

It seems unlikely that God, or even an angel, should seek the blessing of a mere mortal. Unless, of course, this deity was neither angel nor deity but instead an impostor who had everything to gain by convincing Jacob that he was in the grasp of God himself. But who craved Jacob's blessing the most?

Circumstantial evidence points to Jacob's nephew, Reuel, as the mysterious stranger. The encounter took place in Edom, the land of his father, Esau. Reuel would have accompanied his father as part of the four hundred men gathered to ride against Jacob. It would seem poetic justice to Reuel for Jacob to be forced to bless him. His uncle had received his blessing by impersonating Esau. Now Reuel, Esau's son, could reclaim that all-important blessing by impersonating God.

This would not be the last time that Reuel would exhibit hubris enough to take on the very mantle of God.

THE FACE OF GOD

Jacob was convinced that his adversary in the dark had been no mere mortal. "And Jacob called the name of the place Peniel: for I have seen God face to face, and my life is preserved."[21] It seems that a powerful combination of fear and suggestibility had convinced Jacob that he had stared into God's face. Not likely. The taboo surrounding the idea of even glimpsing the features of the Almighty was deeply entrenched. The Israelites believed that even a glimpse of God was sufficient to kill them. This suggests that the stranger's face was hidden from Jacob; all the better to deceive him.

Was the clever Reuel wearing a mask?

As we've seen (Genesis 31) a teraphim, probably a mask, caused a serious conflict between Jacob and Laban when Laban accused Jacob of stealing it. Innocent of the original theft, Jacob had nevertheless immediately grasped its value and had taken the teraphim from Rachel and buried it beneath an oak tree. Did Reuel or one of Esau's spies see Jacob hide the sacred mask? If Reuel had dug it up from its burial place, then its miraculous appearance on the stranger's face would have added a dimension of horror for Jacob who believed that the precious talisman was safely hidden.

The wrestling episode carries the whiff of an elaborate act of illusion. The kind of trick that would be the specialty of an Egyptian-trained master magician. We can't return to the scene of the crime and dust for fingerprints but there is compelling evidence that points to Reuel as the only man arrogant enough to take on the role of God.

VOICE PRINT

Modern criminology utilizes the eccentricities of language and the unique way people express themselves to track criminals. Individuals can be identified not only by the words they use but by the way they express themselves. What we say not only reveals what we mean but also who we are. Richard Elliott Friedman translates the relevant passage in the Torah, "he prevailed not against him" as "he saw that he was not able against him." He notes that this combination of the verbs to be and able occurs in only one other passage in the Torah.[22] This unique grammar (to be able) is used by Reuel (as Jethro) at the foot of the Mountain of God when he tells Moses that he is not able to lead his people alone because the duty is "too heavy" for him.

Reuel's unique voiceprint betrays his identity.

The wrestling match with God was only the opening act in the drama of Reuel's obsession with revenge; a brief bow as he readies to step on stage to play out each act leading to a long-awaited finale. Leading to the day that he can slip into Moses's role and seize the leadership of the children of Israel: the day that he dons a mesmerizing mask and transforms himself into a second Moses.

MURMURINGS

The constant murmurings that emerged against Moses after Reuel stole his identity suggests that some of the tribe suspected that the new Moses, the prophet who hid his face behind a veil, was someone other than their true leader. But for most of the people his transition from a mild-mannered, stuttering shepherd to a terrorizing, ranting egomaniac was accepted with unquestioning resignation.

Reuel was so talented and eliminated Moses by such clever means that most didn't realize that their prophet had been replaced by an impostor. How was he able to murder and then impersonate Moses without the people rising in rebellion? The answer lies in the elaborate set of skills he acquired as an apprentice magician in Egypt, the center of illusion and magic. This was where Reuel finely tuned the elaborate arts he needed to enact his coup. His masterful plot was played out with a series of illusions that wound around what, in their day, were extremely sophisticated tricks.

Jewish folklore testifies that Reuel was so talented that he rose to the sacred position of master magician in that advanced civilization. He made dark use of the secrets skills that the Egyptian priests had honed for thousands of years. It is to the ancient land of the Nile that we must travel to uncover the true source of Reuel's success.

3

———•———

Blueprint for Murder

Egypt was the mother of magicians.

CLEMENT OF ALEXANDRIA, THIRD CENTURY CE

The popularity of the *Lord of the Rings* trilogy and the wild success of the *Harry Potter* franchise have reinvigorated the word *magic*. These new magicians are more than simple illusionists; they are masters—and mistresses—of sleight of hand whose adroit showmanship delights, tricks, and sometimes bewilders. But there remains a chasm of difference between the ancient arts of magic and our common view of the glamorous illusionist and conjuror—spellbinding us with clever tricks—or even that of the common street magician only intent on separating us from our money.

The flamboyant Vegas magician is a pale reflection of his Egyptian precursor whose every word and gesture affirmed a vivid mythological realm.[1] Unlike the modern performer who degrades magic in the service of his act, Egyptian magicians believed that their rituals manipulated the supernatural.

Even the modern use of the wand illustrates the profound difference between then and now. Today, it has been reduced to a flamboyant toy used to misdirect a compliant audience; a far cry from its role in ancient Egypt where they believed that the wave of a powerful wand could invoke the gods.

We still play with remnants of Egypt's sophisticated religion. Every time we pierce our ears or indulge in a tattoo or spray a favorite perfume over our throat we are sharing a diluted hint of a culture that has haunted and fascinated us for thousands of years. The Egyptians believed that the ear was a particularly vulnerable organ, allowing demons easy entrance to capture the soul. Not many women realize as they choose a flattering pair of earrings at the jewelry counter that these sparkling pieces were invented by the Egyptians as amulets to deflect evil forces from entering the body. Powerful magicians were consulted to ensure that the appropriate design was selected to best deter the feared invaders. For those who couldn't afford the elaborate dangling version, ear-piercing was considered better than nothing. There was some comfort for the otherwise unadorned in the belief that "ear-piercing may have been thought to bestow some sort of protection in itself."[2] And sweet-smelling perfume was believed to attract good spirits in contrast to the foul odor of garlic that was used to ward off evil spirits.

Tattoos were also part of a magician's trade. "Early opponents of Christianity accused Jesus of having trained as a magician in Egypt and of working his miracles by means of magical tattoos acquired there."[3] The remnants of Egyptian magic are preserved whenever a modern-day showman uses masks, wands, and sometimes lions, snakes, and "ghosts" in his or her act. Even the twenty-first-century conjurer's choice of a black costume would not have been out of place in ancient Egypt.

EGYPTIAN PUPPETS

Today puppets are almost exclusively associated with children's entertainment. In ancient Egypt, however, they were used for a much less benign purpose—as tools operated by the priests to manipulate the fate of the nation. Puppetry in ancient Egypt was no child's play but a deadly serious business. Evidence from Ethiopia demonstrates how monarchs were selected for succession to power. "Among the most characteristic processes in the consultation of statues is the designation of the Ethiopian sovereigns by the statue of Amon-Ra at Napata. . . . The candidates were brought before the statue of the god, which had been adjured to make its choice known. They filed past the idol, which remained motionless until it 'seized' the candidate it chose. The statue thereupon declared in formal terms that this was the king."[4]

The statue of Amon-Ra was a puppet operated by a priest. This Ethiopian convention was based upon the Egyptian model practiced during the reign of Amenhotep (fourteenth century BCE) and probably long before, whenever candidates for the office of High Priest were selected.[5] They were paraded in front of a priest holding a pole with an idol attached to the top. The pole's hollow center contained a hidden string that the puppeteer pulled when the preordained candidate passed before him. The nodding head of the idol controlled who would gain power.

Myths and storytelling took center stage in the magician's world. Writing and the power of words, including ritualistic chanting, played a forceful part in their repertoire. They loved puns and were obsessed with the purity and perfection of the mythical "First Time"—that time in the golden past when gods lived among humans. It was a time that the Egyptians yearned to re-create. Any possible future could never compare to that idealized past. What was old was good. What was new was suspect.

Despite their powers and respected position, the Egyptian magicians harbored many fears and superstitions. The night, when dark forces and creatures of the desert held sway, was filled with terror for them. "Spells against the dangers of the night were performed at dusk."[6] And magicians always carried staffs to use against lurking demons. But despite this, their relation to nature was much closer than a modern magician's. It spoke directly to them.

THE TERROR OF THE BIRDS

On a gray November day in London's Hyde Park we passed beneath a cluster of leafless trees, their skeletal branches alive with the chatter of hundreds of starlings. Suddenly, the birds fell silent. A long moment passed. And then with a single hum they rose as one body and took flight. We were amazed at the uncanny unison of the flock, alerted by a signal undetectable to us that had pulled them as if by a magnet from the bare branches.

The delight we felt at this wild display would have been denied to an ancient Egyptian. Not because they didn't appreciate the wonders of nature—they were keen observers of the world around them—but their attitude toward birds in flight was thickly layered with superstition and legend. They saw the simultaneous movement of a flock as evidence of control by an invisible, evil force. They used cruel "throwsticks" to break up the flocks, weapons that symbolized the victory of order over chaos. Convinced that imperceptible forces of evil might destroy the peace as suddenly and ruthlessly as a crocodile lunges from calm water to drag an unwary bather to his death, they lived in constant fear that could only be abated with ritual and magic.

An ancient Egyptian would be horrified by the depictions of chaos shown on a modern movie screen. The evil enacted in *The Mummy* or *The Scorpion King* would be deeply shocking to them. The mere process of representing an idea, whether benign or malevolent, through words, dance, music, or drama was considered tantamount to making it a reality. The primary purpose of art was not entertainment. The creative process, in all its manifestations, was respected because it was considered part and parcel of the formative magic that brought the world into existence. The idea of carelessly conjuring up movie-screen size images of evil would be considered reckless, to say the least. To represent evil, even in art, was to enhance its power. When it was necessary to depict malevolent gods, care was always taken to minimize their size. They must never be given more power than they already possessed by allowing the perception to prevail that they were larger than life.

Our currently popular vampire movies would be more easily accepted. Combating demons with rituals and charms was regarded as a natural undertaking. Indeed, the custom of wearing foul-smelling garlic necklaces to ward off an enemy originated in Egypt. The shape of the garlic clove was reminiscent of a demon's fang. Egyptian magic fought like with like.

The startling visions in Alfred Hitchcock's classic *The Birds* would have disturbed an Egyptian's soul. The image of thousands of birds possessed by an invisible, malicious force would speak directly to their greatest fear—that chaos could overwhelm the fragile universe at any time unless kept at bay by the force of magical ritual.

THE PRIEST/MAGICIAN

In the twenty-first century magic, science, religion, and mythology could not be more separate entities. Each is a distinct specialty. Each offers its own experts and practitioners who jealously guard the gates to their individual secrets. In contrast, in ancient Egypt the priest and the magician received the same education. They studied the same myths and called upon the same gods and goddesses in their magic. Priest and magician were, in fact, the same person. When they performed ceremonies and cast spells, they assumed both roles simultaneously.

These roles were only differentiated by whom they served. When they attended to the royal family, especially the pharaoh, they were esteemed as priests and entrusted to perform critical rituals considered essential for the preservation of the kingdom. These duties emphasized what might be called "calendar magic," magic performed at specific times of the day and on special days of the year. When these same priests served the public, they assumed the role of magician. But the same deities were invoked and the same rituals carried out as those enacted in the splendor of the royal temples.

In short, the magician was a priest in private practice.

As we've seen, the modern magician is more showman than storyteller. His stories are rudimentary compared to those of his predecessors. Depending on your religious point of view most would agree that today's conjurer bears little resemblance to a Roman Catholic priest. But ancient magicians played an integral part in orthodox religion, casting spells to protect the royal family as they practiced their consciously optimistic profession. (On occasion, women performed rituals in Egyptian temples.)[7] Although it was accepted that evil would never be conquered, this depressing reality was balanced with the belief that the forces of darkness could be contained through careful ritual, ceremony, and the discreet practice of the sacred secrets held by the esteemed court magicians. Nothing corrupt or degrading stained these duties. The magician/priests were not judged by their glittering showmanship but by how well they served the purpose of goodwill and their pharaoh and how successfully they brought prosperity to the land.

In Jewish folklore, Reuel is repeatedly depicted as performing his magic inside the sanctity of the royal court, which would mean that he was honored as both priest *and* magician. How did a Hebrew-speaking foreigner come to be trusted enough to be accepted as a student of the elite practice of Egyptian magic? What worldview did he embrace and what skills did he absorb in this most dominant and mysterious of ancient civilizations? How did the magic he learned in Egypt help him in his obsession to propagate his "holy"* bloodline?

What were the common mythological assumptions shared by Moses and Reuel? And how much of Reuel's existence involved acts of illusion designed to trick people into believing that the gods favored the practitioner who stood before them? We can all be deceived by the magician unless we know his trade secrets. By pulling back the curtain and revealing the manipulations behind the scenes we can watch a master magician at work.

REUEL IN EGYPT

Nearly 3,500 years ago Thutmose III (1457–1425 BCE) "initiated the practice of bringing the princes of subject kings of western Asia to Egypt to be trained in Egyptian ways to prepare them to replace their fathers upon their death."[8] Ancient texts refer to

---

*"Holy" because Reuel was the first person to be descended from Abraham through both of his sons: Ishmael, the founder of the Arabs, and Isaac, the founder of the Jews.

this hostage and education policy imposed on the eastern colonies: "Now the children of the chieftains and their brothers are brought in order to be hostages of Egypt. Now if anyone of these chieftains die, then his majesty will have his son to assume the throne."[9] In this way the sons became pawns of the Egyptians; pawns who could be anointed kings at the will of their masters. This policy was perpetuated for centuries after Thutmose III and would have been in effect in Reuel's time.

Although Reuel was the only child of the betrayed Esau and his second wife, Basemath, he was not the firstborn son. Esau had three wives and as a result Reuel had an older half brother. Having himself been deprived of his inheritance by the treachery of his mother and younger twin, Esau was determined not to allow his second son, Reuel, to rise above the first. So Reuel, destined never to rule Edom, was forced to make his own fortune. The chance to live and study in Egypt presented him with a rare opportunity to learn the necessary skills to earn a livelihood. Of course, those selected to travel to what was then considered the center of the world did not regard themselves as hostages. It was considered a great honor to be admitted to the temples and learn from the most learned of all men. Egypt was so exciting compared to the life that they'd left behind that many of the young men of the time were as seduced by its splendor as any small-town teenager of today lured by the bright lights of a great city.

Reuel's older brother, Eliphaz, did not go to Egypt even though it was his right. Why give up such a rare chance? The answer, as with so much of our story, involves a bloodline. Eliphaz's mother—Esau's wife—was a Hittite. The Hittites were sworn enemies of the Egyptians. This alone would disqualify Eliphaz from traveling there. The Egyptian priests would never trust the son of a Hittite not to reveal their precious secrets. In contrast, Reuel's mother, Basemath, was the daughter of Ishmael. Ishmaelites were welcome traders in Egypt, which made Reuel an ideal candidate for an Egyptian education at their esteemed school of magic, the "House of Life."

THE HOUSE OF LIFE

Reuel would have begun his studies as a "lector priest." Learning his art through a demanding apprenticeship, the young man would work in the temple beside his mentor, faithfully observing and imitating his actions. Besides acquiring a thorough knowledge of ritual, the novice would be immersed in geometry, mathematics, astronomy, medicine, and a host of other subjects. He would consult the precious "Dream Books" that were used to interpret the strange world of our unconscious. He would copy out existing texts and be encouraged to compose since all magicians were also expected to be creators.

The lector priests weren't permitted to enter the inner sanctuaries of the temples. And there was a limit to how high some could rise in the hierarchy. A foreign-born lector priest like Reuel must have demonstrated an extraordinary aptitude to be allowed access to the sanctuaries of the royal family.

"Knowledge of the major myths is an essential preliminary for understanding Egyptian magic."[10] When the lector priests became scribes, they would spend hour after hour copying out the myths that provided the sacred software for the Egyptian religion.

THE LEGEND OF OSIRIS

The tragic story of Osiris is one of the most ancient of those myths, dating back to a time when the Great Pyramid still rose as a gleaming white monument on the Giza Plateau. Parts of his compelling story are found scattered on walls, pillars, and the ceilings of sacred buildings. The tale of Osiris's life, suffering, death, and resurrection was so familiar to the Egyptians that in Reuel's time it wasn't necessary to repeat it—everyone knew the details by heart,* as well as modern fans might relate the details of the lives of Superman or Batman.

---

*Our modern understanding of the legend relies upon the first century CE Roman biographer Plutarch, who preserved the complete version.

Osiris was esteemed as the god who ruled the critical forces behind the art and science of agriculture, but he is also depicted as the god of the dead and the great civilizer of Egypt and other parts of the world. It was said that after establishing civilization in Egypt he traveled abroad to bestow the gifts of agriculture, music, and culture on foreign lands. While he was away he left his wife-sister-queen, Isis, in charge—unaware that a dark cloud of ruthless ambition hung over his household in the form of his younger brother, Seth. Jealous of the king and queen, he conspired to assassinate Osiris.

With the help of his collaborators, Seth constructed a chest to the exact dimensions of Osiris's body. When Osiris returned from his demanding mission, a banquet was held in his honor. Seth brought the chest to the celebration and challenged the guests to climb inside it. Nobody fit the custom-designed tomb. Osiris took up the dare and effortlessly eased into the confined space. Seth slammed the lid shut, nailed it closed, and threw it into the Nile. The chest floated for days before reaching the Mediterranean and was eventually carried to Canaanite shores where it was entangled in the branches of a tamarisk tree that grew on the outskirts of the ancient city of Byblos.

The growth of the tree was dramatically enhanced by the presence of the chest containing the decomposing body of Osiris and soon it completely obscured the dead king's coffin. The king of Byblos caught sight of the fabulous tree and ordered it felled to serve as a mighty pillar for his new palace.

Using magic, a mourning Isis had learned the fate of her husband. She traveled to Byblos where she disguised herself as a maid to the queen and tended to the royal couple's children. The enchanting story is told that each night while everyone slept, Isis transformed herself into a swallow and swooped around the magnificent pillar, grieving for her husband. Eventually, she broke down and revealed her poignant tale to the queen of Byblos. Taking pity on her, the queen permitted Isis to release the chest from the wooden pillar.

Knowing the danger, Isis cast a spell to hide the chest from further malevolent forces. But Seth had no intention of allowing Isis her small victory. Practicing his own magic, he discovered the secret hiding place of the chest, broke it open, and removed Osiris's body. Dismembering his brother's corpse into fourteen parts, he scattered the remains across Egypt. When Isis discovered this latest treachery, she built a boat of papyrus and sailed along the Nile, scouring the river banks for the remnants of her dead husband. Everywhere she found a body part she built a tomb. His head became the central relic of the royal city of Abydos. Her husband's penis had been swallowed by a fish, but Isis would not be deterred from her mission to completely reassemble his body. So, she called upon the god of science, Thoth, to fashion an artificial penis. With the body completely restored Isis copulated with the corpse and eventually gave birth to a son, Horus, who like his father was said to emit a *shining radiance.*

Horus inherited his mother's determination and when he came of age avenged his father's murder by killing Seth.

Egyptian myths tell us that the circle was completed when Horus died and was resurrected as Osiris. Indeed, the elaborate process of mummification was invented by the god Anubis to preserve the mutilated body of Osiris.[11] From that time forward, in honor of the two dead, every pharaoh was known as Horus while he ruled. After the pharaoh joined the spirits of the dead among the stars of the constellation of Orion he would be renamed Osiris.

The story of Osiris and his hatred of his uncle, Seth, inspired Reuel. The depiction of one brother's sly use of magic to kill another spoke directly to his obsession. He identified with Horus, the son who had avenged his father's shame. The image of the shining faces of Horus and Osiris would haunt Reuel until the day he could transform that dazzling image into his own.

The Osiris myth provided Reuel with a blueprint for murder.

THE FIRST EGYPTIAN MAGICIANS

Our earliest glimpse into the world of the Egyptian magician comes from a time when Semitic-speaking invaders known as the Hyksos

ruled Egypt. We owe the Hyksos dynasty a debt of gratitude for preserving a record of critical events that otherwise might have been lost
forever. Housed in Berlin and known as the Papyrus Westcar, this
fragile, ancient document recounts a conversation held many centuries
earlier between King Kheops, the ruler of Egypt for whom the Great
Pyramid was built, and his three sons. Its pages depict early examples of
the art of illusion. Each tale is introduced by one of Kheops's three sons.
And each tells a story about a famous "chief kherheb" (the Egyptian
name for magician).

The eldest son introduces the collection with the tale of a waxen
crocodile that the chief kherheb, Ubaoner, brought to life before it
seized its victims and pulled them under water. The middle son speaks
of the time when the chief kherheb, Zazamonkh, *parted the waters* of
a lake to retrieve a pendant lost overboard from the royal boat. Finally,
the youngest son tops his brothers' tales by telling their father he knows
of a living kherheb by the name of Dedi, who was just as gifted as these
dead renowned magicians. Historians of illusion have crowned Dedi the
First Magician because of his famous beheading trick.

> And his majesty said: "Is it true, what is said, that thou canst put on
> again a head once cut off?" And Dedi said: "Yea, that I can, O king,
> my lord." And his majesty said: "Have brought unto me a prisoner
> that is in the prison, that his punishment may be inflicted." And
> Dedi said: "But not on a man, O king, my lord! Lo, is not such a
> thing rather commanded to be done to the august cattle." And a
> goose was brought unto him, and its head was cut off; and the goose
> was placed on the western side of the hall, and its head on the east-
> ern side of the hall. And Dedi said his say of magic, and thereupon
> the goose stood up and waddled, and its head likewise. Now when
> one part had reached the other, the goose stood up and cackled.[12]

Restoring the head of a goose was one thing because to humans, of
course, all geese look pretty much the same! A beheaded goose replaced
by a live bird would go unnoticed by most observers. Not so with a

human victim. The fact that Dedi avoided performing his trick on people indicates to historians of magic that the Papyrus Westcar was more than just a collection of fanciful stories. It details the acts of illusion that magicians of the time exploited to ensure their esteemed position.

If the art of illusion is traceable to the time of the construction of the Great Pyramid, as is suggested in the Papyrus Westcar, then Egyptian magicians had enjoyed a long tradition in which to perfect their sleight of hand. A young man named Reuel, the nephew of Israel and future father-in-law of Moses, eagerly drew upon that tradition of a thousand years' duration as he honed his skills as an illusionist in the aid of his lifelong ambition for revenge.

CONFEDERATES

Reuel absorbed every trick that the master magicians could teach him. This arsenal of magic served as his ultimate means to murder Moses. All he needed to complete his deadly plan were a few trusted confederates. He chose them carefully; looking for those who possessed strong agendas of their own that he could manipulate to his advantage.

Among Reuel's key co-conspirators were Levi, Dinah, and Benjamin. Reuel provided them with "legends" and eventually ensnared them in his long-simmering plan to usurp the mantle of "leader of the Jews" from Moses. After he robbed Moses of his power and his very life he transformed the renowned leader's image into that of an angry, newly articulate, and veiled prophet.

But who was the man that Reuel brutally murdered?

Who was the first Moses?

Did his enigmatic story begin, as is commonly thought, with his birth to a Jewish mother?

Or was he, as Sigmund Freud believed, born with all the advantages of a full-blooded Egyptian coursing through his veins?

4

———•———

Deceit and Disguise

And Joseph knew his brethren, but they knew not him.

GENESIS 42:8.

Reuel's scheme relied upon two people—a brother and sister. Dinah was Israel's only daughter. Her disgrace set the stage for Reuel's cleverly planned conspiracy.

After Israel and his family had finally passed through the dangerous territory of Edom into drought-ridden Canaan he found himself with a young and naive daughter on his hands who longed to trade her predictable life of herding animals and tending flocks for more urban delights. Consumed with curiosity the rebellious teenager slipped out of camp to visit the local village.

Dinah's beauty soon captured the attention of Shechem whose "soul clave unto Dinah" and "he loved the damsel."[1] He "saw her, he took her, and lay with her, and defiled her."[2] Shechem pleaded with his father, Hamor, to negotiate with Dinah's father, Israel, to permit a marriage.

When Hamor approached him Israel "held his peace"[3] until he had a chance to consult with his elder sons. As Hamor feared, when they heard about their sister's sexual encounter they "were grieved, and they were very wroth." It was a thing that "ought not to be done."[4] Hamor tried to calm the volatile situation by offering the outraged brothers friendship and land. Israel was prepared to listen, but his sons rejected the bribery outright. Fearing that their father would reach an agreement despite their objections they threw out another challenge, "We cannot do this thing, to give our sister to one that is uncircumcised."[5] They proposed a bold compromise.[6] If Shechem, Hamor, and all the males of the village would submit to circumcision then they would "consent"[7] to Dinah's marriage.

Hamor agreed to the drastic measure and persuaded the other males of the village to endure the bloody procedure, leaving them weak and vulnerable to the brutal vengeance that followed: "And it came to pass on the third day, when they were sore, that two of the sons of Jacob, Simeon and Levi, Dinah's brethren, took each man his sword, and came upon the city boldly, and slew all the males. And they slew Hamor and Shechem his son with the edge of the sword, and took Dinah out of Shechem's house, and went out."[8]

Israel was livid that his sons had gone behind his back to murder in the name of their wounded pride. He knew that the inevitable wrath of Shechem's neighboring tribes would soon be felt. "And Jacob [Israel] said to Simeon and Levi, Ye have troubled me to make me to stink among the inhabitants of the land . . . they shall gather themselves together against me, and slay me; and I shall be destroyed, I and my house."[9] But his sons were unrepentant. One sneered, "should" Shechem "deal with our sister as with a harlot?"[10] This disrespect was a minor vice compared to the viciousness they had exhibited. But which son would have dared to defy their father with sarcasm? Levi the scribe was the more articulate of the two. It seems likely that he would be the most verbally defiant. Who was this man possessed of a razor tongue? And what part did he play in Reuel's dark conspiracy?

LEVI

Dinah's story reveals Levi's ruthless character. Determined to carry out his own agenda of murder he had avenged his sister without consulting her. We will never know the true nature of the relationship between

Dinah and Shechem because after this drama she disappears from the pages of the Torah. Or does she? As we will show there is reason to believe that Israel's daughter adopted a new identity, a new name, and a new elevated role among the children of Israel.

Levi is depicted as haughty, cruel, brutal, deceitful, hot-tempered, and sarcastic. Not exactly the traits expected of the founder of a priestly caste. How did such a scheming man become the forefather of the Levites, high priests of Israel? It's a question that has continually baffled biblical scholars.[11]

Levi's sarcasm speaks forcefully to his embittered nature. Perpetually full of rage he nurtured a special hatred for his half brother, Joseph. Joseph's rags-to-riches story has inspired thousands of imitations. He was Israel's eleventh son but the first child born to his adored wife Rachel. "Israel loved Joseph more than all his children, because he was the son of his old age: and he made him a coat of many colors."[12] This coat, symbolizing Joseph's special place in Israel's heart, inflamed the hatred of his other sons who "saw that their father loved him more than all of his brethren, they hated him, and could not speak peaceably unto him."[13]

Joseph threw fuel on the flames of their antagonism when he told his older brothers about a dream in which they all bowed before him. The brothers "hated him yet the more."[14] Someone (probably Levi) snapped, "Shalt thou indeed reign over us?"[15] Joseph, unperturbed, escalated the situation by relating another dream in which even "the sun and the moon and the eleven stars made obeisance to me."[16]

Shortly afterward Joseph's brothers guided the family's flock into the wild. When Joseph followed he became lost. A "certain man found him"[17] and pointed him in the right direction. Circumstantial evidence indicates that this "certain man" was Reuel.* By now, the elder brothers had reached the end of their patience with their arrogant sibling and rather than welcoming him back into their midst "they conspired

---

*The story involves both Midianites and Ishmaelites. Reuel was Ishmael's grandson and after he acquired his education in Egypt, he became the high priest of the Midianites. Reuel is the *only* character in the Torah to be simultaneously related to Midianites and Ishmaeli.

against him to slay him."[18] Levi, their likely spokesman,* said, "let us slay him, and cast him into some pit, and we will say, some evil beast devoured him." In a whisper he slyly adds, "and we shall see what will become of his dreams."[19]

Reuben, Israel's eldest son, didn't have the stomach for brazen murder, "Let us not kill him" he urged. His alternative was to "shed no blood, but cast him into this pit."[20] The others reluctantly agreed and, stripping Joseph of his prized multicolored coat, tossed the seventeen-year-old into the pit. When Joseph cried out, the guilty brothers "saw the anguish of his soul, when he besought us, and we would not hear."[21]

Unexpectedly, a company of Midianite merchants came upon the scene. Israel's fourth son, Judah, took the opportunity to finesse their crude plan by suggesting that they sell Joseph into slavery to profit from his disappearance. The brothers negotiated a deal with the Midianites, who pulled Joseph from the pit and later sold him to Ishmaelite traders for "twenty pieces of silver."[22] The Ishmaelites then resold Joseph to the Egyptians.

Reuben secretly returned to the pit, possibly with the intention of freeing Joseph but he was gone. Rejoining the others, he despaired, "The child is not; and I, whither shall I go?"[23] As the eldest son, Reuben was justifiably afraid that his father would hold him responsible for Joseph's failure to return. His entire future was at stake, leaving him vulnerable to Levi's latest scheme, which was to pretend that Joseph had died as the result of "some evil beast" that had "devoured him." Reuben had little choice but to go along with the lie.

The brothers wasted no time smearing goat's blood over Joseph's discarded coat before breaking the news to their father about his favorite son's "disappearance."

The image of that blood-spattered coat haunted Israel. "This have we found: know now whether it be thy son's coat or no,"[24] Levi†

---

*Neither Reuben nor Judah ever said a sarcastic word in the whole Torah. Levi and/or Simeon were sarcastic when they retorted to Israel's scolding about the rape of Dinah saying: "Should he deal with our sister as with a harlot?" Genesis 34:31.

†The text doesn't name the speakers in the pit/slavery incident. This is a clue, as we will see, to the motives of the editors of the Torah. It seems likely Levi was the speaker since he was the son most practiced in deception.

prodded. As expected, Israel cried, "It is my son's coat; an evil beast hath devoured him."[25]

Full of hypocrisy, the elder sons tried to console their father but "he refused to be comforted" saying, "I will go down into the grave unto my son mourning."[26] Joseph's mother, Rachel, wept uncontrollably over the loss of their love child. They had waited so long for him. Now he was gone. But not as permanently as they had been cruelly led to believe.

JOSEPH AND POTIPHAR

Joseph had been sold to Potiphar, a high-ranking Egyptian who gradually came to have great respect for his exceptional slave. A Jewish folktale suggests that the young captive's expertise in the use of hypnotism helped him gain such unusual favor with his powerful master:

> One day, whilst Joseph was waiting upon his master, the latter noticed how Joseph's lips were moving silently, and he suspected his servant of being a magician and preparing to cast a spell upon his master.
>
> "What is the meaning of the whispering," cried Potiphar, "dost thou intend to make use of occult arts against me, and to bring magic into Egypt, the land of magic and magicians?"
>
> "Far be it from me," replied Joseph, "to do such a thing."
>
> "Then why are thy lips moving silently?" asked Potiphar, still suspicious.
>
> "I am praying to my God," said Joseph, "imploring Him to make me find favor in thine eyes."
>
> It happened that Potiphar once asked his perfect servant to bring him a cup of hot water, and Joseph hastened to comply with his master's request. Potiphar took the cup and said "I have made a mistake, for it is a cup of tepid water I really want."
>
> And Joseph replied: "The water is tepid, as my master desires."
>
> Potiphar dipped his finger in the water, and behold it was tepid indeed. Potiphar wondered greatly and made up his mind to test Joseph's powers even further.

"It is not water at all I wanted, but a glass of mixed vermouth."

"If my master will drink from the cup in his hand he will find that it contains mixed vermouth," said Joseph.

Potiphar drank, and to his amazement found that the cup really contained a delicious wine. Continuing to Joseph he said again:

"I would rather have absinthe mixed with wine."

And Joseph replied: "My master has only to drink from the cup to find that it contains absinthe mixed with wine."

And indeed, Potiphar convinced himself that the cup Joseph had brought him contained absinthe mixed with wine.

Continuing his test, Potiphar again said: "It is spiced wine I would rather drink," and once more he discovered that his cup contained spiced wine. And when he saw that God was clearly on Joseph's side, and fulfilled all his desires, he honored him greatly, taught him all the liberal arts, and placed before him better fare than the food offered to the other slaves. He also placed the keys of all his possession and treasures in Joseph's hand, appointing him his chief steward.[27]

Under the spell of hypnotism, "A profoundly responsive subject hears, sees, feels, smells, and tastes in accordance with the hypnotist's suggestions."[28]

The Egyptians practiced hypnotism for centuries before the time of Reuel. The earliest evidence of its use comes from an Egyptian papyrus dating from 1552 BCE—one of the oldest medical texts in existence. "In the Ebers Papyrus, a treatment was described in which the physician placed his hands on the head of the patient and claiming superhuman therapeutic powers gave forth with strange remedial utterances which were suggested to the patients, and which resulted in cures."[29]

Some three hundred years later, the Egyptian priests introduced "Sleep Temples" in which patients were treated with the art of suggestion. Unlike Western holy men, who were warned against such indulgences by the Church, the priests of ancient Egypt enthusiastically embraced hypnotism and probably advanced the art well beyond what we have achieved in the last century and a half—the short time that the West has hesitantly experimented with hypnotism.

JOSEPH THE NARCISSIST

Jacob and Rachel spoiled their only son, Joseph. He was special. He was gifted. He was so much better than Leah's sons, his older half brothers. This upbringing turned him into what today we would call a narcissist: a person with "a pervasive pattern of grandiosity, need for admiration, and a lack of empathy."[30] Is this an apt description of Joseph? Certainly, his brothers thought so. And he was a narcissist possessed of a rare skill; the use of the subtle and potent weapon of hypnotism.

Even such a prominent and powerful figure as Potiphar was brought under the sway of the young man from the east. Joseph eventually usurped every aspect of Potiphar's life and ultimately became the master of his master. Potiphar was so entranced that "he knew not ought he had, save the bread which he did eat."[31] Potiphar was not the only member of the family mesmerized by this strange slave. His wife became sexually obsessed with Joseph: "And it came to pass after these things, that his master's wife cast her eyes upon Joseph; and she said, Lie with me. But he refused."[32]

Joseph's refusal only whetted her interest. After arranging for all the other men and servants to be absent, Potiphar's wife again tried to seduce her husband's servant. Once more he spurned her. This time her passion turned to rage, and she charged Joseph with rape. Joseph had made a big mistake. Upon hearing his wife's wailing, Potiphar was shaken from his trance and "his wrath was kindled."[33]

PRISON

Potiphar threw Joseph into prison. But once again he succeeded in casting his amazing charisma over those around him. By exercising his powers of astute observation and his keen instinct for survival, Joseph worked his magic on the Keeper of the Prison and effectively seized control of the jail. He made it his business to befriend new prisoners and earned a valuable reputation as an interpreter of dreams; a talent that was considered priceless.

He discovered that the pharaoh's butler was a fellow inmate and successfully impressed him by predicting that his dreams meant that he would shortly be released; probably a tale he repeated to all the prisoners sentenced to death. If they believed him he succeeded in calming their worries and eliminating behavioral problems. Many probably went to their deaths convinced that they would be spared at the last minute just as Joseph had predicted. And the few who were released became his enthusiastic supporters. This strategy eventually paid high dividends. Before the pharaoh's butler was freed, Joseph planted an autosuggestion: "think on me when it shall be well with thee," he murmured.[34]

JOSEPH AND THE PHARAOH

After the pharaoh suffered two deeply disturbing dreams about the dire fate of the precious corn crop so crucial to his realm's survival he turned to the court magicians to interpret his haunting visions. But the experts were bereft of answers. Their failure, combined with the butler's newly improved circumstances, triggered his memory of the talented Hebrew slave and his canny ability to interpret dreams. He told the pharaoh about the imprisoned man's amazing abilities.

Joseph was promptly summoned to an audience with Egypt's leader. It didn't take long for the pharaoh to become ensnared by Joseph. The stranger from the east offered a logical explanation for his troubling dreams. Seven years of plentiful crops would be followed by seven years of famine and drought.

Joseph advised the pharaoh to store food during the coming years of plenty to ensure a reserve when any deadly famine struck. The pharaoh recognized wise advice when he heard it and immediately appointed his former prisoner to a position of high authority.

Joseph's meteoric rise to power came despite the fact no one could possibly know if his dream interpretations were correct. Seven years of plenty and at least one year of famine had to pass before the prophecy could be tested. This suggests that Joseph had hypnotized the most powerful man alive and lulled him into a vulnerable state of extreme suggestibility.

Is this story of dreams and the malleability of a powerful mind merely a myth? Or is it a phenomenon with roots that lie tangled around a common human weakness?

Even in our times the rich, famous, and influential are often surrounded by sycophants. They can develop a blind spot when a person with Joseph's kind of unbridled entitlement crosses their path. They can even find the experience refreshing in contrast to the kowtowing attitudes of their usual entourage. Always in control themselves, they can dangerously underestimate the ruthlessness of their new friends.

The pharaoh was considered literally a god. To look him directly in the eye could result in death. This made him vulnerable to a stranger who not only didn't hesitate to meet his gaze but showed no fear. And once invited in, the narcissist can subsume the life of his victim. At first the two unusual partners dance the dance of equals. But before long the original positions of power are reversed. All the benefits of power, glory, and fame that the narcissist believes they were born to assume are leached from their more influential mark.

Tales like that of the young Hebrew slave rising to become Egypt's highest-ranking official are staples of other times and places. Rasputin (1872–1916) entranced the royal family of Russia, eventually rising to an unprecedented position of influence for a commoner. His gift for hypnotism convinced a vulnerable Tsarina Alexandra that he held the cure to her only son's life-threatening hemophilia. Eventually, his dominant sway helped topple the Russian royal family.

Rasputin and Joseph were entirely different characters, but they demonstrate how even the most untouchable can fall prey to the influence of a canny narcissist who can expertly wield the little understood and underappreciated art of hypnotics.

DISGUISE

The drought and famine that Joseph had predicted did devastate the entire Middle East. But Egypt, with its plentiful storage of food, remained an oasis in the bleak desert of mass starvation. In Canaan, Israel and his family grew desperate for food. He was forced to send ten sons to Egypt to seek relief: "Behold, I have heard that there is corn in Egypt: get you down thither, and buy for us from thence; that we may live, and not die."[35]

By this time, Joseph's mother, Rachel, had died giving birth to another son whom she called Benoni, meaning "son of my sorrow."[36] But Israel changed the boy's name to Benjamin, meaning "son of the right hand,"[37] which indicated his most favored status. Despite his delight in this new arrival, Israel had never forgotten Joseph and suspected that Reuben, Simeon, Levi, and Judah might have had a hand in his disappearance. So, when he was forced to send them to Egypt he refused to let Benjamin accompany them, "Lest peradventure mischief might befall him."[38]

By now Joseph was the governor of a province that lay at the eastern entrance of Egypt. New arrivals from Canaan had to travel through this territory. When the brothers who had tried to kill him arrived, Joseph hid his shock and coolly and cleverly adopted a disguise. He made "himself strange to them"[39] and enjoyed the satisfaction of watching as his hated brothers "bowed down themselves before him with their faces to the earth"[40] just as he had predicted in the dreams that had enraged them. When the moment passed he promptly accused them of being spies and threw them into jail where they were left to their misery for three days. Spies, then as now, could be subject to torture and were frequently executed. From Joseph's perspective, a few days of terror were mild punishment for those who had plotted to leave him to die a lingering death in a pit before condemning him to an expected short and brutal life as an Egyptian slave.

Time was on Joseph's side. He spent it devising a plot of his own. He had learned that his mother had died giving birth to Benjamin and that his father had forbidden his half brothers to take this new favorite to Egypt. Having nearly died at the hands of these men, Joseph was determined to secure the safety of his younger brother, a boy he had never met. First, he had to break up the cold-blooded team of Simeon and Levi. Second, he must test the trustworthiness of the others.

With these objectives in mind, Joseph had them hauled before him. He used an interpreter to mask his fluent Hebrew. This clever ploy also gave him extra time to carefully consider his responses to their quivering statements. Reuben expressed shame for what they had done to Joseph saying in Hebrew to his brothers, "Spake I not unto you, saying, Do not sin against the child; and ye would not hear?"[41] This was the first indication of guilt from any of them. No doubt Joseph scanned the reactions of his other brothers for a response to Reuben's confession.

Joseph renewed his torture of his enemies. He announced, again through the interpreter, that they could return to Canaan with plenty of corn to satiate the family's hunger. But there was a shocking caveat to his life-saving offer. He "took from them Simeon, and bound him before their eyes."[42] Jewish folklore claims it was Simeon who had thrown the young Joseph into the pit;[43] the logic of revenge demanded an "eye for an eye." Simeon was taken hostage and Joseph declared that he would only be freed when Benjamin was brought to Egypt and presented to him.

This was an unexpected blow to Levi. He was close to Simeon. One can imagine him frantically urging the brothers to race back to Canaan so that they could gain Simeon's release. Speed was imperative because Simeon was being left behind without access to food.* Any delay and he would starve; exactly the kind of cruel death planned for Joseph when Simeon cast him into the pit. When the brothers arrived home and told their father about Simeon's deadly predicament they were shocked at his response. Israel accepted that his second-born son was as good as dead, "Simeon is not,"[44] and refused to send Benjamin to Egypt even if it meant the other son's slow death. Reuben made a valiant effort

---

*The text doesn't say this outright but the urgency with which Reuben and Judah pleaded with Israel to return to Egypt suggests that Simeon was in imminent danger of dying.

to persuade Israel to change his mind, ensuring Benjamin's safety by declaring, "Slay my two sons, if I bring him not to thee."[45] But even this gruesome guarantee failed. Israel retorted, "My son shall not go down with you; for his brother is dead, and he is left alone: if mischief befall him by the way in which ye go, then shall ye bring down my gray hairs with sorrow to the grave."[46]

Levi would have been devastated by his father's refusal to try and save his brother. He knew that if Reuben couldn't persuade Israel to change his mind then his own entreaties would be wasted.

Eventually as the last kernels of corn that the brothers had carried from Egypt were consumed everyone accepted that Simeon must have starved to death. It may have been Levi who persuaded Judah to try once again to change Israel's mind about taking Benjamin to Egypt as a human bargaining chip even though he had no realistic expectation that Simeon was alive. They could have traveled to Egypt and back again twice in the time that had elapsed: "surely now we had returned this second time."[47]

It was too late to save him. But now the life-giving corn was used up and the children of Israel again faced starvation. So, armed with a new argument Judah tried to move his father's cold heart: "And Judah said unto Israel his father, Send the lad with me, and we will arise and go; that we may live, and not die, both we, and thou, and also our little ones. I will be surety for him; of my hand shalt thou require him: if I bring him not unto thee, and set him before thee, then let me bear the blame for ever."[48]

A desperate Israel was forced to relent. Things had changed for the worse. Now they all faced death from hunger. Once again, the brothers set out for Egypt; this time Benjamin was with them.

Upon arriving in Egypt, they immediately asked for a meeting with the mighty governor. Still unaware that it was Joseph who held this esteemed position they were disturbed when a butler invited them to dine with his Egyptian master. It was unprecedented. Egyptians never dined with foreigners. They were uneasy and suspicious, fearing that they might be poisoned. The story of the brothers' return to Egypt with

Benjamin is an established part of the ancient oral tradition.* But we suspect that one phrase was inserted by the Priests serving the agenda of their ancestor, Levi. It reads, "And he" (meaning Joseph) "brought Simeon out unto them."[49]

The text is ambiguous. It doesn't say, "a weak and exhausted Simeon was retrieved from the dungeon." Nor is there any rejoicing that Simeon was still alive after the brothers' long "lingering" in Canaan during which time they could have twice traveled the distance to and from Egypt. Instead, we are left with a bare statement. Was Simeon alive? Or was it a corpse that Joseph presented to them?

Circumstantial evidence strongly suggests that Simeon died as a hostage. He is conspicuously absent from any future accounts. Unlike Reuben, Judah, and the other children of Israel who received rich tracts of the Promised Land, his tribe didn't receive any land. Instead, Simeon's descendants are forced to live under the protection of Judah. It seems that Simeon must have been dead. This fact, we suggest, was something the Priests† censored from the written record because it revealed Levi's powerful motive for acting against Joseph.

Joseph was overcome with emotion when he saw Benjamin for the first time. The long delay in his brother's return may have convinced him that Benjamin had been killed in revenge for Simeon's fate. Joseph left his brothers and temporarily retreated into another chamber to collect his thoughts. He wept,‡ washed his face, and returned to the room

---

*Author's note: This story consists of **E**, **J**, and **JE** of the documentary hypothesis, in which various passages of the Torah are thought to have been written/edited by various authors at different times; these passages are designated accordingly as **E** (oral stories by Hebrews who called God by the name "Elohim"), **J** (non-Levite sources, product of an Edomite scribe), and **JE** (the earliest source). These are also called the "Epic" sources. See appendix 2 for more in-depth discussion of the documentary hypothesis.

†The word *Priest* with a capital *P* refers to the scribes descended from Levi. They held Levi in high regard and constantly tried to enhance his stature by adding text, deleting text, and changing the order of events. Henceforth the term *Priests* is used in this book in the same manner the letter **P** is used by biblical scholars who adhere to the documentary hypothesis. See appendix 2.

‡Joseph's weeping suggests empathy that is uncharacteristic of a narcissist. But was he crying for Benjamin or for himself?

where his uneasy siblings waited. Then he astonished them by offering them bread, "because the Egyptians might not eat bread with the Hebrews; for that is an abomination unto the Egyptians. And they sat before him, the firstborn according to his birthright, and the youngest according to his youth: and the men marveled one at another. And he took and sent messes unto them from before him: but Benjamin's mess was five times so much as any of theirs. And they drank, and were merry with him."[50]

JUDAH'S REDEMPTION

Joseph wasn't finished with his disguise. Although he had discovered that Reuben felt guilty about abandoning him to a life of slavery, he wanted to further test the brothers by laying a final trap. He gave them the corn they so desperately needed but had his men secretly plant a precious "silver cup" inside the sack of corn carried on Benjamin's donkey. As they were crossing the Egyptian border Joseph's men swept down upon the brothers, accusing them of theft. Indignantly, they defended their honor, "With whomsoever of thy servants it be found, both let him die, and we also will be my lord's bondmen."[51] When the silver cup was found on Benjamin's donkey the brothers were rounded up and returned to Egypt.

Once again, the sons of Israel found themselves bowing at the Egyptian governor's feet in fear for their lives. Joseph demanded, "What deed is this that ye have done?"[52] As spokesman, a bewildered Judah asked, "How shall we clear ourselves?"[53] Joseph remained silent. Judah begged for a private audience, pleading that if Benjamin should die then their father would soon follow him to the grave, "For how shall I go up to my father, and the lad be not with me? Lest peradventure I see the evil that shall come on my father."[54] He threw himself on the Egyptian's mercy, offering to take any punishment if the governor would free Benjamin.

Judah's courage persuaded Joseph that it was time to reveal his identity. "I am Joseph," he said, "doth my father yet live? And his brethren could not answer him; for they were troubled at his presence."[55] They had good reason to be troubled, but Joseph assured his brothers that they had been forgiven. He kissed each of them. No doubt Reuben felt released from his shame. We can also imagine Judah's relief that he would not be sentenced to life as a slave in Egypt for Benjamin's "crime" of possessing the "stolen" silver cup. But it is difficult to see Levi embracing Joseph. He had shown no remorse or pity for Joseph's ordeal. And now, with Simeon's death, he had even more reason to hate Joseph. But Levi was in no position to challenge him. Yet.

Levi's archenemy had saved the tribe. The Priests subsequently airbrushed any reference to his explosive reaction when he understood that all Joseph's prophetic dreams of glory had come true. His despised brother, draped in deceit and disguise had risen to the top. These bitter lessons forever doomed Levi's relationship with Joseph's son; a man who was to become the most iconic of all the prophets—Moses.

THE FAMILY TREE

In the Torah, the artificial family tree constructed by the Levites contradicts common sense. As shown in table 4.1, Moses's family tree, according to the Levite scribes, states that he married a woman (Zipporah) from his grandfather's generation.

TABLE 4.1. DESCENDANTS OF ABRAHAM ACCORDING TO THE LEVITES

	By Hagar	By Sarah
1st generation	Ishmael	Isaac
2nd generation	Bashemath	Jacob (Israel)
3rd generation	Reuel	Levi
4th generation	Zipporah	Kohath
5th generation		Amram
6th generation		Moses

According to the Priests, Moses was born six generations after Abraham and married Reuel's daughter, Zipporah, from the fourth generation. Not likely. Even by biblical standards. Nor can the simple insertion of two additional generations account for the extra 430 years of Egyptian bondage that the Levite scribes claim that their ancestors endured. In their account Moses's father lived centuries before the prophet was born.

In contrast to this artificial family tree, if Moses was the son of Joseph he would then be a natural contemporary of his wife, Zipporah.

TABLE 4.2. DESCENDANTS OF ABRAHAM ACCORDING TO EGYPTIAN AND ROMAN SOURCES

	By Hagar	By Sarah
1st generation	Ishmael	Isaac
2nd generation	Bashemath	Jacob (Israel)
3rd generation	Reuel	Joseph
4th generation	Zipporah	Moses

Moses's family tree, as recorded by ancient Egyptian and Roman sources, reveals that the prophet married a woman (Zipporah) from his own generation.

JOSEPH'S SON

The idea that Moses was the son of Joseph comes with an ancient pedigree.

Apollonius Molon (fl. 70 BCE) was a Greek rhetorician whose pupils included Cicero and Julius Caesar. He claimed that "Moses was third from Joseph, which may mean 'third son' or 'the grandson of Joseph.'"[56] The Roman historian Marcus Junianus Justinus (third century CE) declares it as a well-known fact that Moses was the third son of Joseph in his *Epitome,* an abridgment of a lost book written by Pompeius Trogus.* Four

---

*Pompeius Trogus's father was a secretary to Julius Caesar and his grandfather gained Roman citizenship serving under Pompey. Pompeius Trogus lived in the time of Augustus and made his living writing histories.

centuries earlier (in the first century BCE) Trogus had recorded Joseph's time in Egypt during which he "gave his mind eagerly to the magic arts of the place"[57] and "made himself master of the arts of magic."[58] And he adds a rare reference to his son's physical appearance; he was handsome like his father, "His son was Moses, who in addition to the inheritance of his father's wisdom, received also great beauty of person."[59]

Where did Trogus get the idea that Moses was Joseph's son? It seems probable that the Roman scholar had come across the works of Egypt's most famous historian, Manetho. Writing three centuries before the birth of Christ, Manetho's book, *Aegyptiaca,* was a primary source for all ancient scholars studying in Egypt. Unfortunately, only fragments of the document have survived. The short passages relating to Moses come to us from a scholar who was hostile to its contents—the Jewish historian Josephus (c. 37–100 CE).

It seems that Josephus disapproved of elements of the Egyptian story and had no compunction in censoring them. For example, he was hostile to the idea that Moses and Joseph lived at about the same time and criticized the Egyptian librarian Cheremon (fl. first century CE) for holding this belief.[60] *This is a critical point.* The entire foundation of the Hebrew Priests' account of Moses's life rests upon the assumption that the prophet and Joseph lived in different centuries and were not related to each other. The Priests desperately wished to suppress the truth of Moses's paternity because they wanted to claim the famous prophet as one of their own: a Levite, a descendant of Levi.

Manetho's account of Moses is the only Egyptian story about him that survives. The Romans who read it concluded that Moses was Joseph's son. Unlike us, they had the benefit of access to the entire text of *Aegyptiaca.* We can dream that the complete text of *Aegyptiaca* may one day be recovered but for now, we can only rely upon the fragments that Josephus reproduced to understand the Egyptian's view of Moses. Even these remnants reveal evidence that strongly suggests that the Romans got it right when they concluded that Moses was Joseph's third son.

Manetho was a priest of Heliopolis (city of the sun) where Joseph's wife and stepfather had lived centuries earlier. His legacy to Egyptology is his idea of dividing Egyptian history into thirty dynasties beginning with a mythical past full of gods and goddesses and continuing until 323 BCE. These dynastic divisions, with minor modifications, have become the standard time scale used by modern Egyptologists.

Manetho depicted Moses as the leader of a band of lepers who revolted against the Egyptian authorities. If Manetho was fabricating lies about Moses, as Josephus accuses, it seems unlikely that he would claim Moses as a priest of his own order (Heliopolis). If he was creating fiction he would not cast Moses in such an unflattering light. We are confronting a slice of history here, not myth.

Belittling the Egyptian historian, Josephus says that Manetho "introduces incredible narrations, as if he would have the Egyptian multitude, that had the leprosy and other distempers, to have mixed with us, as he says they were, and that they were condemned to fly out of Egypt together."[61] Manetho relates that Moses led the lepers, who were *forced to flee,* out of Egypt—a very different scene from the biblical account in which Moses pleads with the pharaoh to let his people go.

At the time the word *leper* held other connotations besides medical. It also denoted ancient beliefs that were considered corrupted or infected. The charge of leprosy against the followers of Moses could well have been rhetorical: referring to their unacceptable beliefs rather than their health. From Manetho's Egyptian perspective, the Jewish exodus was not a noble journey of former slaves seeking justice and freedom in a new land but rather an ignoble expulsion of unruly rebels who held dangerous views. One belief was considered particularly dangerous—monotheism. The belief that there was only one God was associated with the unpopular reign of the Pharaoh Akhenaten.

Moses was raised as a priest in his mother's city of Heliopolis where centuries later Manetho also practiced as a priest and scribe. It was under the influence of the priests of Heliopolis that the Pharaoh Akhenaten developed the idea of a single god who was symbolized by the rays of the sun. Freud believed that Akhenaten's monotheism had been preserved by the priests of Heliopolis and passed to Moses who in turn became the agent who spread this radical concept to the Jews. Freud wrote that the "kernel" of his thesis was "the dependence of Jewish monotheism on the monotheistic episode in Egyptian history."[62] It seems likely to us that Moses adopted monotheism because of his Egyptian education in the very temple where the idea originated—Heliopolis. Freud never recognized that Moses was Asenath's son. Had he done so then his whole theory about the prophet would have stood on firmer ground.

Conscious of the fact that the Egyptians had repudiated Akhenaten's monotheism and made every attempt to stamp it out, Freud theorized that the idea was driven underground. Monotheism survived, possibly for centuries, among the "School of Priests at On from which it emanated."[63] In the Egyptian account, Moses was born into this priesthood. His grandfather, Potipherah, was the high priest of On.

The prophet-to-be hadn't known his father, Joseph, or his paternal grandfather, Israel. This left his maternal grandfather, Potipherah, as his only male role model. Freud thought that his theory that Moses had adopted monotheism from his Egyptian experience would be verified if there were evidence that Moses was a member of the school of On. He never discovered any proof connecting Moses with On. But we have uncovered Egyptian and Roman sources who claim Moses was not only a member of the school of On but was raised by its high priest, his grandfather. This places Moses firmly at the center of the birthplace of monotheism.

The death of Potipherah might have precipitated Moses's flight from Egypt or a change in leadership could have threatened his status. The Torah informs us, "Now there arose up a new king over Egypt, which knew not Joseph."[64] The new king might not have accepted a Hebrew son enjoying the privileges of the Egyptian priesthood. Whatever the reason, Moses no longer felt welcome.

Despite his exalted position, Moses had always sympathized with the common Hebrew workers. His father, after all, was a Hebrew.* In the Egyptian account, the lepers who worked the quarries revolted and "appointed themselves a ruler out of the priests of Heliopolis, whose

---

*Not a full-blooded Egyptian as Freud assumed.

name was Osarsiph, and they took their oaths that they would be obedient to him in all things."[65]

Osarsiph was a great lawgiver who "was by birth of Heliopolis, and his name Osarsiph from Osiris, who was the god of Heliopolis; but that when he was gone over to these people, his name was changed, and he was called Moses."[66]

Osarsiph "was by birth of Heliopolis" just as Moses would be if, as we propose, Asenath was his mother.

The name *Osarseph** combined the name of the Egyptian god, Osiris (Osar) and the Hebrew suffix (seph) of Joseph, which could translate to "the Hebrew son of Osiris." Osiris, in Egyptian mythology, was murdered by his brother. By naming her son after both Osiris and Joseph, Asenath was pointing an accusing finger at Levi—the man who had murdered her husband. She could hope that her son would one day avenge his father's death.

Manetho wrote that when Osarseph became the leader of the Jews, "his name was changed, and he was called Moses."[67] *Moses* meant "son of" in the Egyptian language; much like *MacDonald* in English means "son of Donald." Perhaps it was his striking resemblance to his father, Joseph, that inspired the people to call their new leader by the unusual title of "the son."

The Priests invented the four centuries of bondage in Egypt and perpetuated the myth that Moses and Joseph lived in different eras. They deployed this clever smokescreen to hide a determined agenda. Clear away the smoke and a new timeline emerges that exposes the true character of two powerful men, Reuel and Levi, who both had plenty of opportunity and more than enough willpower to murder Moses.

---

*Osarseph is sometimes spelled *Osarsiph* with an *i* rather than an *e*.

5

———•———

The Widow's Son

O my soul, come not thou into their secret.

GENESIS 49:6

When his sons finally returned to their native Canaan after their long absence in Egypt, Israel was fainthearted with joy to hear the miraculous news that Joseph was alive. As the carts loaded down with gifts from the long-lost son approached camp he celebrated, "It is enough; Joseph my son is yet alive: I will go and see him before I die."[1]

Ominously, the explosive subject of Simeon's fate isn't broached. Surely, Israel would want to know that his imprisoned son was safe? But there is no mention of a happy reunion between father and second son, strongly suggesting that Simeon was dead. This was a body blow for Levi. Sick with grief, he had to swallow his humiliation over unwittingly bowing before Joseph and fulfilling his younger brother's gloating prophecy. But the worst was yet to come. Soon Joseph and his father would be reunited after their long separation. It was only a matter of time before Levi's pivotal role in Joseph's disappearance would be exposed. Israel's inevitable eruption when Joseph revealed the truth about his brothers' collusion in his disappearance is censored from the Bible. The ever-vigilant Priests kept silent about their ancestor's cold betrayal.

Joseph's gifts were just the start of his generosity. Israel was thrilled to learn that his favorite son was bestowing fertile Egyptian land on his family. At last they were free from the threat of starvation and for the first time could enjoy freedom, peace, and prosperity.

But Israel's pleasure in this turn of fortune was short-lived. He was growing old. He summoned Joseph, his wife, and sons to a private meeting where he honored the sons, Manasseh and Ephraim, by adopting them. He assured Joseph that "thy issue, which thou begettest after them, shall be thine, and shall be called after the name of their brethren in their inheritance."[2]

Why was Israel so confident that Joseph and Asenath would have other children?

While other patriarchs had accurately prophesized the future, Israel was not so astute. He was continually overtaken by unforeseen events—from his mother's conspiracy to steal his father's final blessing from him to his miraculous reunion with Joseph. Perhaps the reason Israel was so confident in this case was because he knew that Asenath was pregnant. Her compensation for losing her first two sons to the "honor" of Israel's beneficence was a guarantee that her unborn child would be immersed in Egyptian ways and would bear an Egyptian name.

Indeed, Asenath's third son was given an Egyptian name—Moses, who as we have seen, rose to become a priest in the temple of Heliopolis where his mother was a priestess. *Asenath* means "devotee of Neith." Neith was an ancient Egyptian goddess dating back to the pre-Dynastic period. She was a war goddess and huntress whose regalia included a deshret, or red crown, which symbolized Lower Egypt and the fertile Nile basin. She brandished a bow and arrow, sometimes a harpoon, and was one of the first deities to create the world from self-generation. In the *Pyramid Texts* and the *Book of the Dead* Neith is depicted as playing an important role in funeral rites—firing arrows at evil spirits who threaten to disturb the safe passage of the dead to the afterlife. She also wears a veil. Like the masked Moses, no one ever sees her face. One of her epithets proclaims, "None ever uplifted my veil."[3]

Sigmund Freud was convinced that the story of Moses being born to a Levite woman was manufactured by the Priests to guarantee the prophet's Jewish credentials. "If," Freud argued, "we take seriously the conclusion that Moses was a distinguished Egyptian, then very interesting and far-reaching perspectives open out."[4] But Freud had missed an obvious conclusion. Asenath *was* indeed Moses's real mother. She was a priestess of the very city, Heliopolis ("On" of the Bible), where Freud believed renegade priests continued to practice the monotheistic religion of the long dead pharaoh, Akhenaten. It was from them, Freud argued, that Moses adopted the notion of a single god and spread the idea to the children of Israel.

Why didn't Freud realize that Moses was Asenath's son and its significance to the work he had obsessed over for decades? It was because he remained firmly in the grip of two strong misconceptions. First, he believed that Moses was a full-blooded Egyptian. This idea was central to his initial work on the subject and once adopted he never questioned this basic assumption. (We believe that Moses was the child of an Egyptian mother and a Jewish father.) The second reason Freud didn't see that Asenath was Moses's mother was because the Priests went to exceptional lengths to separate Moses, their most exalted prophet, from the House of Joseph. All the rights and privileges that they enjoyed in their elite positions as revered priests and scribes could be lost if it was discovered that Moses did not belong to the House of Levi.

It was critical that the Levite scribes conceal the fact that Moses was Joseph's third son. They accomplished this through two clever deceptions. First, they invented a dramatic story of 430 years of Egyptian bondage that served to conclusively separate Moses's lifetime from that of Joseph so that they could not be identified as contemporaries. If 430 years separated the two men, they could not possibly be father and son. Secondly, they fabricated a new genealogy for Moses that cut the prophet from his true heritage and pasted him into one that presented him as a distant descendant of their own ancestor Levi.

Freud recognized that one of the central problems with his theory was that he had no proof that Moses had ever even entered the temple at Heliopolis where Freud believed that a secret cult of priests continued to support Akhenaten's idea of a single god. Freud's problem disappears if Joseph was Moses's father because Joseph's wife was Asenath, a priestess of the temple. Indeed, as we have seen, Moses's only father figure when he was growing up was his maternal grandfather, who was the high priest of the Heliopolis temple. Moses, as we will see below, never knew his real father, Joseph.

Freud didn't recognize Moses's intimate connection with the Heliopolis temple because he accepted the story of 430 years of slavery, perhaps because his people were indeed facing slavery and worse in Nazi-occupied Europe. Had he questioned the four-century timeline then Freud might have been able to see what was clear to Egyptian and Roman writers: Moses was Joseph's son and was raised as a priest within the Heliopolis cult. If Freud had understood this he would have achieved the primary objective of his book, by showing "the dependence of Jewish monotheism on the monotheistic episode in Egyptian history."[5]

ISRAEL'S LAST WILL AND TESTAMENT

Israel's private meeting with Joseph's family was kept secret from the rest of the children of Israel. They had to wait until the public ceremony to hear the patriarch's last will and testament when he delivered their inheritances. He began harshly, characterizing his eldest son, Reuben, as "Unstable as water, thou shalt not excel; because thou wentest up to thy father's bed; then defilest thou it; he went up to my couch."[6]

Reuben was deprived of his birthright not because of his crimes against Joseph but because he had slept with Israel's third wife, Bilhah. But was it true? What evidence did Israel have? The text is suspiciously silent on the details. The Priests, whose loyalties lay with Levi, altered the story to depict Reuben as a son who cuckolded his father. But the real reason for Reuben's disinheritance, we suggest, was that the Priests wanted to excise any reference to Joseph's brutal treatment at the hands of his older brothers. That idea brushed too perilously close to the truth and revealed the brothers' later powerful motive to act against Moses—the son of their great enemy, Joseph. This secret the Priests would conceal at any price.

Instead, they played with the reasons for Israel's harsh judgment of Reuben, inventing a story of adultery by inserting the words, "Reuben went and lay with Bilhah his father's concubine: and Israel heard it."[7] Strangely, the words are inserted into a text that has nothing to do with Reuben and Bilhah. And no details are offered about Israel's response or Reuben's inevitable shame. That shame more probably originated from his involvement in the "disappearance" of Joseph than from sleeping with his father's wife.*

We can imagine Israel's angry words to Reuben:

You are my eldest son and should be the most responsible of my children, yet you failed to save Joseph. You always take the path of least resistance. Unstable as water—how can such a weak man become a leader? You will not receive my blessing. Just as you deprived me of the truth about Joseph's disappearance so now will I deprive you of your inheritance.

Whatever Israel said, and whatever the reasons he gave for his shocking disavowal of his son, the result was the same—Reuben was disinherited.

LEVI

Israel now turned his attention to Levi: "Simeon and Levi are brethren; instruments of cruelty are in their inhabitations. O my soul, come not thou into their secret; unto their assembly, mine honor, be not thou united: for in their anger they slew a man, in their self-will they digged down a wall. Cursed be their anger, for it was fierce; and their wrath, for it was cruel: I will divide them . . . and scatter them in Israel."[8]

It's likely that the Priests, seeking to deflect the historical burden

---

*Bilhah was originally Rachel's handmaid but was given to Israel to provide a surrogate child while Rachel herself was barren. Some researchers prefer the term *concubine* to apply to this arrangement. We use *wife*.

that was about to be dropped on their ancestor, inserted the name "Simeon" into Israel's rant. These harsh words not only disinherit Levi—they curse him; rendering him an open target who could be attacked at will without fear of reprisal. Even in his worst nightmares he never expected to become an *outlaw.** Israel rubbed salt into the wounds. He said to Joseph, "thy two sons, Ephraim and Manasseh, which were born unto thee in the land of Egypt before I came unto thee into Egypt, are mine; as Reuben and Simeon, they shall be mine."[9] Israel had dramatically broken with tradition and given Reuben's rich inheritance and Simeon's share of it to Joseph's sons!

Levi must have been livid. A new and compelling motive was added to his humiliation at being forced to bow to Joseph—revenge. His hate knew no limits. What were the consequences of this game-changing scene? How did Levi live with his all-consuming rage? We aren't told. Instead, we are led to believe that even after the reckless breaking of this traditional trust the children of Israel continued to live in peace and harmony.

When Israel died "Joseph fell upon his father's face, and wept upon him, and kissed him."[10] He then arranged for Egyptian physicians to perform the embalming. After forty days of mourning, the number allotted by Egyptian tradition, Joseph went before the pharaoh and pleaded, "My father made me swear," he said, "to bury him in Canaan," and "Now therefore let me go up, I pray thee, and bury my father."[11] The pharaoh replied, "Go up, and bury thy father."[12] Joseph led the caravan of grieving men, women, and children as they traveled with Israel's body across Egypt and into Canaan where he was probably laid to rest next to his beloved Rachel who had died years earlier giving birth to Benjamin. (Significantly, the Priests imply that Israel was buried next to their ancestral mother, Leah.)

Joseph had fulfilled the traditional duty for the son to bury the

---

*Most biblical scholars assume that Levi's disinheritance and disgrace was a result of his slaying of the helpless males of Shechem when they lay healing from being circumcised after Dinah had been "raped." Although that incident was horrible the real cruelty was Levi's treatment of Joseph. It is very telling that the Torah doesn't explore how Levi instigated the plot against Joseph. Certainly, Israel would have learned the truth from Joseph.

father. When his own time came he swore his brothers to a solemn oath, "God will surely visit you, and ye shall carry up my bones from hence"[13] and bury them in Canaan. Like his father, Joseph's body was embalmed and "put in a coffin in Egypt."[14] But unlike Israel, Joseph's corpse wasn't taken to Canaan by his sons after the traditional forty days of mourning. Instead, according to the Priests, his bones remained interred in an Egyptian coffin for more than four centuries until "Moses took the bones of Joseph with him"[15] when the Israelites embarked upon the exodus.

But it was only decades, not centuries, later that Moses took responsibility for Joseph's bones and by doing so identified himself as his son; not the impression perpetuated in the Torah. Instead, its pages depict merely a dutiful fulfillment by Moses of an ancient obligation to a long dead ancestor; a convenient smokescreen that further obscured the truth about Moses's true parentage.

THE LAST BOOK

Deuteronomy, in the so-called supplementary hypothesis, is now considered to be the oldest source.[16] As a result, Deuteronomy provides us with a valuable alternative explanation for certain events that occur in the early books of the Bible. Significantly, it flatly contradicts the Priestly statement, "And Joseph died, and all his brethren, and all that generation."[17] Near the end of Deuteronomy, Moses addresses the leaders of each of the tribes of Israel with the notable exception of Simeon— because, as we contend, he had died in Egypt. And significantly, when the Promised Land is finally conquered Simeon is never rewarded with life-giving land to nourish his tribe. Instead, his descendants were forced to live under the protection of Judah.

Immediately before ascending the mountain where he will die, Moses gives a farewell speech to the tribe. He begins, "Let Reuben live, and not die,"[18] obviously indicating that he was still alive. But according to the Priests, Reuben had been dead for four centuries before Moses was born. Why then would the prophet speak about Reuben as if he was ill but still very much alive? The answer is that the tale of 430 years of bondage was fiction.

We know Reuben recovered from his illness because his is the first territorial claim on the Promised Land. The children of Israel granted him this first son's privilege even though it contravened Israel's last will and testament, which had disinherited him. (If Reuben lived at the same time as Joseph and Moses then Josephus's mocking of the Egyptian librarian Cheremon's "mistake" in stating that Joseph and Moses lived during the same era was unfounded.)

Reuben was not the only one of the children of Israel who lived in the age of both Joseph and Moses—although some changed their names after they left Egypt.

LEVI'S DISGUISE

Moses's words to Levi are the most telling in his farewell speech. The weak spot in Levi's armor was the treacherous role that he had played when he urged his brothers to kill Joseph. About Levi and Simeon, Israel had said, "O my soul, come not thou into their secret . . ."[19] The "secret" that Levi didn't want exposed was that he had lied to his father about Joseph's fate.

In Deuteronomy Moses taunts Levi by revealing that he was the son "who said unto his father and mother, I have not seen him [Joseph]."[20] This charge was aimed at Levi personally and cannot be rationalized away, as some scholars do, by pretending that Moses's farewell speech was directed to the entire *tribe* of Levi. A tribe wouldn't say, "I have not seen him." These are the words of an individual.

And Moses said something else to Levi, something that reveals what happened long after the Israelites had fled from Egypt, "Let thy Thummim and thy Urim be with thy holy one, whom thou didst prove at Massah, and with whom thou didst strive at the waters of Meribah."[21] The words are enigmatic until we understand the context.

In Deuteronomy Moses is speaking to Levi *as if he is Aaron.* The phrase "thy Thummim and thy Urim" refers to two holy ceremonial objects that the high priest Aaron wore on his breastplate.[22] During the exodus, Aaron was the *only* person permitted to wear these relics. The Israelites arrived at Meribah at a time when, according to the Priests, Aaron was the high priest and a great drought held the land hostage. The tribe reproached Moses for having "brought us up out of Egypt,* to kill us and our children and our cattle with thirst."[23] His response was to strike a rock with his staff, releasing a miraculous flow of precious water. The prophet named the place *Meribah,*[24] which meant "tested" for it was here that the Israelite's faith in him had been challenged and reconfirmed.

The author of Deuteronomy assumes that Levi was the high priest at Meribah.

The Priests assume that Aaron was the high priest at Meribah.

Who is right? Which man was adorned with the ceremonial relics at Meribah? Both biblical sources can't be correct. Or can they?

What was the true relationship between Levi and Aaron? The answer to this critical question lifts the veil on one of the Priests' darkest secrets.

LEVI AND AARON

For centuries biblical scholars have puzzled over the relationship between Levi and Aaron. Julius Wellhausen (1844–1918) one of the founders of the "documentary hypothesis"[25] was confounded by the relationship between the two. Levi showed none of the honorable characteristics expected to be displayed by a founder of the priesthood. "There is not the faintest idea of Levi's sacred calling," Wellhausen wrote, for such "an extremely secular and blood-thirsty character."[26] And this is not the only deep mystery surrounding Levi and Aaron.

---

*Reuel was the high priest of Midian, which lay on the east side of the Gulf of Aqaba, neighboring Edom. We suggest that the expression "up out of Egypt" is an addition by the Levite scribes who wished to focus the story on the hated Egyptians. In our opinion, the expression originally read "up out of Midian." It seems likely that the Midianites had tired of receiving refugees from Egypt and drove Reuel and the children of Israel out of Midian. Their destination was the open lands of Canaan where a century-long drought was easing, and the new improved cisterns were making the land of Palestine a destination for refugees.

The Priests were obsessed with genealogy. They inserted long lists of descendants' names into the Torah, even if it meant breaking the natural flow of the stories.* According to these lists, Aaron was Levi's great-grandson. One of Levi's sons, Kohath, had a son named Amram, father of Aaron, Moses, and Miriam. But this artificial family tree doesn't hold up to scrutiny.† In Numbers, the Priests abruptly stop recording Aaron's descendants while continuing on with Levi's family tree. Aaron was an honored ancestor and high priest. Of all the people, the Priests should have wanted to record his descendants. "The failure to mention the clan of the descendants of Aaron," writes Harvard professor Frank Moore Cross, is "most curious."[27]

The reason for this convenient lapse is that Levi and Aaron are not two different people. They are the *same person* using different names.

Humiliated and disgraced by his father, Levi was an outcast—the children of Israel having been ordered to shun him.[28] How could he ever be a leader or enjoy priestly privileges under the auspices of his original, now disgraced, name? So, ever the pragmatist, Levi adopted a new identity as the high priest Aaron. In taking this bold move, he ripped a page from the book of his most hated enemy, Joseph. Levi had witnessed Joseph transform himself from an adolescent dreamer into an esteemed Egyptian leader—even relinquishing his Hebrew name in the process. The Egyptians knew him as *Zaphnath-paaneah*,[29] a name bestowed by the pharaoh meaning "revealer of secrets."[30] Joseph's change of name and identity had been successfully concealed from his brothers until the last possible moment. His identity change had given him total control over his destiny. And that of his enemies.

Levi not only reinvented himself, he took the lesson of Joseph's triumph a step so much further that it changed the historical record. While Joseph's role as an Egyptian governor had only a relatively short run, Levi remained in disguise as the High Priest Aaron for the rest of his life.

Identity change is one of the subterranean themes of the Torah.

---

*A fact that so annoyed Goethe.
†For instance, three generations is insufficient to account for 430 years between the death of Joseph and the birth of Moses.

Changing names was an Israeli custom, and still is to some extent. New settlers quickly Hebraize their names, and others select new names almost at will signifying qualities they admire or wish to possess. One joke suggests that the Israeli social register should be called "Who Was Who."[31] A change in name may be just as simple as that: the same person is called by another name. Jacob changed his to Israel. There is nothing suspicious or even unusual about it. What is more sinister is when the same character's identity change is hidden. Aaron was such a case. But he was not Israel's only child in desperate need of a new identity.

DINAH AND MIRIAM

In line with the barbaric custom of the time, Levi's sister Dinah had been disgraced when she was raped by Shechem. She isn't mentioned by Israel when he reveals his last will and testament even though, as his only daughter, she was entitled to a substantial dowry. She then disappears from the pages of the Torah.

But did she?

We suggest it is far more likely that Dinah followed her brother's example and changed her identity after the Israelites left Egypt. She eagerly shed her role of shamed victim and became "Miriam." As Miriam she was a "prophetess"[32] and adopted the persona of older sister to Moses. In fact, she was related to Moses. She just wasn't his sister—she was his aunt.

The Israelite women knew her real identity and accepted "Miriam" as the leader of "all the women." They felt sympathy and respect for her. She had suffered and might never marry because of her rape. As the prophetess, she plays an active role in the story of the exodus. In the Priest's fantasy, told in the second book of Exodus, Miriam is the caring sister who watches over the infant Moses as he drifts down the Nile in a woven basket. She intervenes with the pharaoh's daughter, assuring that Moses's Levite mother is hired as the baby's wet nurse.

After the children of Israel cross the sea, escaping the Egyptian armies, "Miriam, the prophetess, the sister of Aaron, took a timbrel in her hand; and all the women went out after her with timbrels and with dances."[33]

Later in the Torah, "Miriam and Aaron spake against Moses because of the Ethiopian woman whom he had married."[34] As punishment for this daring opposition, "Miriam was shut out from the camp seven days: and the people journeyed not till Miriam was brought in again."[35] The people loved their prophetess so much that they refused to leave camp until she returned safely from her desert banishment.

The eminent Israeli authority on biblical history Elias Auerbach (1882–1972) was skeptical about the relationship between Miriam and Moses. He notes that Miriam "is mentioned only in connection with Aaron." She "is called Aaron's sister, a curious designation. It eliminates not only the possibility that she was Moses's sister but also that Aaron was Moses's brother."[36]

Like Auerbach, we don't accept that Aaron and Miriam were Moses's brother and sister. That is a further fiction created by the Priests and designed to erase any evidence of Moses's lineage from the House of Joseph and place him firmly in their own House of Levi. The battle between these two houses continued long after the main characters were dead. The Priests tampered with the Torah—among other things designating new names for characters that would better fit their agenda: an agenda that would ensure glory was showered on their ancestors.

AFTER ISRAEL'S DEATH

When the children of Israel returned to Egypt after their father's burial, Joseph's brothers were troubled. "And when Joseph's brethren saw that their father was dead, they said, Joseph will peradventure hate us, and will certainly requite us all the evil which we did unto him."[37]

Without Israel's protection they feared that Joseph might take revenge. The situation is reminiscent of the scene in *The Godfather II* in which Michael Corleone discovers that his brother, Fredo, has betrayed him. As any movie fan knows, the scene takes place in Cuba on New Year's Eve, 1958, as Fidel Castro is about to seize power. The brothers are jostling among a drunken crowd in a Havana club when Fredo accidentally incriminates himself. When he realizes that he's been exposed

Fredo flees into the anonymity of the crowd rather than face Michael's wrath. Michael ostensibly forgives his older brother. But it's a ruse. He's only waiting for their mother to die before taking his revenge. After she's buried, Michael wastes no time in ordering Fredo's murder.

With Israel dead, Levi found himself in the same precarious situation. But Levi didn't make the same fatal mistake as the weak Fredo. He didn't linger, foolishly believing that Joseph would spare him. He was a man of swift action—having proven that by his violent reaction to Dinah's relationship with Shechem. At that time, defying his father's specific command, Levi had not hesitated to turn to his first problem-solving choice—murder.

We suggest that in this kill-or-be-killed situation, Levi resorted to type and struck first. Joseph's fate was sealed.

THE ASSASSINATION OF JOSEPH

Jewish folklore has preserved the colorful details of a plot to kill Joseph. The pharaoh's son was not only jealous of Joseph but desired his wife, Asenath. Before we explore the consequences of this triangle we must appreciate the unique role that folklore played in ancient Jewish society.

After the Promised Land was divided among the tribes of Israel, they enjoyed a short period of peace as a single nation. But soon the tribes who considered themselves loyal to the memory of Joseph formed a nation of their own that they called "Israel," which encompassed the northern half of the Promised Land. To the south lay another nation, Judah, named after Levi's brother. Even though they shared a common language and a common heritage the two nations held different theological points of view. They had their own priests, their own sacred places, their own rituals, and their own stories about the exodus.

For two centuries they lived peacefully alongside each other. Then in 722 BCE, armies from the Assyrian Empire, invading from the north, captured and destroyed Israel. This is the origin of the so-called ten lost tribes of Israel. Many were killed. Some were taken as slaves. But some escaped. A good number fled to Judah where they could still worship Yahweh and speak Hebrew. But there was a catch. Their nation status was gone. They were now the poor cousins having to rely upon the good will of the kings and priests of Judah.

The theological differences between the two peoples had been peacefully maintained, as long as Israel had retained its own territory. But now as war refugees the tribes from Israel, who held a special loyalty to the memory of Joseph, had to take a back seat to the theological supremacy of the Levite priests of Judah.

Judah, holding the refugees from Israel, continued as a nation for another century. It was during this time, with the priests of Judah enforcing their theological view, that the refugees began to share folktales. These tales were recited under a totalitarian regime somewhat akin to Stalin's Soviet Union. Self-censorship was essential. Historical circumstances had created a political climate where stories that put the descendants of Levi in a bad light were quickly repressed.

The refugees from Israel had a strong desire to keep alive their own stories and their own versions of the common stories. So how did folklorists tell their tales so that the people understood the intent without revealing the true facts to any malevolent forces that might be listening? We suggest that one way was with the adept use of body language, especially visual clues. They might roll their eyes or place tongue-in-cheek or cross their fingers as the tale unfolded. These visual hints encouraged the audience to become complicit in the understanding that everything they heard could only be properly understood by assuming the opposite meaning of the words that were being said.

Those who are forced to bend beneath the dual whips of censorship and fear often find creative ways to ease the boot of oppression from their necks—whether it is Aleksandr Solzhenitsyn's *One Day in the Life of Ivan Denisovich* (quickly banned by the powers-that-were, followed by the author's arrest and deportation) or the struggle of modern-day film makers in Iran to slip past omniscient prohibitions.[38]

The story of the Egyptian prince's conspiracy with Levi to murder Joseph probably began with just such covert clues. One such is the following ironic passage, "Asenath had conceived a great respect and liking for Levi, for he was a very intelligent man. But Levi was more than an intelligent man. He was a saint and a prophet, could read the heavenly writings, and instructed Asenath in them."[39]

How flattering to Levi! But surely Asenath hated him? To her he must have been little more than a thug. Married to Joseph, she knew the real story about Levi's role in throwing her husband into the pit. She knew that Levi wanted her husband dead, and she would never have accepted a moral lecture from such a man. The idea was laughable—and this passage probably enjoyed suppressed chuckles from the crowd.

The story continues, tongue-in-cheek, yet containing enough truth to keep the audience's rapt attention. The prince (speaking to Levi and Simeon*) reveals: "I hate your brother Joseph, because he took Asenath to wife, the maiden who ought to have been betrothed to me. If you will help me kill Joseph by the sword, so that I can marry Asenath, you will always be unto me like my brothers and trusted friends. Should you, however, refuse to fulfill my request, you will certainly regret it."[40]

"We are God-fearing men," replied the brothers, "and our father is a servant of the Lord, and our brother, too, is a God-fearing man. We will commit a great sin before the Lord, if we consent to accomplish such a wicked deed. Shouldst thou, however, persist in thy design, know that we will fight for our brother and if needs be die fighting."[41]

The folklorist was really saying that the prince and Levi had formed a conspiracy to assassinate Joseph. Under the watchful eyes of the Priests, the speaker claims that two of Joseph's other brothers took up the plot purportedly refused by Levi. They are not descendants of Levi's mother, Leah, but the sons of Israel's other wives: the handmaids, Bilhah and Zilpah. Their names are Dan and Gad.

By substituting Dan and Gad for Levi and Simeon the folklorist knew that with this wink to the audience he could freely proceed with his story. "Dan had been very jealous of Joseph, and more than once the evil spirit had stirred him up to take his sword and slay Joseph, crush him as a leopard crusheth a kid."[42] The audience knew that it was Levi

---

*The folklorist was obliged to maintain the fiction that Simeon was alive.

(not Dan) who was jealous and wished to kill Israel's favorite son when Joseph was young—"a kid."

At this point the folklorist shares details of the actual plot. Dan (Levi in the eyes and ears of the audience) says to the prince, "tomorrow Asenath is going down to the country and will be accompanied by an escort of six hundred valiant men, whilst Joseph will go to town to sell corn. Now, if my lord will send with us a greater number of warriors, we will start this night, lie in ambush in the ravine, and hide in the thicket, whilst thou wilt proceed us with a vanguard of fifty spearmen. When our sister-in-law approaches our hiding place, we will fall upon her escort, kill all the men and let Asenath escape, so that in her flight she will fall into thy hands for thee to do unto her as thou pleasest."[43]

The plot fails when Levi and Simeon intervene, saving Joseph's life. But that interpretation was merely propaganda designed to let the audience hear the story without censorship. *The real intent of the folktale was to blame Levi for the murder of Joseph.* The dark secret of Joseph's assassination was kept alive through folklore—a slowly burning ember of truth.

Levi's murder of Joseph was the real reason that the Israelites left Egypt. When the Egyptians learned of his murder they took revenge by evicting them. Manetho, the Egyptian historian, had claimed that the "exodus" was really an expulsion rather than a flight to freedom. Far from being free, the children of Israel were condemned to live under the brutal theocratic rule of Reuel and Levi. Under the names *Jethro* and *Aaron* they were the same cruel people—this time, as will see, masquerading as pious priests. The cousins were now allies—an alliance forged in hell.

Meanwhile, Asenath returned to Heliopolis to give birth to her son, Osarseph, a name we suggested earlier meant "Hebrew son of Osiris." In Egyptian mythology, Osiris was murdered by his brother. By choosing *Osarseph* as her son's name, Asenath was telling the world that her husband had been murdered by his brother. The sibling who most likely carried out the dark deed was Joseph's ruthless and secretive brother—Levi.

6

———•———

A Family Divided

Thou shalt have no other gods before me.

Exodus 20:3

Before he left Egypt, Moses fought a deadly battle with an evil magician. Although Jewish folklore and Josephus, the historian, have a lot to say about the conflict, the Levite scribes repressed any record of it. The seeds of the fateful encounter were planted when Moses was given control of the army after the Egyptians suffered a disastrous defeat at the hands of their aggressive southern neighbors, the Ethiopians. These ferocious warriors marched into Egypt without effective opposition. Fearing utter ruin, the Egyptian pharaoh sought advice from his counselors who in turn consulted oracles. Their prophecies foretold that only Moses could save Egypt. He was quickly designated an Egyptian general and assigned troops to take on the Ethiopians.

Rejecting the safest but slowest route, via the Nile, Moses moved swiftly overland across a desert where his men feared disturbing the deadly serpents that lived in the area. Josephus tells us:

Moses invented a wonderful stratagem to preserve the army safe, and without hurt; for he made baskets like unto arks, of sedge, and filled them with ibises, and carried them along with them; which animal is the greatest enemy to serpents imaginable. . . . As soon, therefore as Moses was come to the land which was the breeder of these serpents, he let loose the ibis, and by their means repelled the serpentine kind . . . [and] proceeded thus on his journey, he came upon the Ethiopian before they expected him.[1]

By this clever use of the snakes' lethal enemy, Moses assured his army's advancement against the Ethiopians. But his final victory came because of a secret, romantic ally. Watching from behind the high walls of the fortress, overlooking the battlefield, the "daughter of the king of the Ethiopians" fell in love with the victor and wasted no time in dispatching a servant carrying a marriage proposal. Moses accepted—with one condition. He used her infatuation to successfully "turn" her and with her cooperation Moses was victorious. When she became the queen of Ethiopia, Moses stepped into his place as her king.

Jewish folklore relates the same tale but adds an intriguing twist. Here, the original king of Ethiopia, Kikanos, leaves his chief city of Saba in the hands of the magician Balaam and his two sons:

> The wily wizard, however, powerful magician that he was, succeeded in bewitching the people by his enchantments and persuaded them to forget their allegiance to the king. The inhabitants deposed Kikanos and chose Balaam as their king, appointing his two sons as commander-in-chief of the armies.
>
> The city of Saba was already almost impregnable, surrounded as it was by the Nile and Astopus, or Astaboras, but Balaam took steps to make the city absolutely unapproachable, so as to prevent Kikanos from entering it on his return. He raised the walls of the city on two sides, and dug numerous canals on the third side, between the city and the Nile. Into these canals he let run the waters of the rivers, so that none could approach the city of Saba even after crossing the rivers. As for the fourth side, Balaam, thanks to his magic power and his enchantments, assembled poisonous serpents which were very numerous on the roads between Egypt and Ethiopia.[2]

King Kikanos enlists Moses to save Saba. Drawn to his radiant appearance, "his countenance shone as the morning sun, and his strength was equal to a lion's," the old tale relates that, "So deep was the king's affection for him, that he appointed him to be commander-in-chief of his forces."[3]

Again, Moses instructs each Ethiopian soldier to carry a hungry stork to devour the snakes. He wins the day, but Balaam and his two sons escape before the city falls. As a prize, Moses is given Kikanos's widow as a wife but his new queen hates him and incessantly plots against him. After forty years of ruling Ethiopia beside an antagonistic queen, Moses leaves for Midian.

Why did the Levite scribes suppress the compelling story of Moses's Ethiopian adventures? We know that the idea of Moses as a loyal Egyptian leading the charge to defeat an important enemy would have been repugnant to them. Even more alarming, the depiction of Moses dueling with a magician such as Balaam would have veered far too close to the explosive truth: the fact that Moses was murdered by a magician, Reuel—and that their ancestor (Levi) was an accomplice in that plot.

MOSES LEAVES EGYPT

In the early days of biblical archaeology there was a lot of optimism that the new science could verify the existence of Moses by proving that there was indeed a great migration of people from Egypt who eventually conquered and settled Canaan. This premature optimism was dashed by the stark reality of subsequent excavations.

In *The Bible Unearthed*, Israeli archaeologists Israel Finkelstein and Neil Asher Silberman dispelled any illusions that their digs had verified the story of the exodus.

> The process that we describe here is, in fact, the opposite of what we have in the Bible: the emergence of early Israel was an outcome of the collapse of the Canaanite culture, not its cause. And most of the Israelites did not come from outside Canaan—they emerged from within it. *There was no mass Exodus from Egypt.* There was no violent conquest of Canaan.

Most of the people who formed early Israel were local people—the same people whom we see in the highlands throughout the Bronze and Iron Ages. The early Israelites were—irony of ironies—themselves originally Canaanites![4] [Italics added]

Their conclusion was a severe blow to those who believed that Moses had been a real person. But the question of the prophet's existence— whether he was indeed a flawed flesh-and-blood man, or a fictional character forced to jump through his creator's hoops is a thorny one, not easily dismissed or answered. The biblical story of the great man is full of contradictions and puzzles. Unlike the story of Joseph, which has a discernable beginning, middle, and end, Moses's narrative is scattered and disjointed. At first, we are led to believe that he is a first child; only for it to be revealed later that he has older siblings. We're told he was adopted by an Egyptian princess, but no details of his childhood are offered. The only account of his death is sketchy to say the least and no one knows where one of the most significant figures in history is buried. These troubling mysteries led scholars to doubt his existence.

We believe that Moses was a real person whose pedigree offended Levi's descendants. Unable to explain his Egyptian education, appearance, and accent they were compelled to obscure his family tree. If the truth that Moses belonged to the House of Joseph was ever to be leaked the scribes might be separated from their significant priestly rights and perks. It was imperative that the great prophet not only be from their own House of Levi, but be *seen* to be from it. In their desperate, self-serving tampering with the memory of Moses the scribes could never have guessed that one day the patchy biography of Moses that they had cobbled together would convince scholars that the great prophet was nothing more than a myth.

IN MIDIAN

In our reconstruction, the children of Israel were expelled from Egypt because of the murder of Joseph. Moses was born to Joseph's widow, Asenath, and raised as a priest in the temple of Heliopolis where many years earlier the Pharaoh Akhenaten had created monotheism. Born after the expulsion Moses was the sole Israelite living in Egypt. Did this sense of singularity plant a psychological propensity towards Egyptian monotheism in him?

We've seen that the Egyptian historian Manetho believed that Moses was associated with dangerous beliefs. The Egyptians experienced monotheism as a great threat; a religion that vowed to destroy their many gods. Did Moses receive his belief in a single god from the priests of Heliopolis or from Reuel's god, Yahweh? The Levites voted for Yahweh. Freud favored Heliopolis. We agree with Freud.

We know Moses was an Egyptian priest/magician but unlike Reuel, who also trained in the same arts, Moses had no restrictions on his education. Akhenaten's monotheism is not something that the priests of Heliopolis would be likely to reveal to Reuel. No matter how talented—he was still a foreigner. In contrast, Moses was the high priest's grandson.

During this time, perhaps twenty years or more, Moses's Hebrew family was living in the oasis of Midian under the rule of its high priest, Reuel. Moses had no contact with them. It was only after he was fully grown, had become a general in the pharaoh's army, and successfully reclaimed Ethiopia that Moses left Egypt. The reason for his departure may very well have been the rise of a new pharaoh who "knew not Joseph."[5]

But what was the fate of Moses's Hebrew family during this time? How had their religion changed from the days when they had enjoyed a life of peace and prosperity in Egypt before they were expelled?

MIDIAN AND THE KENITES

It was a time of great upheaval.* Drought had killed hundreds of thousands of people. Canaan, present-day Israel, may have lost more than

---

*As to exactly *when* Moses lived we retain an agnostic position. Biblical scholars have argued over this question for decades with no end in sight. For our purposes, the main idea that is important is our questioning of the Levite insertion of 430 years between the time of Joseph and Moses. This is false. Otherwise, we leave open the question of when these biblical events occurred. We note that the stories assume droughts, but these have been common in the ancient Middle East. For an exploration of the question when the exodus might have occurred, see Hoffmeier, *Israel in Egypt*.

half its population. Even the Egyptians began to tighten their belts, resulting in the expulsion of colonists from the homeland. During these hard times they resented sharing their precious crops with foreigners, especially the children of Israel, whom they considered ungrateful and treacherous. Deprived of fertile land, the Israelites were forced to seek refuge with their cousin Reuel, who had access to one of the few remaining watering holes. Refugees from the climatic disaster flocked to the Midian oasis where Reuel was high priest.

Levi and Dinah were just two of the stream of refugees who fled to Midian. Their forced emigration offered a golden opportunity to adopt new identities as Aaron and Miriam. It would be a great relief—the end of their disgrace. But there was one very big fly in the ointment. Their cousin, the magician Reuel, was in charge.

New refugees could only settle in Midian at the magician's pleasure. The price of admittance was loyalty to one of the tribes of Israel. Reuben, Judah, and each of the remaining sons of Israel adopted refugees into their clans. Levi (as Aaron) claimed authority over all the newcomers' firstborn sons thus ensuring the expansion of his power. The ranks of the children of Israel swelled. The two biggest winners in this emerging confederation were the tribes of Judah and Aaron's "Levites." Judah had been forgiven by Israel and was blessed. Ultimately, after the Promised Land was settled, he seized political control.

Years later Reuel became Moses's father-in-law but at this time he was immersed in the task of educating Israel's sons in the religion of the mountain god, Yahweh. Professor of theology, Karl Budde (1850–1935) noted that Moses's father-in-law is described as a "Kenite."[6] The Kenites were "the original worshippers of Yahweh"[7] under the direction of Reuel.

The biblical scholar Gene Rice believes that the Kenites were a clan of priests and notes that "there are striking similarities between the Kenites and the Levites." Both were scribes/priests. Both "were zealous champions of the pure worship of Yahweh." Rice asks, "Did, in fact, the Levites absorb and take over the function of the Kenites as a priestly order?"[8]

Yahweh was Reuel's god. It is Reuel, not Moses or Aaron, who makes the first sacrificial offering to Yahweh when the Israelite left

Midian and arrived at the Mountain of God. "And Jethro, Moses' father-in-law, brought a burnt offering and sacrifices, and Aaron and all the elders of Israel came to partake of the meal with Moses' father-in-law before God."[9] Reuel was to the Kenites what Aaron became to the Levites: the esteemed founder of a religious order.

Knowing nothing of Levi and his scandalous past the new "Israelites" had no problem accepting Aaron as their high priest. They also accepted Miriam as a respected prophetess. And they would come to accept an Egyptian refugee named Moses as their prophet. There wasn't a lot of questioning going on while the people quenched their thirst at Reuel's wells. It was only much later, as they wandered through the desert (led by Moses) that murmurings about the leadership of the Jews began to drift through the tents.

The conflict between Moses's Egyptian monotheism and Reuel's temperamental mountain god, Yahweh, is a recurring theme in the life of the great prophet. The Levite scribes largely succeeded in erasing the truth about his childhood and replacing it with a version more suitable to their agenda.

Fortunately, Jewish folklore was never subject to their cut-and-paste editing.

JEWISH FOLKLORE

One folktale offers us a remarkable account of Moses's arrival in Midian and his introduction to Reuel, a story the Levite scribes would have quickly censored if they had known of it. The tale revolved around "a staff made of sapphire which the Almighty had created in the twilight of the first Sabbath eve. When Adam was driven out of the Garden of Eden, he carried this staff with him, as one of the gifts he had received from the Creator. He handed it to Enoch, who transmitted it to Noah, who again handed it to Shem. The staff reached Abraham, who transmitted it to his son Isaac. He later gave it to Jacob, who brought it with him to Egypt and handed it to his son Joseph. When the Viceroy [Joseph] died, the Egyptians pillaged his house and took away this sapphire rod which they brought to Pharaoh. Reuel, who was one of the counselors of Pharaoh, saw this rod and made up his mind to possess it. His desire was so great that he did not hesitate to steal it and carry it away when he left Egypt."[10]

Reuel had brazenly stolen a precious symbol of Hebrew leadership that had been passed from father to son from the time of Adam until the age of Joseph. After his audacious theft he fled to the land of the Midians where he rose to the position of high priest to these Bedouin-like nomads based at an oasis. The folktale told how one day, as Reuel was walking in his garden, his precious sapphire rod became rooted in the ground and couldn't be dislodged. He decreed that the man who freed the rod could claim his beautiful daughter, Zipporah, as his wife.

Like the later story of King Arthur and the magic sword Excalibur, many eager contenders took on the challenge. But unlike the Arthur story, when Zipporah's unfortunate suitors touched the precious staff they vanished. They would not be the only characters to suddenly disappear from Reuel's orbit. Vanishing acts seem to have been one of his specialties. The rod story hints of hidden pits triggered by touching the rod. As we know, modern magicians perform their vanishing acts by making use of built-in stage trapdoors and a puff of smoke to conceal the magician's secret subterranean world.

When he arrived in Midian, Moses encountered Zipporah and her sisters watering their animals at their father's well. He made an indelible first impression by saving them from the gang of thugs who were harassing them. When Moses's romance bloomed with Zipporah, Reuel's attitude toward him changed and he "bound Moses with chains and cast him into a dungeon." Reuel assumed that Moses would die of exposure.* But the story took an unexpected twist:

> Soon Reuel . . . forgot about Moses, who would have perished in the pit had it not been for the love the gentle and fair Zipporah bore him. She had loved Moses from the very moment she had set eyes upon him, and could never forget his kindness to herself and

---

*Echoing the story of how Joseph was initially left in a pit to die.

her sisters, when he saved them from the shepherds of Midian. She thought of ways and means how to provide the prisoner, not only with food and drink, but also with various dainties and to lighten his confinement.[11]

In the folktale, Moses is held captive for seven years while Zipporah secretly brings him food. During this time, Reuel grew "prosperous, and princes and magnates came to ask his daughters in marriage. It was especially the noble and fair Zipporah who had many suitors for her hand. She loved Moses in secret, but she dared not confess it to her father, for fear that, remembering the existence of the stranger, he would put him to death."[12]

The folktale assumes that *Reuel wished Moses dead.*

When Zipporah finally confessed to Reuel that Moses was still alive her amazed father,

> Immediately he set him free, cut his hair, gave him a change of garment, and set food before him. Moses thereupon went out into Reuel's garden, which was at the back of the house, to pray to the Lord and to give thanks to Him for the many wonders He had done unto him. Then he lifted up his eyes and suddenly beheld the sapphire staff planted in the ex-high-priest's garden. Approaching this wonderful staff he saw that the Ineffable Name, the name of the Most High, was engraved upon it, and he stretched out his hand to take it. Moses uprooted the staff as easily as one lifts up a branch in a dense forest, and it became a rod in his hand. When Reuel came into the garden and saw the staff in Moses' hand, he was amazed, for none had hitherto been able to uproot or even touch it. . . . [Reuel] immediately gave him (Moses) his daughter Zipporah to wife, whose secret wish had thus been fulfilled.[13]

Releasing the staff required only the trained eye of an Egyptian magician to see through the trick. Moses possessed those skills and so the sapphire rod came full circle, back into the hands of its rightful owner, Joseph's son, Moses.

The story of the sapphire rod assumes that no great time passed between the death of Joseph and the arrival of Moses in Midian; contradicting the familiar story of the fabled 430 years of Egyptian bondage. It also reveals that Reuel felt himself to be the rightful leader of the Hebrew people. The story is only chronologically coherent if Moses was Joseph's son (as we discussed in chapter 4). Under these circumstances Joseph, Reuel, and Moses are all assumed to be alive around the same time. Moses and Zipporah are from the *same generation*. And the folktale assumes that Reuel was hostile to Moses; a fact covered up in the Torah account.

So, what really happened when Moses penetrated Reuel's oasis of Midian?

MOSES IN MIDIAN

If Moses *was* Joseph's son, as the evidence suggests, we can imagine how Reuel and Levi might react to the arrival of the adult Moses in Midian. Levi, in his new persona as Aaron, would want to dispose of the son of his greatest enemy. But Reuel, who was in charge at the oasis, was a subtle character. A master magician who had honed his skills in Egypt, he had developed the fine art of patience and was prepared to wait for the best opportunity to seize command. Reuel had a much longer game in mind.

Reuel also had a genetic agenda in mind. By arranging for Joseph's son to marry his daughter the crafty magician was creating what he believed to be a holy bloodline. Only after Moses gave Reuel two grandsons did the magician decide that he could now afford to turn on his son-in-law. Reuel knew that the people might follow the Egyptian-born son of their hero, Joseph, especially if he bore a striking resemblance to his father.

Reuel had reason to worry about retaining his esteemed position. His authority had not gone unchallenged. In the Koran we learn that the people grew weary of Reuel, who in the Islamic tradition went by the name, *Shu'aib*. Shu'aib had made the mistake of accusing the Midianites of using false weights to measure out the precious commodities that were necessary for all to survive and thrive. For a people who lived by trade the accusation was a serious one punishable by death.

By this time, in our reconstruction, the refugees from Egypt who had been adopted by the tribes of Israel now outnumbered the locals. The Midianites said to Shu'aib, "But for your tribe, we should have stoned you. You shall on no account prevail against us."[14]

They no longer needed or wanted Reuel's services as high priest. This was his "get out of Dodge" moment. But where could he go? Fortunately for Reuel, the rains had returned and the fiery blanket of drought that had devastated Canaan was lifting. Word reached him that good land was available for the taking. But how was he going to get the children of Israel, whose population had swollen, to leave the relative safety of the Midian oasis to undertake a long, dangerous march across the barren desert to Canaan?

Moses may have provided his answer.

As we've seen, indications are that Moses resembled his father, Joseph. Both are consistently described in Jewish folklore as being exceptionally attractive. If Moses did look like Joseph, then Israel's surviving sons might have been more inclined to follow him. After all, Joseph had led the children of Israel out of Canaan when that land was suffering a sustained drought. His son might tap into that old memory to lead them again to a promised land.

It was the perfect opportunity for the magician Reuel. Rather than kill Moses, he could use him to lead the long, risky journey. The tribes loyal to Joseph would welcome his son's direction. Others would have to bide their time until Reuel decided when Moses had outlived his usefulness.

The constant strife between Moses and Aaron that biblical scholars have found so baffling, reflected the continuing struggle between the House of Joseph and the House of Levi. That grim conflict was suspended only for as long as it took to guide the children of Israel from Midian to the Mountain of God.

7

———•———

Psychic Dynamite

I AM THAT I AM.

YAHWEH TO MOSES, EXODUS 3:14.

One of the most perplexing passages in the Torah occurs early in Exodus. After entrusting him with the most critical of missions, Yahweh the Lord suddenly and violently turns against Moses and tries to kill him! Why would Yahweh seek out the prophet, reveal to him the precious secrets of magic, task him with the sacred job of freeing the Jews, and then determine to kill him? And why would the Architect of the Universe fail in his attempt to dispose of a mere mortal?

We take up the story with Moses and his wife on the road to Egypt: "And it came to pass by the way of the inn, that the Lord met him, and sought to kill him. Then Zipporah took a sharp stone, and cut off the foreskin of her son, and cast it at his feet, and said, Surely a bloody husband art thou to me. So he let him go: then she said, A bloody husband thou art, because of the circumcision."[1]

Why did this speedy circumcision of the boy satisfy the enraged "Lord"? Why does Zipporah call Moses "a bloody husband"? And what becomes of her after this frightening episode? These questions have haunted biblical scholars for centuries. In his *Commentary on the Torah,* the noted American scholar Richard Elliott Friedman wrote, "No one knows what the episode at the lodging place means."[2] And the German biblical scholar Martin Noth (1902–1968) wrote that the "obscure" incident provided no adequate reason "why in the face of the threat Zipporah should resort to the act of circumcision."[3]

Jewish folklore links Reuel (here using his title "Jethro") with this story:

> On the road to Egypt, Satan appeared to him in the guise of a serpent and swallowed up his body down to his feet, but he was saved by his faithful wife Zipporah. She knew that this was a punishment because their second son had not yet been circumcised, Jethro having made it a condition that one half of the children should be Israelitish and the other Egyptian. Swiftly Zipporah took a sharp flint stone, circumcised their son Eliezer and touched the feet of her husband with the blood of circumcision. Immediately a heavenly voice called out: "Spew him out," and the serpent obeyed.[4]

We suggest that this anomalous incident provides the key to unlocking our prime suspect's goal. Far from being an obscure, inexplicable, and baffling incident this story reveals a precise, coherent, secret plan. What was that plan? And how did the circumcision of Moses's second son expose it?

Why was Moses helpless to defend himself during the attack? Not because he felt powerless before the Creator of the Universe but because he was enveloped by the hypnotic fugue of Reuel. The Egyptian magician was "playing God" again. As we've seen in chapter 2, Reuel took on this ultimate role when he was a young man and wrestled with his uncle, Jacob. He received Jacob's blessing and pronounced that his uncle's name would thenceforth be changed to Israel. But now Reuel is older and is father-in-law to Moses. He fears that Moses might disappear to Egypt with his wife and his precious grandchild. He must ensure that from now on, he can control the sons of Moses. This, we suggest, is not a tale of supernatural force: it is a story of a grandfather protecting his prized bloodline. It is the story of a breeder of people protecting his investment.

How? Why?

The answer takes us back to Reuel's own bloodline. Isaac, his paternal grandfather, was the founder of the Jews. Ishmael, his maternal grandfather, was the founder of the Arabs.

Reuel was the first person to carry both Jewish and Arab blood within his veins. Much of the story of the exodus can best be understood from the narcissistic point of view of Reuel as he relentlessly pursues his obsessive goal of preserving and enhancing what he believed to be the noblest bloodline of all: his own.

The marriage between Reuel's parents had been opposed by Isaac.[5] Why? The feud had originated generations before—in the time of Isaac's parents, Abraham and Sarah, Reuel's great grandparents.

GOD AND HIS ANGELS

Sarah was infertile; considered a shameful state for any woman in those primitive times. To supply Abraham with a son, Sarah gave her Egyptian handmaid Hagar to her husband as a surrogate mother. But when the child, Ishmael, was born Sarah regretted her decision. She told Abraham, "I have given my maid into thy bosom; and when she saw that she had conceived, I was despised in her eyes."[6] A fierce hatred grew between the two women.

Abraham faces a crisis. He doesn't want to come between Sarah's rage and Hagar's desperate concern for her status. He needs a way out. Conveniently, God soon speaks to Abraham ordering him to "hearken" unto the voice of Sarah. The stressed husband tells his wife of many years that she can deal with Hagar however she wants.

Sarah wastes no time in making life intolerable for her former maid. Hagar is pushed to the breaking point by Sarah's harsh treatment and flees the camp rather than suffer more indignities. She and her unborn child face death by exposure but miraculously she is chosen to be one of the first biblical characters to encounter an angel. The apparition saves her by supplying water:

> And the angel of the LORD found her by a fountain of water in the wilderness, by the fountain in the way to Shur. And he said, Hagar, Sarai's maid, whence camest thou? and whither wilt thou go? And she said, I flee from the face of my mistress Sarai. And the angel of the LORD said unto her, Return to thy mistress, and submit thyself under her hands. And the angel of the LORD said unto her, I will multiply thy seed exceedingly, that it shall not be numbered for multitude. And the angel of the LORD said unto her, Behold, thou art with child, and shalt bear a son, and shalt call his name Ishmael; because the LORD hath heard thy affliction.[7]

Hagar is promised that her descendants will form a new nation, the Arabs. Despite being the *only witness* to the angel's appearance this event secures both Hagar's status in camp and her destiny.

Years later, as Ishmael entered puberty, another angel was invoked. At the age of ninety, Sarah became pregnant and gave birth to Isaac who could certainly qualify as a miracle baby. We can imagine the rumors spreading through camp as fast as through any twenty-first-century small town about the infant's true paternity. The gossip burned Sarah as surely as any flare from the campfire. And then her stepson, Ishmael, made the mistake of casting a "mocking" stare in her direction. "And Sarah saw the son of Hagar the Egyptian, which she had born unto Abraham, mocking. Wherefore she said unto Abraham, Cast out this bondwoman and her son: for the son of this bondwoman shall not be heir with my son, even with Isaac."[8]

Once again Abraham faces a crisis over Hagar and Ishmael. He knows that Sarah wants him to kill Ishmael so that Isaac will be the only heir. But Abraham is fond of his firstborn son. Once again, the Voice of God is conjured; this time instructing him to make a brutal sacrifice. He is commanded to sacrifice the child to God. But, just as in the case of Hagar's imminent death by thirst, at the last moment an angel appears and stops the killing by replacing the boy with a sacrificial ram. Abraham is the only witness. His son, who didn't see the angel, is saved.

Hagar's angel and Abraham's angel are only visible to them. The belief in the existence of these supernatural creatures is based entirely upon the readers of the Torah accepting the stories that Hagar and Abraham tell about them. Today, most of us require a lot more proof before we'll accept the existence of angels. We suggest that both Hagar and Abraham invented the angels to fulfill their *own* needs. Hagar desired respect and got it. Abraham saved his son's life.

Only Abraham witnessed what really happened on the mountain. But Abraham still had to explain the strange episode to Sarah. Desperate to mollify his wife's anger when she discovered that he had not gotten rid of her mocking stepson he offered a compromise. He introduced the practice of circumcision to demonstrate to Sarah that he had after all, drawn blood, if not ended (human) life. The biblical scholar Arthur Frederick Ide wrote, "Circumcision was a surrogate sacrifice of their infant males to their gods. The cutting off the penis' foreskin of the child took the place of an actual murder of the Semitic child which commonly occurred in Palestine."[9]

To continue to ameliorate his heartsick wife, Abraham had to ensure that his other son, Isaac, was bloodied as well. And so, two separate traditions of circumcision were introduced. The Ishmaelites would undergo the ritual at the time of puberty or marriage, but for Isaac's descendants, the Jews, another time was prescribed, "And ye shall circumcise the flesh of your foreskin; and it shall be a token of the covenant betwixt me and you. And he that is eight days old shall be circumcised among you."[10]

Circumcision on the eighth day after birth became the custom for the sons of Isaac. It was on this day, we suggest, that Reuel caught up with Moses's family at the inn. Playing God, Reuel ensured that their second son, Eliezer, was circumcised as a Jew. Reuel then took his daughter and her son back to his homeland. Moses had no choice but to continue to Egypt without his family.

Reuel's grandfather, Isaac, was rattled by Sarah's curse against the children of Hagar. It placed Ishmael in danger. And so, when his son, Esau, married Ishmael's daughter, the founder of the Jews was upset, to put it mildly. Their union violated the curse that Sarah had placed on Ishmael.

TABLE 7.1. REUEL'S BLOODLINE

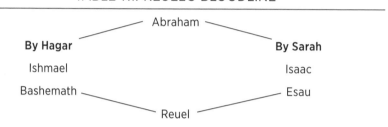

Reuel was descended from Abraham through both his mother (Bashemath) and father (Esau).

As we learned in chapter 2, Isaac had twin sons. His favorite was the firstborn, Esau. Isaac's wife, Rebekah, devised a scheme involving *her* favorite, the younger twin, Jacob, to trick Isaac into bestowing his final blessing on Jacob by having him impersonate Esau. As a result, Esau was left with nothing. He rebelled and became a warrior—conquering a mountainous region of present-day Jordan (then called Seir), which he renamed Edom. Esau became a king and his wife, Bashemath (the daughter of Ishmael), was mother to Reuel, a prince of Edom who received an elite education as a magician in Egypt.

REUEL'S WIFE

We know the names of Reuel's parents, grandparents, great-grandparents, his uncle, and thirteen of his cousins. Also, his sons and daughters, his half brothers, and even one of his half brother's illegitimate sons. But the identity of one major character is conspicuous by her absence. Nowhere in the Torah are we told the name of Reuel's wife. His daughter married Moses. Her mother's identity is crucial. Who, then, was she?

Jealous of his noble bloodline, Reuel must have thought long and hard about his choice of wife. We suggest that he decided on his cousin Dinah, known in Midian as "Miriam," the prophetess.* By marrying Miriam he sealed his alliance with Levi (Aaron) but he nurtured a more long-term aim. While his cousins made a living by breeding sheep and goats, Reuel's preoccupation was with human bloodlines. By linking his genealogy with Miriam's, he created children who were genetically linked to Israel, Judah, and Levi, as well as to his own already impressive list of powerful relatives, including Abraham, Ishmael, and Isaac.

When Reuel gave his daughter Zipporah to Moses the final piece in the genetic puzzle fell into place with the birth of their sons, Gershom and Eliezer. Reuel had almost perfected his bloodline. His own name, as well as that of Joseph's, through his son Moses, could now be added to the list of ten patriarchs whose nobility flowed through the veins of Reuel's grandsons.† Moses's sons represented a great prize. (It is possible that in the centuries that followed this bloodline remained pure. And it remained a secret: a secret preserved for a thousand years to the present. As we will see in the epilogue, today over a million people carry on Reuel's pedigree.) But to fulfill the ultimate objective of his secret genetic agenda Reuel had to seize control of the children of Israel.

MOSES IN MIDIAN

The adventure, turmoil, and trouble Moses endured as an Egyptian warrior in Ethiopia was airbrushed from the Torah. Instead, his story jumps abruptly from that of the child we encounter in Exodus 2:10 to full adulthood in the next verse:

> And it came to pass in those days, when Moses was grown, that he went out unto his brethren, and looked on their burdens: and he spied an Egyptian smiting an Hebrew, one of his brethren. And he looked this way and that way, and when he saw that there was

---

*Further evidence of the marriage of Reuel and Miriam will be presented in chapter 9.
†The ten patriarchs are Abraham, Ishmael, Isaac, Esau, Jacob (Israel), Levi (Aaron), Judah, Reuel, Joseph, and Moses.

no man, he slew the Egyptian, and hid him in the sand. And when he went out the second day, behold, two men of the Hebrews strove together: and he said to him that did the wrong, Wherefore smitest thou thy fellow? And he said, Who made thee a prince and a judge over us? Intendest thou to kill me, as thou killedst the Egyptian? And, Moses feared, and said, Surely this thing is known. Now when Pharaoh heard this thing, he sought to slay Moses. But Moses fled from the face of Pharaoh, and dwelt in the land of Midian.[11]

Moses's destination has caused much consternation among biblical scholars: "We learn nothing about the reason Moses turned to Midian"[12] and "No reason is given for Moses' choice of the land of Midian as his goal."[13] What was there about this place that drew him?

Moses knew the legend of the devastating drought that had forced his father's people from Egypt before he was born. He also knew that Midian was located at a rare, life-saving oasis ruled by Reuel, cousin to all the children of Israel. For more than two decades while Moses was growing up,* the Israelites had lived in Midian where Levi, reinvented as Aaron, was Reuel's apprentice in the teachings of the mountain god, Yahweh.†

Tales about the fate of his father's tribe would be carried by traders passing through the Egyptian city of Heliopolis, the capital of the northeastern province of Goshen where the Israelites had once lived. Having been raised in the city as an Egyptian priest he must have been curious about his Jewish relatives in Midian.

The tipping point came when a new pharaoh arose "who knew not Joseph."[14] During the reign of the pharaoh who knew Joseph, Moses was safe in Heliopolis, thriving under the tutelage of his grandfather, the high priest. But the new pharaoh, reinforcing the bigotry of ages, might well have objected to a man who was half-Jewish practicing within the sacred temple of Heliopolis. Moses, we suggest, didn't just

---

*Moses must have been at least twenty when he first left Egypt.
†As we have seen in chapter 6, Reuel's priests were called *Kenites* while Aaron's were known as *Levites*. Only the names were different: the worshipped God was the same.

wander into Midian accidentally. The new homeland of his uncles and cousins would have been a natural destination.

Compared to the colorful sapphire rod folktale, the Torah's account of Moses's meeting with his future wife, Zipporah, is brief:

> Moses fled from the face of Pharaoh, and dwelt in the land of Midian: and he sat down by a well. Now the priest of Midian had seven daughters: and they came and drew water, and filled the troughs to water their father's flock. And the shepherds came and drove them away: but Moses stood up and helped them, and watered their flock. And when they came to Reuel their father, he said, How is it that ye are come so soon to day? And they said, An Egyptian delivered us out of the hand of the shepherds, and also drew water enough for us, and watered the flock. And he said unto his daughters, And where is he? why is it that ye have left the man? call him, that he may eat bread. And Moses was content to dwell with the man: and he gave Moses Zipporah his daughter.[15]

Reuel is portrayed as a generous and wise man who took pity upon an Egyptian fugitive. But knowing Reuel's obsession with his bloodline it seems improbable that he would marry his precious daughter to the first man who showed her kindness. The story is more complex than the text reveals. Aware that Moses was Joseph's son—the one honorable son of Israel whose blood was missing from Reuel's genetic agenda—he was keen to welcome him into the family. It wasn't Moses's impressive fighting abilities that persuaded Reuel to marry him to his daughter. It was his genetic inheritance that Reuel coveted.

The account of Moses at the well with Reuel's daughters assumes he was a formidable fighter. He had just completed a grueling journey across unforgiving mountains and deserts that would have left an ordinary man unfit for any battle. But the contemporary audience through their folktales knew that Moses had been a great warrior in Ethiopia even if the tales of his adventures would later be cut from the Torah. The Israelites knew that simple shepherds were no match for Moses's experienced sword.

Reuel's daughter assumed Moses was Egyptian because his face and head were shaven in the manner of the Egyptian priests. The iconic image of Moses, complete with long, flowing hair and generous beard depicts him as decidedly Hebrew but the Moses who first arrived in Midian was clean shaven.

Reuel and Moses broke bread together. The meal represented more than just sustenance. In those distant times, the breaking of bread implied "an unsaid promise of protection."[16]

Moses believed he had found sanctuary. Little did he suspect that he had just fallen into a deadly trap rigged by a mortal enemy.

REUEL AND MOSES

Moses's conniving father-in-law went by two names in Midian. To his family he was known as Reuel. But the Midianites for whom he acted as high priest knew him as *Jethro,* meaning "his excellence,"[17] a formal title. But it might have meant something much more. Jethro might well have been the name of Reuel's larger-than-life persona adopted whenever he assumed the role of spokesman of God to the Midianites. On these occasions he may have even worn a special costume and feature-concealing mask. This was high drama and with his Egyptian training, Reuel knew how to put on a mesmerizing show.

Kirsch writes that "Jethro was a sorcerer and Moses was his apprentice."[18] We suggest that is was Levi who was Jethro's actual apprentice. Moses was known as Reuel's shepherd. At the time, the term *shepherd* carried a more complex meaning than our modern notion of a solitary man tending a flock of sheep. The "'shepherds,' along with the 'priests,' were groups of religious personnel . . . they were servants of the temple and its high priest."[19]

Moses was well tutored in the nuances of Reuel's religion. Reuel taught him how to speak with God using prayer, meditation, and hypnotism—three powerful naturally linked forces. William J. Bryan Jr. in *Religious Aspects of Hypnosis* wrote, "One best learns to pray from someone who already knows how to pray in the same manner that one best learns hypnosis from someone who already understands it. As with hypnosis, prayer takes practice; and . . . consists of concentrating the mind on one central focus of attention, namely a deity, and relaxing the rest of the voluntary musculature."[20]

He continues, "in no state of prayer in any religion in the world is the fist ever clenched . . . the muscles of the body are always relaxed." Bryan also writes, "Many elements of hypnosis remain in our religion today. The chanting, testimonials, the flickering candles and the cross as a fixation point for our vision; the relaxation of the rest of our body; the bowing of our heads in supplication. . . ."

There is even an element of autosuggestion in the modern prayer; "most praying is done with the eyes closed, and as the prayer ends it is usually brought to a close by the saying of a familiar phrase (e.g. the *Amen* used in Christian churches), which serves as a wakeup signal and allows the parishioner to then open his eyes. It is exactly the same in hypnosis."[21]

Prayer, as we understand it today, is a much more recent technique of communicating with God than what was practiced in Reuel and Moses's time. Their moments of contemplation were more closely related to what we would call meditation. As the two men meditated, clever Reuel likely took the opportunity of using his hypnotic voice to implant suggestions into the mind of his novice. Moses was used to absorbing knowledge from his grandfather at Heliopolis. It was easy for him to transfer this same respect and devotion to his father-in-law in Midian. It is probable that Reuel gave Moses a key word or phrase to trigger an immediate trance. The phrase might have been, "put off thy shoes from off thy feet, for the place whereon thou standest is holy ground;" words that Reuel may have repeated to Moses before their meditation sessions. Such an autosuggestion would prove critical during their extraordinary meeting on the Mountain of God.

On a subterranean level, the relationship between Reuel and Moses dominates the remainder of the Torah. Traces of Reuel's fingerprints can still be discerned in various scenes despite the persistent attempts of the Priests to erase them from history.

Moses lived the isolated life of a shepherd tending to Reuel's flocks in the wilderness of Midian. Many a prophet in the Bible would spend time alone with nature. Winston Churchill recognized that "Every prophet has to come from civilization, but every prophet has to go into the wilderness. He must have a strong impression of a complex society and all that it has to give, and then he must serve periods of isolation and meditation. This is the process by which psychic dynamite is made."[22]

Every time Moses returned to Midian he spent more time with Reuel. The American writer Jonathan Kirsch in his award-winning biography *Moses: A Life* wrote of Reuel, "only God enjoyed a more intimate and influential relationship with Moses."[23]

Reuel was even brazen enough to impersonate the Almighty.

THE BURNING BUSH

The day came when Moses "led the flock to the backside of the desert, and came to the mountain of God"[24] where he experienced the extraordinary vision that stands as one of the most famous passages in the Old Testament. If we look at this exchange without the blinkers of familiarity or religious dogma it strikes the reader that "God" chose a rather bizarre manifestation:

And the angel of the Lord appeared unto him in a flame of fire out of the midst of a bush: and he looked, and, behold, the bush burned with fire, and the bush was not consumed. And Moses said, I will now turn aside, and see this great sight, why the bush is not burnt. And when the Lord saw that he turned aside to see, God called unto him out of the midst of the bush, and said, Moses, Moses. And he said, Here am I. And he said, Draw not nigh hither: *put off thy shoes from off thy feet, for the place whereon thou standest is holy ground.* Moreover, he said, I am the God of thy father, the God of Abraham, the God of Isaac, and the God of Jacob. And Moses hid his face; for he was afraid to look upon God.[25] [Italics added]

The Voice spoke directly to Moses, ordering him to stay away from the burning bush. Why? Did a concealed speaker not wish to be seen? Was this really the Voice of God or was it just a simple act of ventriloquism by a master magician demonstrating his supreme command of hypnotism? Did the words "put off thy shoes from off thy feet, for the place whereon thou standest is holy ground" place Moses into a hypnotic trance?

Not a god, rather an Egyptian-trained magician spoke to Moses from behind that burning bush. The prophet tried to discover the mysterious deity's name. "And Moses said unto God, Behold, when I come unto the children of Israel, and shall say unto them, The God of your fathers hath sent me unto you; and they shall say to me, What is his name? what shall I say unto them? And God said unto Moses, I AM THAT I AM."[26]

I AM THAT I AM has been translated as "Yahweh." Not a name at all. More a refusal to divulge a name. Like the mysterious stranger/god who wrestled with Jacob, the burning bush deity kept his identity secret.

In both cases the powerful, hidden being was none other than the magician Reuel playing the role he intended to master—God.

Moses was terrified to learn that God had chosen him to undertake a holy mission. He protests that he's not worthy of the task because he is "not eloquent" and is "slow of speech." At this point Yahweh, the supposed Supreme Creator of the Universe, has a temper tantrum, shouting, "Is not Aaron the Levite thy brother? I know that he can speak well. And also, behold, he cometh forth to meet thee."[27]

This is Aaron's first appearance in the Bible. Why and how did he suddenly materialize at the Mountain of God? Was he following Moses "to the backside of the desert"[28] as the shepherd tended to his sheep? It seems unlikely.

Aaron's abrupt manifestation suggests a more insidious scenario. His appearance was part of a setup. But for what purpose? Why would Reuel and Aaron go to such extremes to convince Moses to return to Egypt? What was it that they really wanted but couldn't get their hands on without Moses's unique help?

The answer, we suggest, is Joseph's bones.

The last line of Genesis tells us that the Egyptians embalmed Joseph's body and "he was put in a coffin in Egypt."[29] The normal Egyptian practice was to conceal the location of tombs. Because the Israelites had been expelled from Egypt following Joseph's death none of them knew the secret location of his tomb. Jewish folklore says, "Moses was greatly perplexed, for he knew not the place where the coffin of Joseph could be discovered."[30] But Moses had the right to know the whereabouts of his father's grave. The Egyptians could not object to a son safeguarding his father's bones. It was a normal, even expected, part of their culture. And Moses's shaved head and face, as well as his Egyptian dress and accent, wouldn't raise an eyebrow from the authorities. As far as they were concerned, Moses was Egyptian. Undisturbed by the powers-that-be, he could remove Joseph's coffin from Egypt.

But why would Reuel want to possess Joseph's bones?

The answer is to be found, once again, in Jewish folklore. We recall how Rachel stole the image that Laban worshipped. This image, called teraphim, a gruesome Jewish folktale tells us, "was really the head of a man, a first born, whom the worshipper had slain, pinched off his head and salted it with salt and balsam. The name of an unclean spirit and incantations were then written upon a plate of gold and placed under the tongue of this head. The head was then placed in the wall, lamps were lit in front of it, and the worshipper, bowing down before the head, asked it to tell him oracles."[31]

Possessing the skull of a famous man was believed to be a way of contacting and influencing the spirit world. As an Egyptian-trained magician, Reuel believed that possessing Joseph's skull would help him in his quest to take control of the children of Israel. He knew the Israelites would celebrate the recovery of Joseph's coffin and that they would willingly follow the coffin to the Promised Land. It was Joseph, after all, who had saved them from starvation in Canaan during the drought, leading them to prosperity in Egypt. For the Israelites, Joseph was a mythic figure. To possess his bones would be a huge asset for Reuel. But a big hurdle lay between him and his goal. He had no authority to demand that the Egyptians release Joseph's coffin to him.

But one person did—his devoted protégé, Moses.

The mission that Moses was charged with by the deity hiding behind the burning bush could not have been to free his people from Egyptian bondage. The tribe had already been expelled from the land of the Nile and were living without Egyptian restraint in Midian. Instead, Reuel, impersonating Yahweh, ordered the prophet to retrieve Joseph's bones. Moses eagerly acquiesced because he wanted to fulfill the dying Joseph's request to be buried in the Promised Land. Little did he suspect that the real purpose of his journey was to deliver Joseph's remains to Reuel in the aid of black magic.

In his disguise as Yahweh, Reuel taught Moses magic tricks guaranteed to mesmerize the children of Israel. The first was to transform a hypnotized snake into a rod. This was Magic 101 for an Egyptian priest. When the snake was dropped it jolted out of its trance and quickly slithered away. As high priest to the Midians, who were known as "sons of the snake" Reuel would have been familiar with the reptiles—and due to his position—perhaps even an expert snake charmer.

During the second "miracle" Moses shut off the blood flow to his arm, turning his hand white as if it had become leprous. The last trick was to transform water into blood. All three acts were designed to invoke terror. Snakes, leprosy, and the miraculous appearance of blood all evoked great fear in the Israelites. They would want to avoid such terrifying supernatural sights; precisely Reuel's aim since none of the tricks invited close examination.

Today, only at a religious revival complete with dramatic faith healings, would you be likely to find an audience so impressed by magic that they would believe such displays to be acts of God. Most people would need a more spectacular exhibition to entice them to abandon their homes and follow a stranger—no matter how charismatic—into the wilderness. We're reminded of Christopher Marlowe's alleged objections to Moses as a magician, which were touched on in chapter 1, namely that his tricks would only work on the gullible.

Having been given his instructions from Yahweh, Moses returned from the Mountain of God to speak with Reuel, ignorant of the fact that Reuel had been the Voice of the Burning Bush that he had listened to so intently. "And Moses went and returned to Jethro his father-in-law, and said unto him, Let me go, I pray thee, and return unto my brethren which are in Egypt, and see whether they be yet alive. And Jethro said to Moses, Go in peace. And the LORD [Yahweh] said unto Moses in Midian, Go, return into Egypt: for all the men are dead which sought thy life."[32]

It seems that Reuel (Jethro) had no objection to his son-in-law returning to Egypt. But he hadn't foreseen that Moses would take his wife and child with him. To get them back Reuel was forced to play God at the inn and leave Moses to travel on to Egypt with Aaron. One can only wonder with what glee Levi (acting as Aaron) must have felt at the prospect of retrieving Joseph's bones. Fully aware of the script written by Reuel he would play his role to the hilt.

Joseph was an unrivaled hero to the Israelites. The return of his bones inspired great loyalty. As Moses solemnly accompanied his coffin as it was carried before the assembly of Israelites,* the people were satisfied that they'd found their new Joseph. A true son of his father. He would lead them to the Promised Land just as Joseph had saved them from starvation during the drought in Canaan.

The first act of Reuel's coup was complete.

---

*We learn in Joshua 24:32 that Joseph's bones were buried in Shechem.

8

——•——

Into the Wilderness

Whosoever toucheth the mount shall be surely put to death.

EXODUS 19:12.

The image of Moses has been seared into the popular imagination as a bearded hero in flowing robes who took on an evil pharaoh and liberated his people from Egyptian slavery. The story goes that, initially, in a futile attempt to gain their freedom, Moses and Aaron try to capture the pharaoh's favor with bedazzling displays of magic. Their efforts leave him unimpressed. Like the convenient appearance of angels and the commanding voice of God the royal command performance is witnessed only by the few who stand to benefit from this brazen bit of ultimate name dropping. Such a lack of authoritative evidence concerned the Israelites who were puzzled that their esteemed elders weren't present for the display as would have been the custom.

A Jewish folktale tried to address this nagging problem:

Moses and Aaron now invited all the elders of Israel to accompany them to Pharaoh. The elders started out with the leaders, but stealthily, on their way, they dropped off, one by one, and two by two, so that when at last the sons of Aaron reached the palace, they

were alone. And the Lord said: "Since ye have acted thus and abandoned my messengers, ye will be punished." When the hour, therefore, came for Moses to receive the Law on Mount Sinai, the elders
of Israel were not permitted to accompany him, and to ascend the
holy mountain, for they were told to tarry at the foot of the mountain and to wait until Moses returned.[1]

Moses and Aaron were the only members of the tribe present at court
because the elders had lost their nerve when the moment came to face a
pharaoh who held absolute power over their lives. The folktale satisfied
the people's curiosity about their conspicuous absence. But the people
had another problem with the story. They knew that commoners would
never have dared enter the palace. The pharaoh was notoriously ruthless
so how, they wondered, did Moses and Aaron penetrate the substantial
security that surrounded Egypt's leader? Another folktale explains: "But
Moses and Aaron penetrated into the palace, led by the angel Gabriel,
who brought them in, unobserved by the guards."[2]

Since these two "heroes" were the only witnesses to their own
amazing deeds (such as Aaron's rod not only transforming into a
serpent but swallowing the serpents of the Egyptian magicians) we
must keep our skeptic's hat on. Absent our faith in the truthfulness
of Moses and Aaron, we suggest something less sensational but no less
significant took place when Moses returned to Egypt. His sacred mission to retrieve the bones of his father was something the Egyptians
could appreciate. And, as we've established, Moses was a respected
Egyptian priest trained in the holy city of Heliopolis. The holder of
such an esteemed position would have been guaranteed an audience
with the pharaoh.

The Israelites learned about the amazing miracles performed for the
pharaoh as *stories* told by Moses and Aaron. When simple magic fails
to bend the pharaoh's will and they can't convince him to release the
Israelites they are forced to turn to a more powerful display of sorcery.

The trump card that finally influences the pharaoh is Moses's
claim that God had personally warned Moses that a series of devastat-

ing plagues would break over the Egyptians. The prospect of these ten plagues were so terrifying, especially the death of firstborn sons, that the reluctant but fearful pharaoh finally agrees to grant the Israelites their freedom. But at the last moment, perhaps suspecting that he's been tricked, he changes his mind and orders his army to pursue the fleeing tribe. Facing the insurmountable obstacle of the sea, Moses wields his magic staff to part the waters, allowing the Israelites to cross to dry land. After they have safely reached the other side he not only brings the raging water back together but drowns the pharaoh and his army in the process.

These wonderful and colorful events have formed the backbone of the Hollywood version of the prophet's story. What are we to make of them? Are they true? Are they exaggerations of real events? Or are they the stuff of fantastical fiction?

PLAGUES

Sigmund Freud believed that Moses acquired monotheism from the priests of Heliopolis who practiced it in secret. Such secrecy was essential because Egyptians had come to hate the idea of worshipping a single god. The rule of Pharaoh Akhenaten was a time they'd rather forget. Indeed, it is archaeology, not Egyptian history that tells the real story of that age and its beliefs. Egyptian historians wiped clean the whole blasphemous subject of Akhenaten's time. But there were, according to Sigmund Freud and others, a group of priests who remained secretly loyal to the monotheistic teachings of Akhenaten.

Egyptian monotheism began as a counter-religion during a time when the country was suffering from a series of natural disasters. The German biblical scholar Jan Assmann defined a counter-religion as one that "rejects and repudiates everything that went before and what is outside itself as 'paganism.'"[3] But what made it possible for such a radical religion to take hold in Egypt? Was it just because Akhenaten was pharaoh and held the power to enforce his beliefs? Certainly, this was true. But there was another reason why he was able to carry through his reforms: the series of devastating natural disasters had shaken the people's faith in their traditional gods.

Ian Wilson's *The Exodus Enigma* links the story of the exodus and its series of "plagues" with the eruption of a volcano on the Greek island of Thera.[4] It exploded with the force of six thousand nuclear weapons sending a cloud of smoke and ash high into the atmosphere and causing darkness to fall during daylight as far away as Egypt. The volcanic ash asphyxiated animals, destroyed crops, and left a fine dust spread over the land. The red iron oxide within the ash settled in lakes and the Nile River, turning its water the color of blood. As Wilson notes, volcanic eruptions are frequently accompanied by swarming flies, which in turn are swallowed by an ever-increasing population of frogs. All these natural consequences, Wilson argues, are reflected in the story of the plagues that God is said to have brought down upon Egypt to persuade the Egyptian pharaoh to free the Israelites.

Even in the twenty-first century, in April 2010, twenty countries initiated an ATC Zero (Air Traffic Control Zero—all airspace closed), the first since 9/11, after a volcano in Iceland exploded ash over western Europe, affecting the lives of millions. The impact of the eruption of even this minor volcano sometimes left sophisticated media at a loss to process it. We can hardly imagine the devastating effect an eruption would have had on the primitive people brought to their knees by it thousands of years ago. What other cause could they assume was behind this blow besides a magical, malevolent force or the hand of a supernatural power?

As we will see, much later the physical events caused by the volcanic eruption would be attributed to the God of the Israelites: "And the LORD said unto Moses, Stretch out thine hand toward heaven, that there may be darkness over the land of Egypt, even darkness which may be felt. And Moses stretched forth his hand toward heaven; and there was a thick darkness in all the land of Egypt three days."[5] Other plagues related to the volcanic eruption but attributed to God included the death of "all the cattle of Egypt"[6] and "the LORD rained hail upon the land of Egypt"[7] leaving "small dust in all the land of Egypt,"[8] "and all the waters that were in the river were turned to blood."[9] God also sent "swarms of flies"[10] and "frogs came up, and covered the land of Egypt."[11]

In *Act of God,* author Graham Phillips expanded upon Wilson's work. Reviewing changes in radiocarbon dating, Phillips recalibrated the timeline of the volcanic explosion, dating it to just before the rise of Akhenaten who came to power around 1364 BCE. Phillips believes that the resulting catastrophe was so traumatic for Egyptians that they felt abandoned by their gods.[12] Akhenaten manipulated that fear to initiate his revolutionary idea of monotheism.

The priests of Heliopolis played a pivotal role in this religious revolution. According to Egyptian mythology, Phillips explains, the world had once before experienced a near world-ending catastrophe when the goddess Sekhmet had tried "to annihilate the human race. She was the negative aspect of the sun's power, and it was the sun that was being obscured."[13] In the story, the sun god "Re" saves humanity. The priests of Heliopolis, Phillips notes, were "quick to draw attention to this fact."[14] In their theology, Re had been promoted to the role of supreme god. This was henotheism, the "belief in one god without asserting that he is the only God."[15] Having been educated within this Re cult, the new pharaoh, Akhenaten, took the notion one step further and declared that Re was the *only* God! And further, Akhenaten, was his prophet! This was monotheism, the "doctrine that there is only one God."[16]

The idea that Thera's volcanic explosion had a devastating effect on the Egyptian environment is compelling. But the idea that the exodus occurred following the demise of the reign of Pharaoh Akhenaten, as Graham Phillips suggests, can be explained by other forces. Political human forces rather than environmental ones.

As we've noted, Akhenaten's monotheism was a counter-religion, one that declared that the sacred beliefs of the past must be eradicated to satisfy the world-saving sun god Re. But after Akhenaten's seventeen-year reign ended, succeeding pharaohs turned violently against his religion. Akhenaten was deemed a terrible heretic whose influence had to be destroyed once and for all.

The priests of Heliopolis who had championed Akhenaten were

thrown into disrepute. Heliopolis and its temple were considered too sacred to destroy but there was zero tolerance for any expression of monotheism and a fanatic effort at rewriting history succeeded in wiping the slate clean—leaving no trace of Akhenaten's religious reforms. His idea that a single god reigned supreme would have remained unknown to the world if archaeologists hadn't discovered the holy city of Amarna.

THE ENCLAVE CULTURE

Under constant threat of persecution by succeeding pharaohs, the priests of Heliopolis still loyal to the religious reforms of Akhenaten were forced underground. They became what the biblical scholar Mary Douglas called an "enclave culture" where a minority "develops a multitude of purity laws in order not to be swallowed by the majority culture."[17] Having originated as a counter-religion, monotheism was transformed first into an enclave culture that ultimately became a secret society.

Rebelliously, the priests of Heliopolis continued to develop their religion and as part of their lore, we suggest, they integrated the "plagues" that befell Egypt before the rise of Akhenaten into their secret theology. The terrible catastrophes became part of their cult and Akhenaten's single God, Aten, was held responsible for the disaster that had devastated their world. They needed a new prophet to take up their cause.

That prophet was Moses, the grandson of their high priest.

After having fallen under Reuel's spell Moses returned to Egypt to collect the bones of his father, Joseph. It seems probable that he would have visited with the people who had educated him, the priests of Heliopolis who saw in their former colleague a possible prophet who could revive Akhenaten's monotheism. They urged Moses to propagate the powerful story of the plagues as being an integral part of monotheism.

Remember that no other Israelites accompanied Moses when he returned to Egypt and the magic he and Aaron performed before the pharaoh was witnessed by them alone. When Moses returned to

Midian accompanying his father's coffin he also brought with him the stories preserved by the priests of plagues that had devastated the land centuries earlier. Just like the stories that Moses and Aaron had told about the magic that they had performed at the royal court—nobody could challenge their version of events.

Reuel was naturally curious about the secret teachings of the priests of Heliopolis and when Moses revealed them to him he rushed to incorporate them into his emerging teachings. By this time, Reuel had decided to leave Midian where the locals were becoming hostile and lead the children of Israel to the Promised Land. Reuel wanted to turn the miraculous stories Moses and Aaron had acquired in Egypt into a reality for the Israelites. He decided to present them with a vivid miracle— one that they would never forget. One that would confirm the stories Moses and Aaron had brought to Midian from their Egyptian trip.

PARTING THE RED SEA

Hollywood has given us the quintessential Moses scene when Charlton Heston raises his arms and commands the parting of the Red Sea. But scholars have cast doubt upon this spectacle: the roaring wall of water falling back before Moses's magic staff. There is considerable skepticism about where it is claimed that the event took place. The most direct translation of the relevant passage declares that the "miracle" took place at the "reed sea" not the Red Sea (as Hollywood would prefer). After Martin Noth explored this mysterious body of water he concluded that we "can no longer make out where" the "reed sea" was. He notes that the context implies a body of water near where Reuel plied his trade as a high priest: "In I Kings 9:26, as is clear from the context, the *gulf of el-aqaba* on the east side of the Sinai peninsula is described as the 'reed sea.'"[18] Midian was the ancient land directly east of the *gulf of el-aqaba*. The other country bordering the gulf was Edom.

In 2003, Colin Humphreys's *The Miracles of Exodus* made, for the first time, physical sense of Moses's parting of the sea. He began by noting that, "reeds grow in freshwater rivers and lakes and not in saltwater seas . . . *Yam suph* must therefore refer to an inland freshwater reedy lake in which reeds grow: hence the name 'Sea of Reeds.'"[19]

This narrowed the search to a very specific body of water. Following Martin Noth, Humphreys wrote, "Since 1 King 9:26 states that Solomon built his ships at Ezion Geber, near Elath in Edom, on the shore of the Red Sea, and since we can identify ancient Edom as a country adjacent to the Gulf of Aqaba, we can say with reasonable certainty that the biblical Red Sea is the Gulf of Aqaba."[20]

Reuel was a Prince of Edom. The exodus's most spectacular drama took place on his home turf.

But how *did* Moses part the waters? This, according to Humphreys, is entirely possible because of a natural phenomenon known as "wind setdown." The Bible tells us that before the sea of reeds parted, "the Lord caused the sea to go back by a strong east wind all that night."[21] Such a wind blowing from the east in the Gulf of Aqaba creates a phenomenon familiar to oceanographers. Because of a wind setdown the depth of the waters can vary considerably.[22] "For example, a strong wind blowing along Lake Erie, one of the Great Lakes, has produced water elevation differences of as much as sixteen feet between Toledo, Ohio, on the west and Buffalo, New York, on the east."[23]

The situation at the Gulf of Aqaba is ideal for a wind setdown because the prevailing wind is from the northeast* and the gulf extends to the southwest. Since the gulf is over a hundred miles long, the water levels near the shore create ideal conditions for a wind setdown, which forces the waters here to recede by a full mile.[24]

In the gulf near the shore, where the freshwater reeds grow, there are two dips in the water basin that expose a hump of land. The children of Israel might well have seen a vast sea blocking their passage the night before the wind setdown occurred. The hump of land was below normal sea level. In the morning, after the northeast wind had pushed the waters to the southwest, the hump formed a miraculously dry path-

---

*Humphrey notes that the Hebrews only recognized the four cardinal directions (north, south, east, and west) and did not subdivide them into northeast, etc. Hence the account in Exodus is consistent with a "strong east wind."

way. There would indeed be water to the left and right as they crossed over where, the night before, there been sea. And after they crossed over the hump and the winds died down and the waters returned, the pathway was again swallowed by water.

So, the parting of the "reed sea" could have been nothing more than a natural phenomenon familiar to the magician Reuel that he used to amaze his unsophisticated countrymen. And this would not be the only "wonder" of Edom that Reuel would use to frighten and amaze the children of Israel.

There were some skeptics in the crowd. Not all the Israelites were convinced that Moses was a great leader. Shortly after they left the "sea of reeds" and had traveled in the relentless heat for three days, "the people murmured against Moses saying, 'What shall we drink?'"[25] Soon Moses, with the aid of a guide supplied by Reuel, discovered "twelve wells of water,"[26] which put a temporary stop to the grumbling. However, the seeds of discontent had been planted. As the journey continued into the "wilderness of Sin" dragging over two and half months the people became desperate, "And the whole congregation of Israel murmured against Moses and Aaron in the wilderness."[27]

To satisfy the new demands of the dissatisfied Israelites, Moses arranged an encounter with God (played by Reuel) who reassures him, "I have heard the murmurings of the children of Israel: speak unto them, saying, At even ye shall eat flesh, and in the morning ye shall be filled with bread; and ye shall know that I am the Lord your God."[28]

It should come as no surprise that the next public "miracle" was designed to curb the people's relentless hunger and put an end to any further murmurings. In the morning they wake to find a sweet, white, sticky substance, manna, covering the ground. A miracle? Like the parting of the sea, the food delivered at this critical point was provided by Reuel's inside knowledge of the plants found in abundance in his homeland. Manna was a natural product of the tamarisk tree that grows in Edom.[29]

Arriving like magic with the dew in the night it was baked into cakes that satiated the tribe's hunger. Manna has been identified as everything from tamarisk resin to lichen to hallucinogenic mushrooms, which interestingly, considering that this stressed, desperate, nomadic tribe was subject to the eccentricities of a volatile leader, produce spiritual experiences.

The manna satisfied for a short period. It was thirst that set off the next round of murmurings. The people cried, "Wherefore is this that thou hast brought us up out of Egypt, to kill us and our children and our cattle with thirst?"[30] Once again, Moses had to produce a quick miracle. He asks God, "What shall I do unto this people? they be almost ready to stone me."[31] The Lord replies, "Behold, I will stand before thee there upon the rock of Horeb; and thou shalt smite the rock, and there shall come water out of it, that the people may drink."[32]

"The rock of Horeb" provides a clue as to where the tribe is to be found at this time in their travels. They have arrived at the Mountain of God where Moses will receive the Ten Commandments. It is here that Aaron will eventually die and be buried. It is in the heart of Edom, at Petra (in modern-day Jordan)—a location that Reuel would know well. Natural watering holes are plentiful because of its perennial stream and regular flash floods. Reuel would have been aware of such a reliable watering place and it would have been a simple task to order his confederates to cover a well with a frail material that could easily be broken by Moses's "magical" staff.

Today, visitors to Petra will encounter a small domed shrine called *Ain Musa,* which means "Spring of Moses" "located on the west side of the gorge."[33] This "miracle" of water was nothing exceptional at all—a trick designed to impress the children of Israel when they were at yet another vulnerable point: this time desperately afraid of death from thirst.

Still later the Israelites demanded meat. Moses consults with Yahweh. Before long quails "miraculously" fall from the sky.[34] Elias Auerbach reports that travelers in this part of the world tell stories of how "migratory birds, tired of flying across the hot desert, suddenly appear in large numbers; worn out they descend upon the oasis to quench their thirst and thus supply the inhabitants of the oasis with a rare and desired meat dish."[35]

So, far from being a miracle the startling sight of birds falling from the sky was yet another natural phenomenon well known to Reuel.

WHERE WAS THE MOUNTAIN OF GOD?

Around 310 CE, an eighteen-year-old Christian named Catherine of Alexandria had a theological confrontation with the Roman emperor Maxentius. The beautiful, quick-witted woman confounded the powerful man with the force of her arguments. Astounded by her audacity he offered to marry her if she would change her faith. She refused. Maxentius then summoned fifty prominent philosophers who attempted to make a fool of Catherine but to no avail. The enraged emperor ordered the philosophers burned alive before departing on a journey leaving Catherine in the hands of his queen and two hundred bodyguards. When he returned Maxentius discovered that Catherine had converted his wife and bodyguards to Christianity. He promptly had the girl beheaded.

It is at this point that a story that might have been rooted in real historical events veers abruptly into legend. Angels are said to have carried Catherine's head south where they deposit the relic on a mountain in the Sinai Peninsula. Shortly afterwards, the hermits who were living in caves on this mountain saw an opportunity to exploit the tales of miracles. In a shrewd PR move, they renamed their mountain Jebel Musa (Moses's Mountain), establishing a not very subtle claim that it was the sacred mountain of the book of Exodus. They soon "found" further evidence for their bold, self-serving assertion.

The sacred mountain received official approval in 337 CE, when Empress Helen persuaded the Greek Orthodox Church to establish a sanctuary at its foot at the site where the locals claimed the "burning bush" once glowed in all its glory before the amazed Moses. Thousands of pilgrims journeyed to the sanctuary and they, in turn, drew the attention of nomadic tribes who wasted no time setting up a lucrative business raiding and looting distracted travelers. A small chapel was built in 363 CE at the peak known to the Christian world as "Mount Sinai."

In 537 CE the Byzantium Emperor Justinian responded to the outcry of the pilgrims who were by then constantly under attack by the nomads. He dispatched his court architects to supervise the construction of a proper fortress and monastery at the sacred place. Slaves from Romania were dispatched to do the hard labor. Legend has it that when Justinian learned that the fortress was at the *foot* of the holy mountain rather than at its peak, as he imagined, he had the chief architect beheaded. The slaves were freed, and many stayed on to become monks at what was now officially a holy site. Today, it remains protected by its original massive fortifications. Up until the last one hundred years, entry could only be gained by reaching a door located high in the outer walls. Crusaders could be found in the area until 1270 and their tales instigated the wander lust of Christian pilgrims from Europe.

At this dusty, isolated place where the stars shine undimmed in the desert night sky can be found a collection of early codices and manuscripts second only to that of the Vatican's library. The monastery holds Hebrew, Arabic, Greek, Syriac, Georgian, Coptic, and Armenian written treasures.

The remnants of the fortress remain today, and the monastery has been designated a UNESCO world heritage site. The Sacred and Imperial Monastery of the God-Trodden Mount of Sinai, otherwise known as St. Catherine's Monastery, continues to receive thousands of pilgrims who travel by air rather than camel and enjoy all the conveniences of the twenty-first century.

Each morning dedicated pilgrims (those who reject the donkey or camel route), convinced that they are following in the footsteps of Moses, pass the merchants' stalls and start their long climb up the 7,500-foot mountain. Under a brilliant blue Sinai sky, they follow the 4,000 worn steps that have been polished to a smooth hue by thousands of feet over the centuries. It takes three hours to reach the summit of the "Path of Moses" where they are rewarded for their dedication with the cool relief of a small chapel.

The present building was erected in 1934 to replace a sixteenth-century structure badly in need of reconstruction. The older, sixteenth-century chapel had, in turn, been built over the remains of the original chapel of 363 CE. Emperor Justinian I who ruled from 527–565 ordered the monastery constructed to enclose the Chapel of the Burning Bush, which had been built by Constantine I's mother, Helena. The living bush is advertised as a descendant of the original.

Visitors are shown the cleft in the mountain where Moses sheltered while Yahweh passed by. They are invited to examine the rock face from which God cut the tablets upon which he carved the Ten Commandments. The experience is exhilarating for the devout. But is it based upon fact or fiction?

JEBEL MUSA

There is no evidence that Moses ever set foot in this part of the Sinai Peninsula. A legend created in the third century CE by hermits who had a vested interest in promoting their isolated mountain about an incident that supposedly took place many centuries before is hardly a reliable source. Before the hermit's imaginative claim no one believed that the place that came to be known as Jebel Musa (Moses's Mountain) was associated with the prophet.

The subject of the location of the Mountain of God has invited controversy for centuries. Biblical scholar Martin Noth was convinced that the mountain that rose above St. Catherine's Monastery had nothing to do with the story told in the Torah. The biblical text, he argued, pointed to a volcanic mountain, "we should no longer look for it on the present 'Sinai peninsula,' for there have never been any active volcanoes upon it in historical times. . . . On the other side of the gulf of *el-ʿaqaba* in the north-west part of what is now Saudi Arabia, . . . there are volcanoes which are still active today."[36] On strictly geological grounds, Noth thought that the area around Midian (northern Saudi Arabia) and Edom (southern Jordan) was a far more probable location for the Mountain of God.

More recently Harvard scholar Frank Cross took issue with linking the biblical text with a volcano. "Such a tradition surely rests, not on a description of volcanic activity, but upon hyperbolic language used in the storm theophany."[37] And later, "When Sinai or Zion is described as on fire or smoking, we need not send for seismologists. Experienced mountain climbers know well the frequent violence and special danger of the thunder storm in high mountains is not a rare sight, moreover, to see lightning strike high points including often isolated trees near the timber line. Those who bear witness to such sights speak of explosions of fire, smoke and steam."[38] Were the terrifying events that shook the children of Israel the effect of a volcano or a storm?

Whether we should look at the Sinai Peninsula or Midian or Edom as the site of Moses's celebrated experiences on the Mountain of God cannot be determined by geology alone.

Israeli archaeologists rule out the Sinai:

> Except for the Egyptian forts along the northern coast, not a single campsite or sign of occupation from the time of Ramses II and his immediate predecessors and successors has ever been identified in Sinai. And it has not been for lack of trying. Repeated archaeological surveys in all regions of the peninsula, including the mountainous area around the traditional site of Mount Sinai near Saint Catherine's Monastery . . . have yielded only negative evidence: not even a single shed, no structure, not a single house, no trace of an ancient encampment.[39]

THE FIRST EUROPEAN AT THE MOUNTAIN OF GOD

In the summer of 1812, Johann Ludwig Burckhardt* (1784–1817) made his way to the ruins at Petra in present-day Jordan. No other European had risked traveling so deeply into this ancient land. To disguise his real identity Burckhardt dressed as a Bedouin and spoke Arabic. The reason he gave for the deception was recorded in his journal. "I was without

---

*He was also known as John Lewis Burckhardt.

protection in the midst of a desert where no traveller had ever before been seen; and a close examination of these works of the infidels, as they are called, would have excited suspicions that I was a magician in search of treasures."[40]

On August 22 he came across a haunting rock formation that would lead him to the ruins. "I perceived a chasm about fifteen or twenty feet in breadth . . . called the El Syk. . . . The precipices on either side of the torrent are about eighty-feet in height; in many places the opening between them at top is less than at bottom, and the sky is not visible from below."[41]

He walked in the shadows of the towering cliffs until he was stopped in his tracks by a remarkable sight. "On the side of the perpendicular rock, directly opposite to the issue of the main valley, an excavated mausoleum came in view, the situation and the beauty of which are calculated to make an extraordinary impression upon the traveller, after having traversed for nearly half an hour such a gloomy and almost subterranean passage as I have described. It is one of the most elegant remains of antiquity."[42]

What he saw was the Khazneh Mausoleum, the "Treasury of the Pharaoh." It had been carved from the great chasm's red rock. Thousands travel to see this wonder, especially since it was popularized by the movie *Indiana Jones and the Last Crusade*. Indy and his father enter the Khazneh Mausoleum searching for the Holy Grail. The movie ends with father and son riding from between the narrow red walls of what the locals call the Siq.

The word may be derived from the Greek *sakos,* meaning "tomb," or "shrine." But today it refers to the entire length of the crags that enclose a shade-and-sun-darted chasm reminiscent of the Grand Canyon.

The Siq and the Petra ruins lie within the confines of an ancient gorge named the Wadi Musa by the local Bedouins, which means the "Valley of Moses." In 1930, the author George Livingston Robinson (1865–1958) published a detailed description of the Siq and its surrounding tombs and sacred places. Robinson didn't put much stock in the Bedouin's stories of Moses. He begins *The Sarcophagus of an Ancient Civilization* by dismissing "a worthless Mohammedan legend to the effect that Moses died and was buried in this valley!"[43] He was arrogantly discarding the local Islamic tradition passed down through generations that held that Moses died at Petra and that the remains of both Moses and Aaron had once rested there.

The Torah claims that Moses died on a mountain overlooking the Promised Land. His burial spot remained a mystery.

Robinson was most interested in proving that a "High Place" overlooking the Siq was once the holy place of the "sons of Esau." He believed that the ancient ruins of Petra were the sacred remains of the heart of Edom. Drawing upon a journal he had kept thirty years earlier (May 3, 1900) Robinson concluded, "If we mistake not, we have found nothing less than the principal High Place, or sanctuary of the sons of Esau, which henceforth will throw valuable light upon the religion of the Edomites and illumine the whole question of worship in High Places, so frequently alluded to in the Old Testament."[44]

Robinson describes the High Place as being about six hundred feet above the trench known as the Siq. "The whole summit of the mountain on which the High Place is located, does not exceed five hundred feet in length by one hundred feet in breadth. . . . The view obtained from it is superb, commanding not only all of the city site, or valley bottom of the Wadi Musa. . . . So steep are the sides of the whole ridge that without artificial cuttings in the rocks ascent would be well-nigh impossible."[45]

Yahweh refers to the "artificial cuttings in the rocks" when he tells Moses to command the Israelites not to "go up by steps unto mine altar."[46] Robinson noted that, "The *height* of the perpendicular walls which bound the chasm is deceiving, and has deceived many."[47]

Burckhardt estimated the Siq cliffs to be about eighty feet high. Robinson estimated the average height as closer to two hundred feet. He noted, "The *entrance* to the Sik was easily defended. The rocks on either side are so high and the passage so narrow that a dozen men in ancient times could, without very much difficulty, have held at bay a whole army of Arab invaders."[48]

Robinson credits another American traveler for having identified the High Place as being of great religious importance to the Bible.

"To an American editor, Mr. Edward L. Wilson, is due the credit of having been the first to *see* this great, and now celebrated, sanctuary. . . . Mr. Wilson visited Petra in 1882."[49]

But it was Robinson, during his 1900 visit, who recorded the most detailed account of the sacred place of the priests of Edom. The High Place was described as having two pillars, a raised platform and a rectangular altar. Each of these he described, including measurements and speculating upon their various purposes. One thing was paramount to his thinking: he had found the Holy of Holies of the sons of Esau.

Reuel was one of those sons.

Astonishingly, Robinson also speculates that there might have been a cave carved into the walls used to broadcast a hidden speaker's voice. Such a device had been found in Israel at Gezer, another sacred High Place where an "inner chamber was the secret chamber, in which a priest, or a boy, was hidden, in order to serve as the mouthpiece of the god. The human voice issuing from the mouth of the narrow tunnel, connecting the two caves, would be regarded as the voice of a spirit."[50]

In Exodus 20 the Israelites hear, for the first time, the voice of Yahweh as he recites the Ten Commandments. Reuel might well have prepared a cave, like the one found in Gezer, which amplified God's voice* so much so that its sheer volume would have completely cowed the already terrorized Israelites.

Reuel's father had once ruled ancient Petra, a part of Edom. Edom consisted of a thirty-mile wide track of mountains that was over a hundred miles in length. Reuel spent much of his youth there and would have known of all its special features including one that was only recently rediscovered. In *The Moses Legacy,* Graham Phillips suggests that the real Mountain of God was near Petra: "According to the Book of Exodus, Moses first discovered the Mountain of God on the far side of the Sinai wilderness from the land of Midian, which would place it in the land of Edom. This is confirmed by the book of Numbers, which tells us that Aaron was buried on the Mountain of God in Edom. The

---

*As we will see, it may have been Moses who was speaking rather than Reuel.

first-century Jewish historian Josephus confirms the place of Aaron's death as the valley of Edom."[51]

The magician Reuel was an Edomite prince familiar with all the unique features of the Edomite mountain range and particularly the "High Place" that lies above the so-called Wadi Musa—Valley of Moses. It was at this High Place that the Egyptian Moses would disappear and be replaced by the masked Moses.

Until he left Edom to learn his trade in Egypt, Reuel, both as a boy and young man, would have climbed all over the mountainous land of his father. He would use this intimate knowledge to dramatic effect when the children of Israel settled beneath the tall walls of the gorge that hid the High Place. Reuel knew that in Canaanite mythology the sound of trumpets signified the coming of God. And he knew how the wind in this valley created a howling blast that imitated so well the din of trumpets and seemed to cause the claustrophobic walls to vibrate.

Phillips writes, "When there is a strong wind from the east, the Siq and Wadi Musa below act together to create a most unusual phenomenon. The wind howls down the narrow cleft to trumpet, quite literally, through the Wadi Musa gorge. The noise it makes is not only eerie: if you happen to be in the gorge itself it is deafening."[52]

Weather and geology had provided the magician Reuel with ideal tools for the creation of one of his most creative and effective tricks.

THE SETTING

The children of Israel had traveled across the desert until they reached a mountain range where Moses, or more likely his Kenite guide, directed the people through an opening in the mountain. It was the narrow entrance to the Siq and it was the beginning of a nightmare of confinement, claustrophobia, and terror for the long-suffering tribe.

Upon first crowding into the welcome embrace of the cool gorge the Israelites would have sighed with relief as they escaped the merciless heat. But it would not have been long before they realized that they were entering an almost subterranean, alien world. Huddling against the rock walls they were immediately warned by Moses, "And thou shalt set bounds unto the people round about, saying, take heed to yourselves, that ye go not up into the mount, or touch the border of it: whosoever toucheth the mount shall be surely put to death."[53]

Moses announced that Yahweh would speak to the people himself. His Voice would be channeled through the narrow crevice of the Siq's walls.

Imagine for a moment the fear that the people must have felt. They were hungry and thirsty and exhausted from their interminable journey. They had seen wonders that they never dreamed of and now they had been herded into a confined and strange place and warned that if they trespass they will be struck dead. And then the worst happens—the deafening blast of trumpets announces the coming of God. The thundering echo intensifies their claustrophobia, but the children of Israel can't flee their maker's fury. They are trapped. Some begin to whimper, to cry, to wail, magnifying each other's terror. A voice from above shouts commands but the people are far too frightened to comprehend or obey.

Only one man remains calm—Moses.

9

The Masked Moses

The skin of Moses' face shone: and Moses put the veil upon his face.

EXODUS 34:35.

The children of Israel were terrified by the sound of their God's voice as he dictated the Ten Commandments. Never had He spoken to all the people. His words echoed around the walls of the enclosed gorge as they huddled together like a herd of antelope cowed by encircling lions. The Voice had no obvious origin. The historian of ventriloquism Steven Connor explains that a voice that is "immune to the powers of the eye"[1] carries an especially strong psychological force. "Sound, especially sourceless, autonomous, or excessive sound will be experienced both as a lack and an excess; both as a mystery to be explained, and an intensity to be contained. Above all, sound, and as the body's means of producing itself as sound, the voice, will be associated with the dream and the exercise of power."[2]

No wonder the children of Israel were happy to let Moses, the one man who remained calm during this shocking encounter, ascend the Mountain of God. It was possible that he might pacify the invisible Deity who roared over them.

But what was really going on?

What the frightened tribe heard was not the words of the creator of the universe but the amplified voice of an Egyptian-trained magician. Reuel had deliberately brought the children of Israel to this precise location and set in place the necessary boundaries to ensure that no one stumbled across his plan. He told Moses to instruct the people not to approach the mountain any closer. The penalty for disobedience would be death. As always, Reuel needed his privacy. He could not afford to risk anyone catching the behind-the-scenes moves of his ventriloquism act. High above the gorge the master magician had concealed himself in a cave that had been carefully carved to amplify his voice.[3]

But what of the words he spoke? What was the true origin of the Ten Commandments?

ORIGIN OF THE TEN COMMANDMENTS

Of the 613 laws in the Torah only the Ten Commandments demand prime attention from Christians. But their significance lies not only in what they prescribe but also the clues to their origin that are contained within the words. Most people, when they think of the Ten Commandments, refer to passages from chapter 5 of the book of Deuteronomy in which Moses recites the words to the tribe, as he had received them from God, on the sacred mountain. He is God's spokesman. But another source, recorded in Exodus 20, decree that the commandments were spoken directly by God not to a lone individual but to the gathered, terrified Israelites.

The first commandment, "Thou shalt have no other gods before me"[4] doesn't assert that God is the only deity in existence but rather that the people are forbidden from placing any other god on a higher level. As mentioned in previous chapters, we suggest that the adoption of monotheism came from Moses who acquired the belief during his education among the priests of Heliopolis. They were the first to raise the sun god to a level of supremacy over all others without denying their existence. This is what theologians call *henotheism,* "the belief in one supreme god without any assertion of his unique nature," rather than monotheism, "the worship of an omnipotent and singular divinity."[5]

Raised among the priests of Heliopolis, the Pharaoh Akhenaten transformed henotheism into monotheism. But after his death, when the Egyptians turned violently against everything Akhenaten had stood for, the priests who still adhered to his teachings, we suggest, reverted to their original theological point of view in which one god reigned supreme over all others.

In our reconstruction, Reuel spoke the words that Moses revealed to him from the secret teachings of the priests of Heliopolis. Only later would Judaism be transformed into a purely monotheistic religion.*

In its original version, the second commandment is unequivocal: "Thou shalt not make unto thee any graven image, or any likeness of anything that is in heaven above, or that is in the earth beneath, or that is in the water under the earth: Thou shalt not bow down thyself to them, nor serve them: for I the LORD thy God am a jealous God, visiting the iniquity of the fathers upon the children unto the third and fourth generation of them that hate me; And shewing mercy unto thousands of them that love me, and keep my commandments."[6]

This commandment follows the precise guidelines set down by Akhenaten. It was he who would direct the destruction of the statues of the ancient Egyptian gods; statues that had formerly been treated as if they were living gods. The archaeologist Cyril Aldred explains that the Egyptian priests even acted as servants to these sacred statues. Each morning the priests "cleaned, anointed, clothed, fed and put them to rest as though there were living grandees."[7]

Akhenaten rebelled against the idea of worshipping man-made objects. He outlawed their production and their worship and set about destroying them. His hatred for graven images was absolute. This abhorrence is recorded as the second of the Ten Commandments.

The essence of Akhenaten's monotheism was his insistence upon

---

*The priests taken as hostages to Babylon felt the destruction of the homeland happened because Yahweh was angered by the Israelites recognizing other gods. It was only when they returned to Jerusalem, after years in Babylon, that they adopted a strict monotheism.

the existence of only one god and his rejection of all forms of image worship. These two facets of his religion are recorded as the first and second commandments. Akhenaten's fingerprints are all over them.

JOSHUA

When Moses reaches the Mountain of God a new right-hand man acting as his guard, minister, and warrior suddenly appears at his side. His name was Joshua and he would be tasked with leading the children of Israel into the Promised Land. When a character of such importance appears out of thin air our suspicions must be aroused. What is going on? Who was this stranger so strongly favored by Moses?

As he pondered his next move, Reuel was keenly aware of the split between the tribes who favored Joseph versus Judah's loyal followers.* Reuel already had one foot firmly in Judah's camp because of his alliance with Levi. But he couldn't hope to lead the divided tribes without bringing into his ranks a leader loyal to Joseph. One candidate stood out from the others—Joseph's younger brother Benjamin—son of Israel and his beloved wife Rachel who had died giving birth to Benjamin. After suffering the blow of losing Joseph, Israel refused to trust Benjamin's safety to Reuben, Simeon, Levi, or Judah when they traveled to Egypt seeking food. Nor would he risk Benjamin's life to save Simeon. Believing Benjamin was his last link to Rachel he spoiled the boy. Like Joseph, Benjamin grew to manhood cultivating a strong sense of entitlement. Slowly, his father became disillusioned with his son's character. Or lack of it.

Israel was ecstatic when he learned that Joseph had not only survived but had thrived as a powerful ally of the Egyptians. In an instant Benjamin felt overshadowed by the joyful news. All Israel could think or speak about was *Joseph, Joseph, Joseph.* A further insult came with Israel's last will and testament speech during which he depicted his

---

*This division led to a split of the Promised Land into two kingdoms: Israel in the north and Judah in the south.

youngest son in a most unflattering light. "Benjamin shall ravin as a wolf: in the morning he shall devour the prey, and at night he shall divide the spoil."[8]

Benjamin caught a glimpse of his future in his embittered father's words. Like Levi and Dinah, he suddenly found himself in dire need of a new identity.

One of Benjamin's roles is addressed in Moses's farewell speech. "The beloved of the LORD shall dwell in safety by him."[9] This points to Benjamin being a custodian and guardian of Moses's sacred tent. In the Torah only one man fulfilled this critical role. It was Joshua who ensured that no one trespassed into the inner sanctum. We suggest that "Joshua" was simply a new identity adopted by Benjamin. Under the name Joshua, Benjamin was unencumbered by his father's denigration.

> And it came to pass, when Moses went out unto the tabernacle that all the people rose up, and stood every man at his tent door, and looked after Moses, until he was gone into the tabernacle. And it came to pass, as Moses entered into the tabernacle, the cloudy pillar descended, and stood at the door of the tabernacle, and the LORD talked with Moses. And all the people saw the cloudy pillar stand at the tabernacle door: and all the people rose up and worshipped, every man in his tent door. And the LORD spake unto Moses face to face, as a man speaketh unto his friend. And he turned again into the camp: but his servant Joshua, the son of Nun, a young man, departed not out of the tabernacle.[10]

The Israelites were forbidden to enter the tabernacle without Moses's permission. While he was absent Joshua stood guard ready to slay any Israelite bold enough to enter. The Levite scribes attached the phrase "son of Nun" to Joshua's name to conceal the fact that Joshua was Joseph's brother. The character "Nun" was a ruse to confuse the readers of the Torah as to Joshua's identity. The scribes hated Joseph and didn't want any of the conquests attributed to Joshua to be in any way associated with Joseph.

Moses was Benjamin's nephew. How might Benjamin react to once again being overshadowed by Joseph—even if it was only through his son, Moses? Benjamin, in his new role as Joshua, played a waiting game, secure in the knowledge that Reuel would grant him power once Moses was dead. A deal had been cut. Benjamin, in his new persona of Joshua, would keep the tribes loyal to Joseph in line. Reuel now commanded allegiance in both camps. He could divide and rule. Benjamin, under his new persona of Joshua, gained a destiny as a glorious warrior and prophet.

The last time any Israelite saw Moses's face without a mask he was ascending the Mountain of God accompanied by Joshua; possibly the last man to see him alive.

AMALEK AND HIS SPY

Joshua's first battle took place when a tribe of fearless warriors, under the leadership of a man named Amalek, attacked the Israelites for no apparent reason. But there was cause: one that has gone unnoticed until now. The mystery is entwined in the branches of Reuel's family tree.

TABLE 9.1. ESAU'S DESCENDANTS BY HIS THREE WIVES

By Bashemath	By Adah	By Aholibamah
Reuel	Eliphaz	Jeush, Jaalam, and Korah
	Amalek	

Reuel's father, Esau, had three wives. Bashemath was Reuel's mother. Adah, Esau's second wife, gave birth to his firstborn son and heir, Eliphaz. When he grew up, Eliphaz had an affair with a concubine, Timna, who gave birth to Amalek. Korah was the third son of Esau's third wife, Aholibamah.

Amalek's uncle Korah was a son of Esau's third wife, Aholibamah. Amalek and Korah were about the same age and, we suggest, were allied in their hatred for Reuel.

Reuel was on bad terms with his fellow Edomites. After they left the Mountain of God, the Israelites resided at a place called Kadesh. From Kadesh they sent messengers to the king of Edom requesting safe passage through Reuel's native land so that they could cut short their journey to Canaan, the Promised Land. The king of Edom refused, saying, "Thou shalt not pass by me, lest I come out against thee with the sword."[11] The king didn't trust Reuel not to try to capture Edom with his newly-acquired army of Israelites.

Reuel's attempt to travel through Edom was thwarted by his illegitimate nephew, Amalek. The young man knew he would have no place in an Edom dominated by Reuel. He also knew that Reuel was a crafty magician, so he waited until the Israelites were at their weakest before launching his attack. But how did he know when the opportune moment had arrived?

It was likely that Reuel's half brother Korah acted as a spy for Amalek. Both men feared Reuel wanted to conquer Edom, their homeland. Korah was traveling with the Israelites pretending to be loyal to Reuel. This gave him inside knowledge of what was happening at the Mountain of God. In later passages we learn that he led a rebellion against the rule of the masked Moses. (This will be discussed further in chapter 11.)

Once they reached the Mountain of God, Reuel no longer needed Moses. He had served his purpose. He had provided Reuel with a holy bloodline and inspired the children of Israel to leave Midian and travel into the wilderness. The stage was now set for Reuel's most dramatic performances utilizing all the skills he had acquired as a magician in Egypt.

Before Amalek's attack, Reuel made a bold move to take control of the children of Israel under his Midian persona—the high priest Jethro.

JETHRO

While he was the high priest in Midian, Reuel used the name Jethro. He's depicted as a wise and kindly father-in-law to Moses who offers him sound advice on how the Israelites should be organized: "And Jethro, Moses' father-in-law, came with his sons and his wife unto Moses into the wilderness, where he encamped at the mount of God: And he said unto Moses, I thy father-in-law Jethro am come unto thee, and thy wife, and her two sons with her. And Moses went out to meet his father-in-law, and did obeisance, and kissed him; and they asked each other of their welfare; and they came into the tent."[12]

Moses's behavior is peculiar. Rather than greeting his wife, Zipporah, and their two sons, he rushes past them and bows before Reuel. It seems odd that a husband and father would ignore his wife and sons after a separation but by now Moses was lost to the spell of Reuel. This is the first mention of Zipporah and her sons since the incident at the inn where she circumcised one son to satisfy the angry Yahweh. As we have seen earlier, Reuel was playing the role of Yahweh to keep control of his grandsons. The passage above is the last time Zipporah is mentioned in the Torah. She was expendable. From this point on Moses's sons are raised by Reuel.

As Jethro, Reuel takes control of Moses. But the children of Israel still tremble after their experience with Yahweh, the terrifying mountain deity who shouted commandments at them. Reuel must calm their fears by offering a sacrifice to Yahweh before talking with key Israelites about what the future might hold. "And Jethro, Moses' father-in-law, took a burnt offering and sacrifices for God: and Aaron came, and all the elders of Israel, to eat bread with Moses' father-in-law before God."[13]

It is Reuel, not Moses or Aaron who "took burnt offering and sacrifice for God." Martin Noth believed that the Mountain of God must have been a Midianite sanctuary. "The role of the priest of Midian indicates that the holy place on the 'mountain of God' was a proper Midianite sanctuary."[14] Reuel was well acquainted with the Mountain of God and was familiar with all its geological and mystical significance.

Another strange aspect of this scene is that when Reuel goes with Aaron and the elders to eat bread, Moses is not mentioned as being a part of this most important ceremony. Martin Noth commented that it is "striking that he [Moses] is not explicitly mentioned, as it seems now as though we had a cultic meeting only between the priest of Midian on the one side and Aaron and the elders of Israel on the other."[15]

The same passage compelled the Israeli biblical scholar Elias Auerbach to write: "One thing strikes us immediately: Why does the foreign Midianite priest offer up the sacrifice? Why not Moses? Yet even among the guests at the sacrifice Moses is not named; his absence here is even more remarkable. Aaron who is named does not appear as a priest."[16]

The fact that Aaron should stand by idle while another priest (and a foreign one at that) is the first to offer a sacrifice to Yahweh speaks volumes about Reuel's power. The next day he made his bold gambit:

> And it came to pass on the morrow, that Moses sat to judge the people: and the people stood by Moses from the morning unto the evening. And when Moses' father-in-law saw all that he did to the people, he said, What is this thing that thou doest to the people? why sittest thou thyself alone, and all the people stand by thee from morning unto even? And Moses said unto his father-in-law, Because the people come unto me to inquire of God: When they have a matter, they come unto me; and I judge between one and another, and I do make them know the statutes of God, and his laws. And Moses' father-in-law said unto him, The thing that thou doest is not good. Thou wilt surely wear away, both thou, and this people that is with thee: for this thing is too heavy for thee; thou art not able to perform it thyself alone.[17]

The verb *to be able,* as Richard Friedman has noted, is used only by Jethro and the "Angel" who wrestled all night with Jacob changing his name to Israel (Genesis 32:24–33). It appears nowhere else in the Torah.[18]

When Reuel utters "this thing is too heavy for thee," Moses appears to fall into a hypnotic trance. Reuel weaves his spell tighter. "Hearken now unto my voice, I will give thee counsel, and God shall be with thee: Be thou for the people to Godward, that thou mayest bring the causes unto God: And thou shalt teach them ordinances and laws, and shalt shew them the way wherein they must walk, and the work that they must do."[19]

From this point on Moses falls completely under the sway of Reuel who swiftly commands him to impose a paramilitary structure on the Israelites. "Moreover thou shalt provide out of all the people able men, such as fear God, men of truth, hating covetousness; and place such over them, to be rulers of thousands, and rulers of hundreds, rulers of fifties, and rulers of tens: And let them judge the people at all seasons: and it shall be, that every great matter they shall bring unto thee, but every small matter they shall judge: so shall it be easier for thyself, and they shall bear the burden with thee."[20]

In the next line Reuel finally seizes the role that he feels born to— spokesman for God: "If thou shalt do this thing, and God command thee so, then thou shalt be able to endure, and all this people shall also go to their place in peace."[21] Reuel is now presuming to speak *on behalf* of God. Moses, in his suggestible, hypnotized state, accepts the magician's voice as the authentic Voice of God: "So Moses hearkened to the voice of his father-in-law, and did all that he had said. And Moses chose able men out of all Israel, and made them heads over the people, rulers of thousands, rulers of hundreds, rulers of fifties, and rulers of tens. And they judged the people at all seasons: the hard causes they brought unto Moses, but every small matter they judged themselves."[22]

These changes forced Moses to identify his most loyal followers. As Reuel intended, they would shortly become victims of the brutal purges that marked the rule of the masked Moses.

Even though Reuel had proven his dominance over Moses, the children of Israel rebelled and refused to follow Jethro. "And Moses let his father-in-law depart; and he went his way into his own land."[23] Reuel had encountered an unexpected roadblock. His attempt to take direct control of the Israelites (as Jethro) had failed.

HUR

With his Jethro persona no longer of use, Reuel slips back into the camp of the children of Israel under another persona, Hur; the name he used while traveling with the children of Israel.

According to Josephus, Hur was Miriam's husband.[24] Josephus treats the marriage as a well-known fact. But the Torah makes no mention of a marriage between Miriam and Hur, even though this must have been a spectacular event. Miriam was a prophetess and sister to Aaron. Her marriage was important, yet the Levite scribes have erased this relationship from the pages of the Torah. This confirms our holy bloodline idea that Reuel married Israel's daughter. By doing so, Reuel insured that the prophet Israel's blood would run through his grandson's veins.

Reuel's wife had transformed herself from the disgraced rape victim known as Dinah, into the highly respected prophetess and sister of Aaron—Miriam. She knew that her husband, Hur, Jethro, and Reuel were the same person but she kept her head down, for the time being. Only after the masked Moses took an Ethiopian wife would Miriam rebel (as we will see in chapter 11).

MOSES ASCENDS

Reuel was preparing his most spectacular performance unaware that there was a spy within the tribe's midst. The time of his greatest vulnerability was rapidly approaching. Reuel's half brother Korah witnessed these events. He was an Edomite and knew the territory like the back of his hand. While the rest of the Israelites were forbidden to approach the Mountain of God on pain of death, Korah was intimate with all the surrounding trails. It would have been easy for him to slip from camp unnoticed and ride to see his cousin, Amalek. A plan was set in place to rid their homeland of its unwelcome returning son, Reuel. But the perfect moment for Amalek's attack was still days away.

The children of Israel rested within the confines of the gorge while they waited for further instructions from the mountain god, Yahweh. Jethro had provided food by making a sacrifice and water had gushed from their well when Moses had released it with a strike of his mighty staff. The children of Israel had left the privations of their desert ordeal behind. Then Moses received new instructions from Yahweh: "And he said unto Moses, Come up unto the LORD, thou, and Aaron, Nadab, and Abihu, and seventy of the elders of Israel; and worship ye afar off. And Moses alone shall come near the LORD: but they shall not come nigh; neither shall the people go up with him."[25]

Nadab and Abihu were Aaron's sons.* Moses invites them and possibly seventy elders† to climb the mountain to see for themselves,

> the God of Israel: and there was under his feet as it were a paved work of a sapphire stone, and as it were the body of heaven in his clearness. And upon the nobles of the children of Israel he laid not his hand: also they saw God, and did eat and drink. And the LORD said unto Moses, Come up to me into the mount, and be there: and I will give thee tables of stone, and a law, and commandments which I have written; that thou mayest teach them. And Moses rose up, and his minister Joshua: and Moses went up into the mount of God. And he said unto the elders, Tarry ye here for us, until we come again unto you: and, behold, Aaron and Hur are with you: if any man have any matters to do, let him come unto them. And Moses went up into the mount.[26]

Moses expected to return. He says, "Tarry ye here for us, until we come again unto you."[27] But his face was never seen again.

By handing over power and authority to Aaron and Hur, Moses had sealed his fate.

He was murdered as he ascended the Mountain of God. Joshua, who had accompanied him, must have known his fate. And Aaron's sons, Nadab and Abihu, probably witnessed the crime.

For days the children of Israel waited in vain for their leader's return. As time passed, having themselves so recently experienced the threat of death by starvation and thirst, they were forced to accept that without access to food and water Moses must be dead, lost to the ravages of the dry mountain.

---

*Their horrible fate will be explored in Chapter 10.
†The phrase "and seventy of the elders of Israel" was likely added.

And when the people saw that Moses delayed to come down out of
the mount, the people gathered themselves together unto Aaron,
and said unto him, Up, make us gods, which shall go before us;
for as for this Moses, the man that brought us up out of the land
of Egypt, we wot not what is become of him. And Aaron said
unto them, Break off the golden earrings, which are in the ears of
your wives, of your sons, and of your daughters, and bring them
unto me. And all the people brake off the golden earrings which
were in their ears, and brought them unto Aaron. And he received
them at their hand, and fashioned it with a graving tool, after
he had made it a molten calf: and they said, These be thy gods,
O Israel, which brought thee up out of the land of Egypt. And
when Aaron saw it, he built an altar before it; and Aaron made
proclamation, and said, Tomorrow is a feast to the LORD. And
they rose up early on the morrow, and offered burnt offerings,
and brought peace offerings; and the people sat down to eat and
to drink, and rose up to play.[28]

The golden calf was designed to replace the esteemed figure of Moses
at the head of the procession of the children of Israel. Without a true
leader they were even more exposed to the harsh side of nature—and of
human predators. Who would lead them? Who knew the way out? The
Israelites had reached a low point.

KORAH THE SPY

It was likely that Reuel's half brother Korah acted as a spy for Amalek.
Both men feared Reuel wanted to conquer Edom, their homeland.
Korah was traveling with the Israelites pretending to be loyal to
Reuel. This gave him inside knowledge of what was happening at the
Mountain of God. In later passages we learn that he led a rebellion
against the rule of the masked Moses. (This will be discussed further
in chapter 11.) Korah recognized that the Israelites were at a low point.
Moses was missing. It was a perfect opportunity to deal Reuel a deci-

sive blow. Korah slipped from the camp under cover of night to alert Amalek* that it was time to strike.[29]

Joshua heard the battle from where he stood at the peak of the Mountain of God. "There is noise of war in the camp,"[30] he says. He spoke to Reuel because by now Moses was dead.

Acting as Moses, Reuel instructs Joshua, "Choose us out men, and go out, fight with Amalek: tomorrow I will stand on the top of the hill with the rod of God in mine hand. So, Joshua did as Moses had said to him, and fought with Amalek: and Moses, Aaron, and Hur went up to the top of the hill."[31] The hill overlooked the valley where the battle took place.

THE EGYPTIAN PUPPET

This was the most dangerous time for Reuel. With Moses dead the Israelites did not have the courage to fight Amalek's army. So, to calm their fears, and to provide them with inspiration, Reuel, disguised as Hur, along with Aaron (Levi) created a life-size figure of Moses that they operated as a puppet on a hill overlooking the battlefield:

> And it came to pass, when Moses held up his hand, that Israel prevailed: and when he let down his hand, Amalek prevailed. But Moses' hands were heavy; and they took a stone, and put it under him, and he sat thereon; and Aaron and Hur stayed up his hands, the one on the one side, and the other on the other side; and his hands were steady until the going down of the sun. And Joshua discomfited Amalek and his people with the edge of the sword.[32]

Martin Noth refers to the role played by Aaron and Hur as "a very strange helping part,"[33] but not so strange when we consider the

---

*Biblical scholars have never offered a rational reason for Amalek's attack, but we see here that Reuel's illegitimate nephew had good reason to try to kill his uncle and the army of Israelites who followed him. Amalek knew that there would be no place for him in an Edom controlled by Reuel.

important political role played by puppets in ancient Egypt,* the place where Reuel learned his trade. The sudden appearance of Moses on the hill overlooking the battlefield encouraged the children of Israel to fight valiantly against the army of Amalek. They had believed he was long dead but then, in their hour of need, Moses had reappeared on the hill to guide them to victory. The prophet was alive! God was on their side.

Reuel's brilliant puppet show during the battle against Amalek was just a prelude to the magician's most spectacular performance—that of the Shining Faced Moses whose terrible rages would come to dominate the Israelites.

From now on, the name *Moses* belonged not to Joseph's third son, but to the magician, Reuel.

THE SHINING FACE OF MOSES

The battle against Amalek had ended in a stalemate but considering the odds, the Israelites considered that a victory. It was a time of celebration, "And Miriam the prophetess, the sister of Aaron, took a timbrel in her hand; and all the women went out after her with timbrels and with dances. And Miriam answered them, Sing ye to the LORD, for he hath triumphed gloriously; the horse and his rider hath he thrown into the sea."[34]

This passage is usually associated with the death of the Egyptian soldiers who had followed the Israelites into the Red Sea and drowned when Moses released the waters that he had divided to allow safe passage for the tribe to the other side. But what Miriam's "Song of the Sea" was really referring to was a common mythological motif of the Canaanites. In their mythology (the Israelites still retained these beliefs despite Yahweh's commandments) the god Ba'l, a rider of the Clouds, defeats the Sea Prince by clubbing him and throwing him into the sea.[35] This happens just as Ba'l has risen from the dead. We suggest that Miriam's "Song of the Sea" spoke to a raised-from-the-dead Moses

---

*See chapter 3 for the use of puppets as acts of illusion used for political gain.

directing the defeat of Amalek's army, in the same way that Second World War soldiers would sing World War I songs: *It's a Long Way to Tipperary; Pack Up Your Troubles in Your Old Kit Bag.*

Once again Miriam led the children of Israel in celebration. Jubilance swept over the camp as the people, fueled by plenty of liquor, wildly danced around the golden calf and surrendered to the joy of victory over Amalek. The Israelites were now as high as they had formerly been low. This swing of emotion left them vulnerable to Reuel's perfectly timed act—his appearance as the Shining Faced Moses.

> And it came to pass, when Moses came down from mount Sinai with the two tables of testimony in Moses' hand, when he came down from the mount, that Moses wist not that the skin of his face shone while he talked with him. And when Aaron and all the children of Israel saw Moses, behold, the skin of his face shone; and they were afraid to come nigh him. And Moses called unto them; and Aaron and all the rulers of the congregation returned unto him: and Moses talked with them. And afterward all the children of Israel came nigh: and he gave them in commandment all that the LORD had spoken with him in mount Sinai. And till Moses had done speaking with them, he put a vail on his face.[36]

Aaron was unafraid to approach Moses because he knew that this was Reuel in disguise. The phrase "and all the rulers of the congregation" was likely a belated addition to the passage. The children of Israel were afraid of the glowing face for they feared that even the reflection of Yahweh's glory might strike them dead. Moses wore two masks, the shining face and the veil, but fear was his best defense for those who dared to question: is this really Moses? And to make that fear take root Moses, for the first time, exposed his terrible rage, "And it came to pass, as soon as he came nigh unto the camp, that he saw the calf, and the dancing: and Moses' anger waxed hot, and he cast the tables out of his hands, and brake them beneath the mount. And he took the calf which they had made, and burnt it in the fire, and ground it to powder, and strawed it upon the water, and made the children of Israel drink of it."[37]

The smashing of the tablets would have terrified the Israelites. They had never known such anger erupt from their meek and stuttering leader. By making the Israelites drink what they thought to be the gold donated for creating the golden calf, Reuel pulled off one more illusion. He kept the gold. It was precious not just for its obvious value but because—along with the more accessible oil—gold provided the essential ingredient to cover his face and force his subjects to turn away in fear from the shining mask that commanded their obedience.

Then Reuel dramatically upped the stakes. He accused the high priest Aaron of sinning against Yahweh's orders. When Yahweh had shouted the Ten Commandments upon the Israelites' arrival at the Mountain of God, he had added an eleventh law: "Ye shall not make with me gods of silver, neither shall ye make unto you gods of gold."[38] This is exactly what Aaron had done.

> And Moses said unto Aaron, What did this people unto thee, that thou hast brought so great a sin upon them? And Aaron said, Let not the anger of my lord wax hot: thou knowest the people, that they are set on mischief. For they said unto me, Make us gods, which shall go before us: for as for this Moses, the man that brought us up out of the land of Egypt, we wot not what is become of him. And I said unto them, Whosoever hath any gold, let them break it off. So they gave it me: then I cast it into the fire, and there came out this calf.[39]

Scrambling to defend himself, Aaron lies, declaring that when he tossed the gold into the fire it miraculously transformed into a golden calf. This contradicts the early statement in which Aaron "fashioned it with a graving tool."[40] For the high priest to have anything to do with the golden calf was a serious sin for which Yahweh should have punished Aaron. In a rare mention of Aaron's name, the Deuteronomist declares that Moses said, that Yahweh was "very angry with Aaron."[41]

So why *did* Aaron go unpunished?

This question has always puzzled biblical scholars. Martin Noth wrote "it is remarkable that Aaron's confession had no further consequences for his own person."[42] Elias Auerbach writes of the "strange leniency toward Aaron . . . found in the story of the Golden Calf."[43] But this odd incident makes sense when we understand what Reuel and Levi, in their disguises as the masked Moses and Aaron were really about as revealed by the following passage:

> Then Moses stood in the gate of the camp, and said, Who is on the LORD's side? let him come unto me. And all the sons of Levi gathered themselves together unto him. And he said unto them, Thus saith the LORD God of Israel, Put every man his sword by his side, and go in and out from gate to gate throughout the camp, and slay every man his brother, and every man his companion, and every man his neighbor. And the children of Levi did according to the word of Moses: and there fell of the people that day about three thousand men.[44]

The reason that the masked Moses didn't punish Aaron was because Reuel and Levi had planned the entire incident. The golden calf was a setup, providing the two conspirators with an excuse to slaughter anyone loyal to the first Moses. Reuel knew exactly who his enemies were, when, as Jethro, he had suggested a paramilitary structure should be imposed on the tribe, "So Moses hearkened to the voice of his father-in-law, and did all that he said. So, Moses chose able men out of all Israel, and made them heads over the people, rulers of thousands, rulers of hundred, rulers of fifties, and rulers of tens."[45] Moses had naively targeted his most loyal followers making it easy for Reuel and Levi to slaughter them.*

There was no need to punish Aaron—he was never an object of the plot. The true Moses and his supporters were the intended victims. This was not manslaughter—the act of an enraged man swayed by

---

*It is doubtful that three thousand were killed but those capable of resistance to the new regime were murdered.

uncontrollable anger. No. It was a cold, calculated murder of the true Moses and his supporters.

And where was Hur while the slaughter was carried out? Reuel had only adopted the persona of Hur when he realized that the Israelites were not going to accept him as Jethro, the high priest. Now that the real Moses was dead and Reuel had been transformed into the masked Moses, he no longer needed the Hur persona. Hur conveniently disappears from the Torah as suddenly as he appeared.

The reign of the masked Moses had been born in blood and much more would be shed before Reuel had reached his goal. The masked Moses was a very different character from the third son of Joseph. The true Moses who had been born in Heliopolis was a man who believed in one god and led his people by inspiration. His impostor was the cunning Reuel who appeared as the masked Moses and led by fear.

We can't know *how* Moses was murdered. Joshua might have killed him. He might have been poisoned during the final meal before he ascended the Mountain of God. Levi may have thrown him into a pit to die a death befitting the son of Joseph. Or Reuel might have done the job himself.

There are many ways that the execution might have taken place. There is no definite solution to that mystery. But we do have the answer to another ancient puzzle—where is his body?

10

————•————

Skull and Bones

There was nothing in the ark save the two tables of stone,
which Moses put there.

KINGS 8:9

R euel's sensational appearance before the children of Israel as a
shining-faced god mimicked the quintessential Egyptian drama
of Osiris. He adopted the center-stage role of Horus, a main player in
the drama whose Egyptian epithets include "He-of-the-radiant-face"
and "Shining-of-face."[1]

We recall how Osiris's brother, Seth, tricked him into climbing
into a coffin, after which he coldly nailed it shut and tossed it into
the Nile. The coffin was eventually retrieved by Osiris's wife, Isis.
But then Seth stole it again and this time he cut the body into fourteen parts before burying them in different locations. One by one,
Isis retrieved her husband's mutilated bones and, with the help of the
god Thoth, reassembled Osiris. Thoth fashioned an artificial penis
for Osiris since this vital body part had been swallowed by a fish. Isis
copulated with the Frankenstein-like remains of Osiris and gave birth
to Horus who then took revenge on Seth, by slaying his evil uncle
in battle.

During their Egyptian sojourn the children of Israel had become familiar with the story of the dysfunctional quartet of Osiris, Isis, Seth, and Horus. An association between Moses and Horus would have seemed natural to them. Both heroes were widow's sons: Horus being born to Isis after Osiris's death, and as we believe, Moses was born to Joseph's Egyptian wife after he was murdered. Both displayed shining faces.

As a young lector priest in Egypt, Reuel found that the story of Osiris spoke to his unique family circumstances. It didn't take long for his enflamed sense of justice to spin the ancient drama into a blueprint for the murder of Moses. In Reuel's mind he was Horus. Osiris represented Isaac, and Jacob embodied Seth. This was the reason Reuel changed Jacob's name to *Israel* meaning "struggles with god," a name that could not be more different than *Reuel,* which means "friend of god."[2]

Jacob had tricked Isaac just as Seth had tricked Osiris. Seth's trick ended in murder while Jacob's impersonation cost Reuel's father, Esau, and in his turn, Reuel the leadership of the Jews. The only way to rectify such an unforgiveable crime was for Reuel to seize that lost position of power by murdering and impersonating Moses.

The murder of Moses had one more parallel with the Egyptian tale that he wished to re-enact. The first order of business the shining-faced Moses undertook, after all opposition had been purged, was to order the construction of a holy coffin—the Ark of the Covenant.*

In it he placed the skull and bones of Moses.

It was Reuel's final salute to the Osiris story and offered the perfect culmination of his long-sought revenge.

THE ARK OF THE COVENANT

The Ark's dimensions[3] are typical of the Egyptian chests known as *tabots.*[4] Its cubic capacity is virtually identical to the famous "coffer"

---

*It was called the Ark of God, the Ark of the Testimony, the Ark of the LORD, the Ark of the Covenant of the LORD, the Ark of the Covenant of God, the Ark, and the Ark of the Covenant.

inside the King's Chamber of the Great Pyramid.[5] But the thing that anyone seeing a replica of the Ark of the Covenant would notice right away is that it is not big enough to hold a human body. Unless, like the corpse of Osiris, that body had been dismembered.

Earlier (in chapter 7) we suggested that Reuel sent Moses to Egypt on a mission to retrieve Joseph's bones. Reuel's belief, common to his era, was that the possession of the skull of a great man helped its possessor to communicate with the supernatural world. This was especially true if the victim had died unexpectedly or had not been buried properly. A murder victim was believed to be wandering aimlessly in a kind of twilight zone. Such a spirit would be compelled to follow his own skull and could be forced to do the bidding of the magician who possessed it. The skull's ghost was thought to have the additional ability of summoning other useful ghosts or demons.*

JOHN THE BAPTIST

The most famous biblical skull is that of John the Baptist. The New Testament story takes place centuries after Moses's time yet throws a revealing light upon the mystical use of skulls. The drama unfolds during the tyrannical reign of King Herod, the monarch who ordered the death of Jewish babies born in Bethlehem. The infant Jesus escapes Herod's cruel edict and as an adult is mentored by John the Baptist.† Not long after John baptized Jesus, King Herod married his brother's wife, Herodias. The union was sinful in John the Baptist's eyes and he doesn't hide his opinion from Herod, "It is not lawful for thee to have thy brother's wife."[6] Herodias is furious that John dares to question the marriage and she persuades King Herod that John should be "cast into prison."[7]

Herod manages to forget about John but his embittered wife, Herodias, had a long memory. She lays a trap for her husband. Her plot

---

*See Shakespeare's *The Tempest* as an example of this belief.
†In the beliefs of the Druze, Reuel was the mentor to Moses just as John the Baptist had been the mentor to Jesus. See epilogue, "The Secret Religion."

unfolds during the king's birthday celebrations when Herodias's beautiful daughter (Herod's stepdaughter and niece) dances for the king. So enchanted is King Herod that he invites her to sit beside him and swears a most generous oath. "Ask of me whatsover thou wilt, and I will give it thee. And he sware unto her, I will give it thee, unto the half of my kingdom."[8]

Herodias's daughter was wise enough to beg to leave the court while she considers his incredible offer and seeks out her mother for advice, saying, "What shall I ask?"

"The head of John the Baptist,"[9] is the unhesitating reply.

Rushing back to court before the King's guests, witnesses to his promise, can leave, his niece announces, "I will that thou give me by and by in a charger the head of John the Baptist."[10]

King Herod is shocked. "And the king was exceedingly sorry; yet for his oath's sake, and for their sakes which sat with him, he would not reject her. And immediately the king sent an executioner, and commanded his head to be brought: and he went and beheaded him in the prison. And brought his head in a charger, and gave it to the damsel: and the damsel gave it to her mother."[11]

Herodias's willingness to turn down half a kingdom for John's head suggests that she had more than just revenge in mind. She may have been a witch who believed that the prophet's skull would give her power over demons.

When Herod heard of the miraculous cures that Jesus was performing he was terrified, saying, "It is John, whom I beheaded: he is risen from the dead."[12]

In the same century, Diodorus Siculus describes how the head of a great man was frequently embalmed "in cedar oil and carefully preserved in a chest."[13] In his compelling *The Head of God,* Keith Laidler writes, "These heads were so highly valued that they would not be sold for their weight in gold, for they were said to possess powers of prophecy. . . . In short, the severed head symbolized divinity."[14] He continues, "the tribe of Benjamin was more implicated in the ritual of head worship than any distinct kin-group among the Hebrews."[15]

We suggest that Benjamin, assuming his Joshua persona, was present when Moses was decapitated.

Laidler identified a head-worshipping cult among ancient Israelites in which "the embalming of the head and its reverence was reserved solely for those who had shown great powers of leadership and mystical abilities. In addition, the secret teachings were never revealed to the mass of the Jewish people and remained the preserve of an initiated elite."[16]

In Jewish folklore, Reuel's nephew Amalek is depicted as an Egyptian-trained magician "who mutilated the bodies of the Israelites."[17]

Reuel had shamanlike reasons for wanting to possess Moses's skull. But secrecy was essential. If the children of Israel ever learned that the Ark of the Covenant contained not the Ten Commandments engraved on stone, as they were told, but rather the remains of their esteemed leader, then Reuel's reign as the masked Moses would come to an abrupt and brutal end. To prevent falling to such a fate Reuel built a mystique around the Ark of the Covenant that kept the tribe as far away from the holy relic as possible.

The construction of the Ark is detailed by the Levite scribes. Moses instructed the craftsmen,* "thou shalt overlay it with pure gold, within and without shalt thou overlay it, and shalt make upon it a crown of gold round about it. And thou shalt cast four rings of gold for it, and put them in the four corners thereof; and two rings shall be in the one side of it, and two rings in the other side of it. And thou shalt make staves of shittim wood, and overlay them with gold. And thou shalt put the staves into the rings by the sides of the ark that the ark may be borne with them."[18]

The addition of the staves ensured that the Ark could be transported untouched by four men. This turned out to be a potentially dangerous duty when it was announced that Yahweh was present *inside* the Ark!

Perched atop the ark were two winged cherubim. Between them was the "mercy seat" where Yahweh sat when he spoke face-to-face with

---

*The Druze claim their ancestors constructed the Ark of the Covenant.

Moses: "And when Moses was gone into the tabernacle of the congregation to speak with him, then he heard the voice of one speaking unto him from off the mercy seat that was upon the ark of testimony, from between the two cherubim: and he spake unto him."[19]

Later, the power of the Ark was used as a secret weapon during battles. "And it came to pass, when the ark set forward, that Moses said, Rise up, LORD, and let thine enemies be scattered; and let them that hate thee flee before thee."[20]

So, who was brave enough to come near such a dangerous chest? Who could be trusted? Deuteronomy informs us, "At that time, the LORD separated the tribe of Levi, to bear the ark of the covenant of the LORD."[21]

Reuel kept close tabs on the ark. The magician could not risk anyone getting too near his precious chest. But only a fool would make such an attempt. Just like the hidden face of the prophet, the contents of the Ark of the Covenant were protected by fear.

What was the origin of the gold that lined and covered the ark? Reuel had melted down the golden calf. Deuteronomy relates Moses's words, "I took your sin, the calf which ye made, and burnt it with fire, and stamped it, and ground it very small, even until it was small as dust: and I cast the dust thereof into the brook that descended out of the mount."[22] But did Reuel really dispose of all the gold? Gold was essential, not only for embellishing the Ark of the Covenant, its rings and staves, but also to add to the oil the magician used to disguise his face. Oil was commonly smeared over features to make a person's "face to shine."[23] Add gold dust and a radiant face that would be awe inspiring to any audience is guaranteed.

When it was not being transported, the Ark resided inside Moses's sacred tent, which included other ceremonial objects: a table, a candlestick, an altar, and a place to wash hands and feet.[24] Joshua stood guard outside prepared to kill any uninvited guests. We think the Midianite nobleman Hur (Reuel) joined Joshua in supposed "sentry duty." But the Levite scribes erased Hur's name from this vital function. A veil-like curtain surrounded the ark concealing it from the rest of the tent and providing a private space for Reuel. He could see out, but no one could see in. When the Ark was finally placed inside King Solomon's Temple the veiled area was called the "holy of holies."[25] Only the high priest was permitted inside this most sacred territory. When the Ark was traveling with the Israelites, Moses alone could pass through the veil that concealed the Ark of the Covenant. Others did so at their peril.

NADAB AND ABIHU

Nadab and Abihu were Aaron's oldest sons. Along with two other brothers they were responsible for the maintenance of the Ark and the sacred tent that the Levites called the tabernacle. They alone were unafraid of handling the sacred chest. Josephus reveals an intriguing detail about the garments Aaron's sons wore while performing their rituals—tiny gold bells had been sown into the hem of their robes so that there would be no mistaking the direction of their movements.[26]

A limited number of people were permitted inside the tent. Moses, Joshua, Aaron, and his four sons were among those select few. As Miriam's husband, Reuel was permitted private access to the ark. The nature of the surrounding veil allowed Reuel to see out while concealing his own activities. Such secure privacy permitted quick costume changes, application of make-up (including the essential gold dust), and the fitting of his mask.

Not even Aaron's sons could see what Reuel was up to. Inevitably, Nadab and Abihu grew curious about what was inside the Ark of the Covenant. One day, believing themselves to be alone the boys entered the sacred tent. They paid a high price for that teenage curiosity. Fulfilling the ritualistic requirements, they had purified themselves by washing and applying a special ointment to their bodies before acting on their private dare. "And Nadab and Abihu, the sons of Aaron, took either of them his censer, and put fire therein, and the incense thereon, and offered strange fire before the LORD, which he commanded them not. And there went out fire from the LORD, and devoured them, and they died before the LORD."[27]

The two young men were incinerated. Moses instructed Aaron's younger sons, Eleazar and Ithamar, to remove the corpses. Amid his grief Aaron is threatened by Moses. "And Moses said unto Aaron, and unto Eleazar and unto Ithamar, his sons, Uncover your heads, neither rend your clothes; lest ye die, and lest wrath come upon all the people: but let your brethren, the whole house of Israel, bewail the burning which the LORD had kindled. And ye shall not go out from the door of the tabernacle of the congregation, lest ye die: for the anointing oil of the LORD is upon you."[28]

Moses warns that the men were covered by the same combustible "anointing oil of the Lord" that had killed Nadab and Abihu. When it came to protecting secrets, Reuel's ruthlessness knew no boundaries.

We suggest that from his hidden position behind the veil Reuel heard the warning jingle of the bells sewn into the boys' clothes. He watched while they washed and applied the combustible "anointing oil" before they entered the intriguing forbidden territory. Egyptian magicians were expert in handling fire. The sun god, Re, placed upon his brow "a protective cobra to spit fire at his enemies."[29] Utilizing his pyrotechnic skills Reuel had set a fatal, painful trap for Nadab and Abihu. But why did he want them dead?

The answer takes us back to the Mountain of God on the day that Moses was murdered. Nadab and Abihu were present when Moses ascended the mountain to receive the tablets engraved with the Ten Commandments. Also present were Aaron, Hur (Reuel), and Joshua. As part of the tight inner circle Nadab and Abihu would already know too much for Reuel's liking. And now, by trying to access the Ark of the Covenant they had proven themselves reckless. They might stumble over the magician's secrets. They had to die.

Nadab and Abihu's agonizing deaths made it clear to all the children of Israel that the Ark was strictly off limits—dangerously so. If the high priest's sons could be burned to death simply for trying to enter the holy of holies, then who would dare to lift the lid on the Ark of the Covenant?

Terror ensured that Reuel's chest of magic tricks was safe from scrutiny.

THE ARK OF THE COVENANT IN WAR

In popular culture the Ark of the Covenant has been magnified to comic book status and has even been portrayed as a technological device for communicating with God. This was brought vividly to life in *Raiders of the Lost Ark* where Indy's mission was to prevent Adolf Hitler from obtaining the supposedly invincible weapon that was the Ark.

The true danger posed by the Ark was no less colorful. Its role as the store case for an evil magician containing objects of black magic like Moses's skull and props for the magician's diabolical acts of illusion—gold dust, oil, costumes, and a mask[30]—caused a degree of real life chaos and death that could never be captured on film.

Long after Reuel had hung up his mask and, as we will see, had adopted a new persona, Jericho became the first city "conquered" by the children of Israel. Reuel had mentored Benjamin in the arts of illusion. In his new role as Joshua, Benjamin made practical use of the Israelites' faith in the power of the Ark.

The Israelites surrounded Jericho from a safe distance.[31] No one was seen coming or going from the city. For seven days the priests marched around their target, blowing trumpets and horns—the Ark carried high at the head of their procession. It was understood to be the critical force in their display; without it, the accompanying shouting and trumpets were mere props. At a critical moment Joshua orders his men to emit a mighty roar. Famously, the walls of Jericho then collapsed. When the Israelites entered the city it was in ruins. Only a "harlot," Rahab, and her family had survived. Earlier, she had hidden the trusted spies that Joshua had sent into Jericho. She was rewarded by being allowed to join the victorious children of Israel, which she no doubt welcomed as an umbrella of security in the harsh world she and her children inhabited.

Did the Ark of the Covenant really cause this devastation?

Today, thanks to the work of archeologist Kathleen Kenyon, we know that the crumbling walls of Jericho were already in ruins for centuries before Joshua's arrival. We suggest that Rahab was bribed to pretend that the city had collapsed around her. The only people living in Jericho were her family. It wasn't the influence of the Ark of the Covenant that brought down Jericho's walls—it was just one part of a greater illusion that served Reuel's grand plan. When the children of Israel entered the city the shock and awe of the ruins convinced them that the Ark was a formidable weapon.

The legend of the mighty Ark grew but the day came when the Israelites relied upon its legendary power once too often. Long after Joshua, a new leader named Samuel faced a losing battle with the Philistines. He sent for the Ark. "And when the ark of the covenant of the LORD came into the camp, all Israel shouted with a great shout, so that the earth rang again."[32]

At first the Philistines were struck with fear but their abhorrence at the thought of being conquered was stronger than their fear of death. They fought valiantly, defeated the Israelites, and "the ark of God was taken."[33]

The spell of the invincible weapon was broken.

The Philistines kept the Ark for seven months. Unlike the Israelites they had no qualms about looking inside it. What did they find? Only the biblical account remains. "When the Philistines took the ark of God, they brought it into the house of Dagon, and set it by Dagon."[34] The statue of Dagon was regarded as a god.

These few words and the event that happened immediately after its seizure offer a strong suggestive clue about the secret contents of the Ark of the Covenant. Something extraordinary happened to the statue of Dagon overnight. In the morning, when the Philistine priests entered the temple, "behold, Dagon was fallen upon his face to the ground before the ark of the LORD; and the head of Dagon and both the palms of his hands were cut off upon the threshold; only the stump of Dagon was left to him."[35]

Dagon's mutilated body, like that of Osiris, symbolized the contents of the Ark of the Covenant—the skull and bones of Moses. The Philistine god Dagon was a "famous maritime god or idol, as generally supposed to have been like a man above the navel, and like fish beneath it."[36] The thigh bones couldn't be represented because

Dagon didn't have legs. They had to make do with severed hands.

For centuries, the mutilated statue of Dagon remained a clue to the secret contents of the Ark of the Covenant. But then, around 1100 CE, Christian crusaders took control of Jerusalem. They had a secret mission of their own.

WHAT THE TEMPLARS FOUND

Numerous writers have explored the question of what exactly the Templars were trying to excavate from beneath the remains of King Solomon's Temple. The descendants of Reuel, the Druze,* claim that they were responsible for constructing the famous temple. If true, they would have been familiar with all its subterranean features. They may have even been in league with the crusaders. The French historian Gaetan Delarforg contended that, "The real task of the nine knights was to carry out research in the area in order to obtain certain relics and manuscripts which contain the essence of the secret traditions of Judaism and ancient Egypt, some of which probably went back to the days of Moses."[37]

Keith Laidler's *The Head of God: The Lost Treasure of the Templars* presents some of his key findings:

> Three vital facts are now incontestable. First, there is definite, documentary evidence that treasure of some kind was hidden beneath the temple. Second, there are ancient, man-made tunnels and vaults carved from the rock under the Temple Mount. And finally, the Templars spend much time and energy excavating at least some of these tunnels, as evidenced by the Templar artifacts discovered in passageways under the Temple Mount. Taken together, this makes the argument that the Templars found a treasure of some sort during the early years of their formation extremely persuasive. And there is one other piece of evidence that not only strengthens the argument

---

*See epilogue, "The Secret Religion."

outlined above, but also makes plain an early Templar connection to
the worship of sacred heads—the startling and gruesome change in
the burial habits of the Templar initiates.[38]

After the temple excavations, it became the custom for senior Templar
officials to be buried in ark-sized coffins, which were far too short
for normal Christian burials. Laidler describes what an opened
Templar coffin revealed of the corpse, "The arms were left intact. It
was only the lower limbs that were disarticulated and laid cross-wise
over the trunk. The severed head was likewise placed on the trunk,
just above the crossed limbs. This is, of course, the classic skull and
crossbones."[39]

We suggest that when the Templars opened the Ark of the
Covenant they found a skull and bones. Because the Ark was so closely
associated with Moses and because no one knew where the prophet
was buried, the Templars concluded that the skull and bones found
inside the sacred relic must belong to him. They weren't prepared to
make their shocking discovery public. But they did honor the famous
prophet by emulating his fate in their burial rituals.

After the excavations in Jerusalem, skull worship became a central
part of the Templars' secret rituals. Laidler writes, "There is no doubt
that a preserved, severed head was involved in Templar ritual, and that
it was regarded with great veneration and awe . . . [and] one relic stood
pre-eminent—the long-haired, bearded head that was seen almost exclusively at the Paris temple. Many tales centered around the worship of
this severed embalmed head whose name, as many Templars admitted
after their arrest, was *Baphomet.* . . . The translation of this word is
Father of Wisdom."[40]

Laidler contends that the skull of the Father of Wisdom, belonged
to Jesus. But Jesus was the *son* of God. As Sigmund Freud made clear,
the *father* figure of the Jews was Moses.

The priests of Jerusalem despised Jesus but revered Moses. They
never would have permitted the skull of the "unholy" Jesus to reside
beneath their sacred temple. But when they saw that Jerusalem was

about to fall to the conquering Babylonians, the priests hid the Ark of the Covenant in a secret location beneath the temple.

Even so many centuries after the death of Moses, the Jerusalem priests dared not open the Ark. They believed that they were preserving the tablets with the Ten Commandments engraved upon them. When the Templars recovered the Ark of the Covenant they promptly pried opened the relic, confiscated the skull of Moses, and abandoned the Ark like a husk.

What became of the coveted skull is unknown. Some say it was transported to Paris and remained there until 1307 when the mighty Templar regime was overthrown by the French king after which the Ark of the Covenant was transported to Rosslyn Chapel in Scotland before finally being taken to a secret hiding place in America.[41]

For now, the fate of Moses's skull can only be traced in works of fiction.

11

———•———

The Spy and the Leper

And the earth opened her mouth, and swallowed them up.

NUMBERS 16:32.

Amalek's attack had failed but the spy Korah persisted in trying to foil his half brother's plans. Korah knew he would suffer if Reuel ever ruled Edom. Forced to lay low during the bloody purge that followed the golden calf apostasy, he had marveled at the audacity of Reuel's performance in his role as the shining-faced Moses. His keen eye also noted the vulnerability of the troubled Israelites who found themselves oppressed by an endless set of harsh rules and regulations.

The Levite scribes did not want it revealed that Korah was kin to Reuel. They created the perfect cover-up—a false family tree. Elias Auerbach writes,

> According to the description in our text Korah is a Levite and contests Moses' and Aaron's privileges. This is a flaw in the account; *the original source could never have reported it in that way*. For, what are the privileges of the leader which Korah rebels against? The priesthood? But, according to all the ancient sources, all the Levites are priests. . . . In reality Korah cannot have been a Levite at all; the

rebellion is, rather, an attempt of the non-Levites to assail the priest-hood of the Levites.[1] [Italics added]

In Genesis 36:5 we learn that Korah was Reuel's half brother, an Edomite. But who were the non-Levites who conspired with him "to assail the priesthood of the Levites"? One tribe was ripe for the picking—the descendants of Reuben.

Korah had identified two susceptible men from Reuben's tribe, Dathan and Abiram. About them Martin Noth writes, "It is completely unknown how in particular these two otherwise completely unknown Reubenites came to rebel against Moses."[2] We can suggest two reasons. First, their ancestor Reuben had been disinherited by Israel, leaving them in the same situation that Reuel had once faced: forced from the line of succession that led to the leadership of the Jews. Second, their hatred for the reign of the masked Moses.

Josephus's depiction of Korah tells us that he was "very skilful in making speeches, and having this natural talent, among others, he could greatly move the multitude with his discourses."[3] We can imagine a gathering of disgruntled Reubenites gathered around the dying embers of a fire while Korah whispered his carefully prepared incitements:

O how the mighty have fallen. Reuben is Israel's firstborn son, yet you are all degraded. Levi has become the high priest and has taken a new name, Aaron. He pompously parades around issuing orders while my brother, an Edomite, wears a mask pretending to be Moses. Oh, how Israel must be turning in his grave! Have you no pride? What has become of your nobility? Join with me to rid ourselves of these pretenders! *

Part of the story of Korah's rebellion was preserved from the ancient oral tradition but most was told by Levite scribes. The "official" version states that,

---

*This is an imaginary quote based upon our research.

Korah, the son of Izhar, the son of Kohath, the son of Levi, and Dathan and Abiram, the sons of Eliab, and On, the son of Peleth, sons of Reuben, took men: And they rose up before Moses, with certain of the children of Israel, two hundred and fifty princes of the assembly, famous in the congregation, men of renown: And they gathered themselves together against Moses and against Aaron, and said unto them, Ye take too much upon you, seeing all the congregation are holy, every one of them, and the LORD is among them: wherefore then lift ye up yourselves above the congregation of the LORD?[4]

Why, Korah argued, should Moses and Aaron hold exclusive domain over the people? Had not all the children of Israel been chosen by Yahweh? By his bold challenge of Moses's and Aaron's presumption that they are more holy in the sight of God than the rest of the tribe, Korah compares to Luther who railed against the priests of Rome.

According to Jewish folklore a telling conversation followed between Moses and Korah.

[Moses said,] "I have heard that ye are not satisfied with me, and are accusing me of pride and arrogance. Have you forgotten that I went from Midian to Egypt for your sake, but never asked any reward for all my trouble and my labours? If I am now supposed to be ruling over you, it is not because I have sought greatness and been ambitious. It is the Lord who has commanded me to be your leader, and I have never done anything except what the Lord has commanded me to do." Thus spoke Moses, but Korah replied, "Thou has done but little for us. Thou hast taken us out of Egypt, where we lived in plenty, but has not brought us to Canaan, the land thou didst promise to give us." And when the followers of Korah heard his words, they rose against Moses and were almost on the point of stoning him.[5]

The tribe's bitter complaint that Moses hadn't fulfilled his promise to give them precious land to compensate for leaving their lives of "plenty"

in Egypt hardly seems the natural reaction of a people said to be trau-
matized by terrible memories of centuries of cruel bondage.

Korah's challenge was a serious one. Reuel was forced to play for
time. He ordered the rebels to bring incense to his tent the following day
at which time, he declared, Yahweh (the LORD) would be the sole judge
of their complaints. In the non-Levite segment of the story Dathan and
Abiram refuse. "We will not come up: Is it a small thing that thou hast
brought us up out of a land that floweth with milk and honey, to kill us
in the wilderness, except thou make thyself altogether a prince over us?
Moreover, thou hast not brought us into a land that floweth with milk
and honey, or given us inheritance of fields and vineyards: wilt thou put
out the eyes of these men? we will not come up."[6]

The text then abruptly switches back to the Levite account in which
Moses successfully commands Korah and his supporters to report the
next day and face Yahweh.

Reuel had one night to prepare his trap.

WHEN THE EARTH OPENED HER MOUTH

We know the motives of the rebels. The Reubenites wanted fertile land,
to be rid of Reuel, and to restore their family name. Korah wanted to
prevent Reuel from using the army of the children of Israel to conquer
Edom. Reuel stood in everyone's way.

The brilliant magician faced danger from some very determined foes.
All the tricks of his trade had to be spun into immediate action. This
was a battle that must be won. It demanded his artistry in the application of two powerful illusions. The confusion and fear brought with fire
and smoke spewing from Yahweh to serve as misdirection from hidden
trapdoors must be played perfectly if Reuel hoped to remain in control.

He plotted and prepared all night. His tent stood outside the camp
and as we've seen was guarded night and day by Joshua.[7] This isolation and security provided Reuel with an opportunity to dig a large
pit within the tent, complete with trap door. When it was finished, he
ordered the tent moved away from the hole, leaving the invisible trap

door in front. The next morning Korah's rebels waited before the tent's entrance beside Moses and Aaron. Excitedly anticipating Yahweh's first appearance the rest of the tribe gathered at a distance.

The text offers scant details of their God's first appearance, simply describing the holy figure as "the glory of the LORD." But the anxious people hardly had time to concentrate on the entity's features. A thundering voice riveted them to where they stood. The billowing smoke and flashes of fire that emanated from the sacred tent erased any doubt that they were in the awe-inspiring presence of Yahweh.

But whose impressive voice really inspired such terror? Moses and Aaron were outside the tent. Only Joshua was left inside to speak on behalf of Yahweh. Joshua may have feigned Yahweh's voice, lit the fireworks, and fanned the smoke. "And Korah gathered all the congregation against them unto the door of the tabernacle of the congregation: and the glory of the LORD appeared unto all the congregation. And the LORD spake unto Moses and unto Aaron, saying, Separate yourselves from among this congregation, that I may consume them in a moment."[8]

Ominously, "Yahweh" commands Moses (Reuel) and Aaron (Levi) to move away from the rebels. Obeying, the two go to their knees, on either side of the entry where they seem to be worshipping the voice of God. But their true purpose is much more nefarious than the act of prayer.

Moses hammers home the message that it is the all-powerful Yahweh who is responsible for the tragedy that is about to unfold:

And Moses said, Hereby ye shall know that the LORD hath sent me to do all these works; for I have not done them of mine own mind. If these men die the common death of all men, or if they be visited after the visitation of all men; then the LORD hath not sent me. But if the LORD makes a new thing, and the earth open her mouth, and swallow them up, with all that appertain unto them, and they go down quick into the pit; then ye shall understand that these men have provoked the LORD.[9]

Moses (Reuel) and Aaron (Levi) seize the ropes that release the trap-door to send Korah and his rebels plummeting to a certain death at the bottom of the pit.

> And it came to pass, as he had made an end of speaking all these words, that the ground clave asunder that was under them: And the earth opened her mouth, and swallowed them up, and their houses, and all the men that appertained unto Korah, and all their goods. They, and all that appertained to them, went down alive into the pit, and the earth closed upon them: and they perished from among the congregation. And all Israel that were round about them fled at the cry of them: for they said, Lest the earth swallow us up also.[10]

When the earth splits open the children of Israel flee in terror. No witnesses are left as Reuel's confederates kill the rebels where they lie helpless in the yawning pit. The purge is complete when the trapdoor is lowered, locked above, and soil thrown across it. With this standard magician's trick, the disappearing act, Reuel had successfully annihilated Korah's rebellion.

After the pit engulfs its victims it closes as quickly as it opened—suggesting the very real presence of a cleverly designed mechanical device rather than supernatural intervention. (The non-Levite text* states that the rebels' tents and households also disappeared into the great pit. This was probably an exaggeration added to enhance the impression of Yahweh's glory and might.)

How did Reuel learn of Korah's rebellion in time to prepare his defence? It is probable that there was a spy embedded within the ranks of Korah's conspiracy. A likely candidate was the Reubenite "On," who is mentioned in the opening lines of Numbers 16 as being one of Korah's rebels. According to Jewish folklore, On's wife persuaded him not to participate in the rebellion:

---

*The **J** source of the documentary hypothesis—see appendix 2, "Research Methodology."

One man, however, had a lucky escape, owing his salvation to his wife. His name was On, the son of Peleth. His wife was a clever woman, and when she saw Korah talking to her husband and persuading him to rebel against Moses and Aaron and depose them from both leadership and priesthood, she did not approve of the plot. On had given his promise to Korah to join him, but when the leader of the rebellion left, and On was discussing the matter with his wife, the latter said to him:

"I do not approve of this plot, and as for thyself, my dear husband, no benefit will ever accrue to thee from the rebellion, whether it be successful or not. If Moses gains the victory and is master, thou wilt be subject to him, and if Korah is successful, thou wilt be subject to him."

"Thou are right," admitted On, struck by the truth of his wife's argument, "but what can I do now? I have given an oath to Korah to join him when he comes to our tent to fetch me, and it is incumbent upon me to keep my oath."

"Do not worry," said On's wife, "and leave the matter to me."[11]

It transpires that her urgent advice was compelled by more than just political savvy and wifely worry about her husband's fate. On's wife was Reuel's spy. She plies her husband with wine so that he is too drunk to participate in the rebellion. By alerting Reuel to the coming rebellion she gives him time to construct his trap. Like the man-sized puppet wielded by Hur and Aaron during the Israelites' battle with the Amalekites that was designed to trick the tribe into believing Moses was still alive, Reuel again made canny use of illusion for political rather than religious or entertainment ends. The ultimate magician had still more deadly acts of illusion to retrieve from his precious cache of tricks, which we will see in chapter 12.

Korah's insistence that all the children of Israel were chosen by Yahweh and that Moses and Aaron had no divine right to rule was ignored. The death of the rebels was proof to the people that their stance was anathema to Yahweh. But Korah's cause still held some life. Another revolt would present an even more serious challenge to Reuel's rule when two of his inner circle, Aaron and Miriam, rose against him.

THE LEPER

The immediate cause of the fresh revolt was a reaction to Moses's marriage to an Ethiopian woman. "And Miriam and Aaron spake against Moses because of the Ethiopian woman whom he had married: for he had married an Ethiopian woman."[12]

Central to this book is our suggestion that Reuel, using the name Hur, was married to Miriam. He held a dual identity—*Hur* during his normal activities and *Moses of the shining face* when he prophesied. Today, we're all familiar with the fantasy dual identities of characters like Batman, Spiderman, and of course, Superman. But in the biblical era such a disappearance into another persona was an extraordinary event even if survival could depend upon it.

The name *Miriam* means "rebellion"[13] in Hebrew, which further suggests that Miriam was not her original name. Her parents would hardly have the foresight to see that their daughter would grow up to become a rebel. At that time obedience, not rebellion, was the critical sign of a woman's piety. Miriam's original identity was that of the rape-disgraced daughter of Israel, Dinah, who had already been reinvented as a prophetess. But in adopting this new façade a serious problem was thrown her way. In the eyes of the children of Israel she was married to Hur, not Moses, so she had to advance another reason for rebelling against Moses besides a new marriage. So, she persuaded her brother, Aaron, to join her in challenging Moses's claim to exclusivity as the sole spokesman for Yahweh. "And they said, Hath the LORD indeed spoken only by Moses? hath he not spoken also by us? And the LORD heard it."[14]

Korah had made the bold claim that any of the chosen people might know the wishes of God through their personal visions and dreams. Miriam and Aaron weren't buying it. They were not interested in such an egalitarian approach. They insisted that they too must belong to the elite chosen to speak for Yahweh. They dared to seek parity with the masked Moses.

Sharing power was hardly in the magician Reuel's nature. Caught off guard by the duo's outrageous public challenge, he was forced to think fast. He slipped into the sacred tent and whispered instructions to Joshua. While Reuel ducked behind the curtain that concealed the Ark of the Covenant Joshua quickly dressed in Moses's garments and pulled his mask over his face. Appearing as Moses, Joshua rejoined Miriam and Aaron before the assembled Israelites while Reuel lifted another costume from among the collected treasures to be found within the Ark—he would become Yahweh.

As the Israelites are manipulated by the magician, Joshua, disguised as Moses, remains silent. Using the power of his voice to "become" Yahweh, Reuel makes his entrance as God incarnate:

> And the LORD spake suddenly unto Moses, and unto Aaron, and unto Miriam, Come out ye three unto the tabernacle of the congregation. And they three came out. And the LORD came down in the pillar of the cloud, and stood in the door of the tabernacle, and called Aaron and Miriam: and they both came forth. And he said, Hear now my words: If there be a prophet among you, I the LORD will make myself known unto him in a vision, and will speak unto him in a dream. My servant Moses is not so, who is faithful in all mine house. With him will I speak mouth to mouth, even apparently, and not in dark speeches; and the similitude of the LORD shall he behold: wherefore then were ye not afraid to speak against my servant Moses? And the anger of the LORD was kindled against them; and he departed. And the cloud departed from off the tabernacle; and, behold, Miriam became leprous, white as snow: and Aaron looked upon Miriam, and, behold, she was leprous.[15]

Miriam did not suddenly contract the curse of leprosy. Her bloodless complexion was the result of fear. Speechless. Defenseless. Shame had rekindled her terrible memories of the time as a young girl (Dinah) when her rape by Shechem had become public knowledge. Aaron knew how traumatic this experience had been for his sister:

> And Aaron said unto Moses, Alas, my lord, I beseech thee, lay not the sin upon us, wherein we have done foolishly, and wherein we have sinned. Let her not be as one dead, of whom the flesh is half consumed when he cometh out of his mother's womb. And Moses cried unto the LORD, saying, Heal her now, O God, I beseech thee. And the LORD said unto Moses, If her father had but spit in her face, should she not be ashamed seven days? let her be shut out from the camp seven days, and after that let her be received in again. And Miriam was shut out from the camp seven days: and the people journeyed not till Miriam was brought in again.[16]

The reference to her father spitting in her face was a bitter reminder of how Israel must have punished Dinah when he learned of her rape. Martin Noth comments that Miriam's penance is one "in which a girl is punished who is guilty of an offense which is shameful."[17] The terrible "leprosy" she experienced disappeared as quickly as it came, suggesting that humiliation and fear, not disease, was its source.[18] The women of the camp were full of sympathy for Miriam and refused to abandon the area where the prophetess was forced to spend her seven days of penance.

Biblical scholars have long been bewildered by the "strange leniency toward Aaron" in the wake of his open rebellion.[19] Just as guilty as Miriam—he receives no punishment. Richard Elliott Friedman asks, "Why does Miriam suffer while Aaron does not?"[20] His explanation is that Aaron's exalted status would be in peril if he was seen to be accountable for such a revolt. "In that position he cannot suffer any direct punishment from God, which would both disqualify him and demean the office of high priest."[21] But the actual explanation is much simpler once we realize that both Levi and Dinah had assumed new identities—as Aaron and Miriam.

Reuel had struck at the weakest point in the rebels' armor—their hearts.

Aaron feared that Miriam's shame would so overwhelm her that she might become like a miscarried child, "of whom the flesh is half consumed when he cometh out of his mother's womb."[22] This is a subtle reference to Dinah's rape—the shame that Reuel knew had secretly dominated her for so long. Levi's affection for his sister was so strong that he had sacrificed the love and respect of their father when he defied him by slaughtering the men of Shechem in revenge for her rape. His plea with Moses on Miriam's behalf once again reveals that side of his character. Even if Aaron's prestige provided a shield against more dire consequences for his actions he was forced to endure his sister's further humiliation.

The next we hear of Miriam she has died in Kadesh.[23]

The religious complaint of who could or couldn't be Yahweh's prophet was a secondary impetus for Miriam and Aaron's rebellion.[24] They were enraged that Reuel had taken a wife as the masked Moses. In this regard their rebellion is very different from Korah's. But their audacity sealed Reuel's determination to display the extent of his power once and for all. The magician would not tolerate another uprising. His appearance as Yahweh would announce his last word about prophets. It would be made clear that none could equal, or should attempt to challenge, Moses. It was critical to establish that he alone embodied the authority to speak face-to-face with Yahweh.

WHO WAS MOSES'S ETHIOPIAN WIFE?

There is no agreement among biblical scholars about the identity of the woman Moses married who so incited the siblings to such anger that they openly rebelled. Richard Elliott Friedman believes that she was "probably Ethiopian."[25] Martin Noth initially favors the "Cushites," a tribe like the Midianites, as her original people but in a later work concludes that "all possible conjectures are without any certain foundation."[26] He does not believe that she was Moses's original wife, Zipporah.[27] Frank Moore Cross disagrees, suggesting that Moses's new wife was indeed the Midianite, Zipporah.[28] If he is correct, then our conviction that Zipporah was Miriam's daughter puts the story in a new light.

Knowing that her husband had married their daughter could well have been too much for Miriam—she exploded. Also, if Reuel had married his daughter then Zipporah's conspicuous absence from the rest of the Torah makes sense. Why else would the wife of the greatest prophet disappear unless there was something so unsavory about her that it warranted that she be erased from the holy text? We can't know if Zipporah became the masked Moses's new wife, but we do know that she was last seen alive in the company of Reuel.[29]

12

———•———

Balaam and the War
against the Midianites

A cloud stood over him on the sudden, and he disappeared.

Josephus on Moses's death in
The Antiquity of the Jews, 4.8.48

The children of Israel refused to decamp while Miriam was undergoing her penance in the desert. Her ordeal took a heavy toll. The next we hear concerns Miriam's death and burial in Kadesh.[1] Kadesh was not far from Edom. It was from this oasis that the masked Moses had sent messengers to the Edomite king seeking safe passage through the King's Highway. This north-south road had been constructed originally for the use of Egyptian troops. It bisected Edom, making it the most direct route to Canaan—the Promised Land. Reuel negotiated with the Edomite king, promising to keep strictly to the agreed route and to pay for any water the tribe consumed. But the king not only refused to grant passage—he threatened war if Reuel trespassed on the highway.[2]

Biblical scholars have puzzled over why the Edomites denied the children of Israel passage through their land. Noth writes,

"Accompanied as it is by a threat, the rejection of this modest request is given no foundation."[3]

We suggest that the Edomite king considered his hostility towards Moses to be built on a very solid foundation indeed. Its bedrock was the death of Korah, an Edomite prince. The rage ignited by that blow had been further inflamed when blood was spilt in the battle against Amalek, another Edomite. Reinforcing his darkest suspicions was the king's deep mistrust of his kinsman Reuel. The Edomites knew that it was the disgruntled, embittered figure of the magician Reuel who lurked behind the mask of "Moses." The valuable spy Korah had kept them well informed about the critical events transpiring in the Israelite camp. The king of Edom was not going to make it easy for such a dangerous enemy to lead a potential army across his land.

AARON'S DEATH?

Never at a loss for a plan B, Reuel found a loophole in the determined king's prohibition. The Mountain of God stood within Edomite territory but given its isolation was unlikely to have been patrolled regularly like the well-traveled, essential King's Highway. Not long before, Moses had sent spies to the Promised Land.[4] They were gone for forty days.[5] They could only have traveled such a great distance and returned in such a short time if they had crossed Edomite territory. During that journey they could have passed the Mountain of God and seen that it stood relatively unguarded.

Armed with this intelligence the children of Israel left Kadesh and arrived at Mount Hor, a mountainous hilltop that stood next to the Mountain of God. It was here in Edom that Aaron was said to have died; a story that enjoys a long tradition. Josephus mentions that the mountain where Aaron perished is near Petra.[6] Graham Phillips records the local Bedouin belief that "It is still called Jebel Haroun—'Aaron's Mountain.' Like the spring of Moses, the local inhabitants still venerate Jebel Haroun as the site of Aaron's tomb. Just below the summit, on a flat ridge overlooking a sheer cliff, there perches a little whitewashed mosque that stands over a cave where the prophet is said to have been laid to rest."[7]

But *is* this the true location of Aaron's grave?

We don't believe that Aaron died at this point in the story. This was a staged death.

Biblical scholars consider the accounts of Aaron's last hours to be curious. Noth notes that the account of the high priest's death "has been made to resemble as closely as possible the corresponding story of Moses' death" and "oddly enough says nothing about the burial and the grave."[8] Remarkable when you consider that Aaron was the Israelis' first high priest. Even Miriam had a gravesite. Only two witnesses testify to the manner of Aaron's end. The account comes to us from the pen of the Levite scribes, who take up the story at Mount Hor:

> And the LORD spake unto Moses and Aaron in mount Hor, by the coast of the land of Edom, saying, Aaron shall be gathered unto his people: for he shall not enter into the land which I have given unto the children of Israel, because ye rebelled against my word at the water of Meribah. Take Aaron and Eleazar his son, and bring them up unto mount Hor: And strip Aaron of his garments, and put them upon Eleazar his son: and Aaron shall be gathered unto his people, and shall die there. And Moses did as the LORD commanded: and they went up into mount Hor in the sight of all the congregation. And Moses stripped Aaron of his garments, and put them upon Eleazar his son; and Aaron died there in the top of the mount: and Moses and Eleazar came down from the mount. And when all the congregation saw that Aaron was dead, they mourned for Aaron thirty days, even all the house of Israel.[9]

Aaron was denied entry to the Promised Land for the same reason as Moses. Both had failed to follow Yahweh's precise instructions about how to retrieve water at Meribah.*

---

*This "reason" seems petty considering all that Moses and Aaron are supposed to have achieved for Yahweh.

Although the people see Aaron, Moses, and Eleazar ascend Mount Hor, only Moses (wearing his mask) and Eleazar return.

The people grieve but have no corpse or grave to grieve over. What is the explanation for this rare lack of ceremony? We suggest that Aaron was wearing Moses's costume and mask when he descended with his son. He used the unquestioned authority of the masked Moses to take revenge on Reuel for Miriam's death. How exactly did this retaliation play out on Mount Hor?

There are two possibilities:

In the first case, Reuel, aware of Aaron's (Levi's) grief and anger over Miriam's (Dinah's) shame and subsequent death, seizes the chance to escape Aaron's wrath. Familiar with the contours and pathways of Mount Hor (Edom was his native land) he abandons his Moses disguise and takes his daughter, Zipporah, along with Moses's sons, and a generous share of the gold donated by the Israelites to create the golden calf, and flees.

Aaron and his son Eleazar, left behind on Mount Hor without Moses must face the awkward and potentially dangerous task of explaining the disappearance of the prophet. They were aware that the children of Israel would not tolerate finding themselves yet again bereft of their leader. Aaron and Eleazar took one of the few choices left and told the people that it was Aaron who had died and was buried somewhere on the mountain. The people could accept this more easily than the idea of Moses's death. They knew how much Aaron had loved Miriam and how hard her death had been on him. Given his intense grief his death would not have been so unexpected.

In the second case Reuel and Aaron could have agreed to the switch. They might have dissolved their partnership. Reuel agrees to assist the Israelites in navigating the country beyond Edom and into the plains of Moab—the territory immediately east of the Promised Land. He tells Aaron that his plan will accomplish their safe passage through Moab and avoid war. But the scheme involves Aaron faking his own death and taking over the role of the masked Moses. Reuel may have threatened to vanish with or without Aaron's agreement.

Once Reuel left camp, his allies, the Midianites, became vulnerable to Aaron in his new role as the masked Moses. Reuel had no reason to want to murder Midianites. He had been their high priest and his daughter, Zipporah, was born there. But Aaron, enraged as he was prone to be, and especially over any shame that befell his sister, felt justified in ridding himself of them all. He may have felt ashamed that he hadn't done more to save Miriam and was compelled to atone with his usual displays of violence.

Midianites who had priests of their own, the Kenites, lived among the children of Israel. As leader of the Levites, Aaron determined to rid himself of these rival priests. A war against the Midianites was the perfect excuse to clean house. The consequences of that war will be explored shortly but first we will follow Reuel as he leaves Edom and takes up his persona as the magician Balaam.

THE MAGICIAN BALAAM

No sooner has the magician Reuel disappeared than a new conjurer, Balaam, enters the story. Balaam's prophetic powers were superior to Moses. He knew exactly when Yahweh was going to speak to him and he could even initiate such a conversation. Reuel also seems to possess such profound prophetic powers. This, we suggest, is no coincidence. Jewish folklore claims that Reuel and Balaam were both magicians serving the Egyptian pharaoh around the same period. Reuel would have been familiar with Balaam's appearance, character, and magical skills. Like a modern-day pseudo guru or fifteen-minute celebrity reinventing himself after squeezing all use from his current identity, it was time for Reuel to move on from his masked Moses persona. It was time to assume the cloak of the magician Balaam.

It is suspicious that Balaam becomes such a vociferous proponent of the god Yahweh. Why? He wasn't associated with the Mountain of God where Yahweh was the presiding deity. Why would he want to claim a mountain god who hailed from Edom as the ultimate deity? Because Reuel, an Edomite, was playing Balaam.

The Israelites were camped outside Moab, the territory that lay east of the Jordan River. It was critical that they gain passage through Moab to enter the Promised Land. The king of Moab, Balak, who was entertaining a delegation of noblemen from Midian, was afraid that the Israelites might conquer his land. He sought advice from the magician Balaam and sent princes of Moab to beseech Balaam to curse the Israelites. "Come now therefore, I pray thee, curse me this people; for they are too mighty for me: peradventure I shall prevail, that we may smite them, and that I may drive them out of the land: for I wot that he whom thou blessest is blessed, and he whom thou cursest is cursed."[10]

But Balaam (Reuel in disguise) did not respond immediately. Instead, he invites the princes of Moab to spend the night under his roof while he consults with Yahweh. "And Balaam rose up in the morning, and said unto the princes of Balak, Get you into your land: for the LORD refuseth to give me leave to go with you. And the princes of Moab rose up, and they went unto Balak, and said, Balaam refuseth to come with us."[11]

When Balak learned that Balaam was not willing to curse the Israelites he was distraught. He sends more esteemed princes to beg Balaam's assistance. Even with the promise of great riches, Balaam (Reuel) once again refuses to go to Moab and again asks the noble messengers to stay overnight while he consults with Yahweh. This time, however, Balaam (Reuel) performs an elaborate act of ventriloquism for the benefit of the noble messengers:

And Balaam rose up in the morning, and saddled his ass, and went with the princes of Moab. And God's anger was kindled because he went: and the angel of the LORD stood in the way for an adversary against him. Now he was riding upon his ass, and his two servants were with him. And the ass saw the angel of the LORD standing in the way, and his sword drawn in his hand: and the ass turned aside out of the way, and went into the field: and Balaam smote the ass, to turn her into the way. But the angel of the LORD stood in a path of the vineyards, a wall being on this side, and a wall on that side.

And when the ass saw the angel of the LORD, she thrust herself
unto the wall, and crushed Balaam's foot against the wall: and he
smote her again.[12]

Ventriloquists know that setting their puppet up as a foil further creates
the illusion that the puppet is real. In his history of ventriloquism, Steve
Connor points out that Balaam's donkey is worked like a puppet.[13] The
hapless animal's "conflict" with Balaam is only the beginning of a grand
illusion:

And the angel of the LORD went further, and stood in a narrow
place, where was no way to turn either to the right hand or to the
left. And when the ass saw the angel of the LORD, she fell down
under Balaam: and Balaam's anger was kindled, and he smote the
ass with a staff. And the LORD opened the mouth of the ass, and
she said unto Balaam, What have I done unto thee, that thou hast
smitten me these three times?[14]

So now the donkey speaks! Reuel has created an enticing performance
for his audience, the noble princes of Moab. Soon the stakes are raised.
They witness a "conversation" between the animal and the magician:

And Balaam said unto the ass, Because thou hast mocked me: I
would there were a sword in mine hand, for now would I kill thee.
And the ass said unto Balaam, Am not I thine ass, upon which thou
hast ridden ever since I was thine unto this day? was I ever wont to
do so unto thee? And he said, Nay. Then the LORD opened the
eyes of Balaam, and he saw the angel of the LORD standing in the
way, and his sword drawn in his hand: and he bowed down his head,
and fell flat on his face.[15]

Balaam's puppet has played his role. The donkey is no longer needed.
Instead, the magician Balaam addresses an angel that *only he can see*
and the "conversation" continues:

And the angel of the LORD said unto him, Wherefore hast thou smitten thine ass these three times? behold, I went out to withstand thee, because thy way is perverse before me: And the ass saw me, and turned from me these three times: unless she had turned from me, surely now also I had slain thee, and saved her alive. And Balaam said unto the angel of the LORD, I have sinned; for I knew not that thou stoodest in the way against me: now therefore, if it displease thee, I will get me back again. And the angel of the LORD said unto Balaam, Go with the men: but only the word that I shall speak unto thee, that thou shalt speak. So Balaam went with the princes of Balak.[16]

So what are we to make of this strange episode? Why didn't Balaam accompany the first messengers sent by Balak? Why this elaborate delaying tactic? What was the purpose of the ventriloquism?

The answers are straightforward once we realize the perilous position that Reuel was in at this stage of the story. First, he did not want to travel to Moab and risk that the visiting elders of Midian might recognize him and reveal his act as the magician Balaam. So, he delayed the trip by twice refusing to accompany messengers, which allowed time for the elders of Midian to leave Moab.

The ventriloquism act ensured his safety while he was with the king of Moab. The princes would testify that Balaam was only a spokesman for Yahweh. He was merely Yahweh's puppet. He could not be held responsible for not acquiescing to the king's wish to curse the Israelites.

Balaam's interactions with King Balak repeatedly saw the magician "falling into a trance, but having his eyes open."[17] During these "trances" Reuel made ominous predictions that the Israelites would be victorious in all their battles against the Moabites. Not what King Balak wanted to hear: "And Balak's anger was kindled against Balaam, and he smote his hands together: and Balak said unto Balaam, I called thee to curse mine enemies, and, behold, thou hast altogether blessed them."[18] But Balaam continued relaying grim prophecies of defeat awaiting Balak and his allies at the hands of the Israelites.

Through these insidious messages Reuel demoralized the Moabites, which eventually allowed the Israelites to gain safe passage through their land. By a simple act of ventriloquism Reuel was able to pave the way for them to cross what otherwise would have been the dangerous land of Moab. It was one of his last acts and he played it out consummately.

BAAL-PEOR

While Reuel was playing the role of Balaam at the court of King Balak, the Israelites were camped on the outskirts of the king's territory (Moab) at Shittim:

> And Israel abode in Shittim, and the people began to commit whoredom with the daughters of Moab. And they called the people unto the sacrifices of their gods: and the people did eat, and bowed down to their gods. And Israel joined himself unto Baal-peor: and the anger of the LORD was kindled against Israel. And the LORD said unto Moses, Take all the heads of the people, and hang them up before the LORD against the sun, that the fierce anger of the LORD may be turned away from Israel. And Moses said unto the judges of Israel, Slay ye every one his men that were joined unto Baal-peor.[19]

Since Reuel was still in Moab playing the part of Balaam (and disturbing their king with doomsday scenarios) he could not have been simultaneously playing the masked Moses at the Israeli camp. As we have already suggested, the "Moses" of this episode was Levi who was so disturbed that the sons of Israel were having sex with the daughters of Moab that he ordered the culprits slowly tortured to death. Yet another example of his violent temper. But it would not be his last act of wanton slaughter.

PHINEHAS

Not long after the Baal-peor incident, a plague broke out among the Israelites. The people feared that Yahweh was taking revenge upon them. During the plague a man and a woman were discovered having sex on holy territory. Phinehas, Aaron's grandson, "took a javelin in his hand; And he went after the man of Israel into the tent, and thrust both of them through, the man of Israel, and the woman through her belly."[20] When Moses (Levi in disguise) learned of the deed he was delighted with Phinehas, saying: "Behold, I give unto him my covenant of peace: And he shall have it, and his seed after him, even the covenant of an everlasting priesthood; because he was zealous for his God, and made an atonement for the children of Israel."[21]

For this vicious act of murder, Phinehas and his descendants are granted a covenant of "everlasting priesthood." This is curious, especially when one considers that as a Levite, Phinehas already had this right.

The text of the Phinehas incident is entirely written by Levites whose account must be taken with a grain of salt. They claim that the man was a Simeonite and the woman a Midianite. This incident signals a shift in the direction of the Israelites' rage from the Moabites to the Midianites. This abrupt change has long confused biblical scholars. The confusion is alleviated when we realize that Levi has become the masked Moses. Levi wanted the status and perks of the priesthood to go entirely to his descendants, the Levites, but was threatened in his ambition by the rival priesthood, the Kenites, who came from Midian. Levi used the incident at Baal-peor to turn the Israelites against all Midianites. Acting as the masked Moses, he sends the Israeli army against Midian.

This not only rids him of the rival priesthood but also enacts revenge against Reuel. Reuel had been the high priest of the Midianites and now that Levi had turned against Reuel, they were fair game. The Levite scribes describe what happened: "And they warred against the Midianites, as the LORD commanded Moses; and they slew all the males. And they slew the kings of Midian, beside the rest of them that were slain; namely, Evi, and Rekem, and Zur, and *Hur*, and Reba, five kings of Midian: *Balaam* also the son of Beor they slew with the sword."[22] (Italics added)

With just these few lines, the Levite scribes effectively erased from history two of Reuel's secret identities, Hur and Balaam. They both, according to the text, were slain during the war with the Midianites. Wishful thinking. Reuel escaped the trap and lived to a ripe old age before meeting his end in a cave overlooking the Sea of Galilee.

After their victory over the Midianites, the Israeli army took many women captives. When the masked Moses (Levi) learned that the women had been spared he was "wroth" with the officers, instructing them to "kill every woman that hath known man by lying with him"[23] but to keep as slaves the female children.[24] With the war with the Midianites over, the Israelites were now ready to cross the Jordan River and capture the Promised Land.

The leader of this invasion would not be Moses. It was time to end the rule of Moses and make way for a new leader, Joshua.

THE DEATH OF MOSES

It's a curious fact that though they lay claim to Moses as their ancestor, the Levite scribes offer no account of the death of "their" prophet. The only description of his end appears in the last pages of Deuteronomy. Moses is climbing Mount Nebo, which overlooked Jericho and the Promised Land. From here, "the LORD said unto him, This is the land which I sware unto Abraham, unto Isaac, and unto Jacob, saying, I will give it unto thy seed: I have caused thee to see it with thine eyes, but thou shalt not go over thither. So Moses, the servant of the LORD died there in the land of Moab, according to the word of the LORD. And he buried him in a valley in the land of Moab over against Beth-peor: but no man knoweth of his sepulchre unto this day."[25]

So, there are no witnesses to the death of the great prophet. He simply disappears. Just like Aaron, Moses ascends the mountain but doesn't come back. The account of the Deuteronomist assumes that God took care of his body, hiding it from the Israelites.

The Jewish historian Josephus offers a different version of the death of Moses. It happens shortly after his farewell address to the tribes of Israel. The people weep, knowing that the great prophet is about to die:

> Now as he went thence to the place where he was to vanish out of their sight, they all followed after him weeping; but Moses beckoned with his hand to those that were remote from him, and bade them stay behind in quiet, while he exhorted those that were near him that they would not render his departure so lamentable. Whereupon they thought they ought to grant him that favor, to let him depart, according as he himself desired: so they restrained themselves, though weeping still towards one another. All those who accompanied him were the senate, and Elezar the high priest, and Joshua their commander. Now as soon as they were come to the mountain call Abarim (which is a very high mountain, situated over against Jericho and one that affords, to such as are upon it, a prospect of the greatest part of the excellent land of Canaan), he dismissed the senate; and as he was going to embrace Elezar and Joshua, and was still discoursing with them, a cloud stood over him on the sudden, and he disappeared.[26]

Like a Vegas magician, Moses disappears in a puff of smoke.

13

———•———

The Deadly Secret

Every secret you've kept will become known.[1]

JESUS TO THE PRIESTS OF JERUSALEM

For more than a thousand years the people lived in desperate hope that Moses would somehow return to lead them and restore the balance of their history. Freud believed that Moses had assumed the supreme role of father figure to the Jews. It followed that they would ultimately be compelled to sacrifice a son in atonement for the murder of that father.[2] Jesus became that sacrificial figure, "the son of God" who died for their violation and inspired the New Testament.

Freud's reading of the German Egyptologist Ernst Sellin convinced him that the traumatic murder of Moses "was the basis of all the later expectations of the Messiah."[3]

Jesus saw himself as the heir to the legendary prophet, saying, "For had ye believed Moses, ye would have believed me: for he wrote of me."[4]

Numerous scholars have noted the uncanny similarities between the two men:[5]

> Like Moses, Jesus's parents hid their child from a vicious ruler determined to slaughter male infants.

Both spent time in Egypt, though to deflect the charge that Jesus was a magician, Matthew would only acknowledge that he had spent time there as a child.

The fathers of both men were named Joseph.*

Jesus matched Moses's ten plagues with ten miracles.

Moses received God's laws on the Mountain of God. Jesus presented his moral blueprint during the pivotal Sermon on the Mount.

Both men spent forty days and forty nights in the wilderness.

Both men emerged from their encounter with God with glowing faces.

Their contemporaries believed them to be Egyptian-trained magicians.

The classic work making the case that Jesus was an Egyptian-trained magician is *Jesus the Magician* by Professor Morton Smith.† He reveals that during the first millennium, "hundreds of thousands of believing Christians" regarded Jesus as a magician.[6] At the time, magic was understood to be a "private religion" used to manipulate "angels and demons" for personal ends.[7]

The gospels represented Jesus as the new Moses. Matthew, Mark, Luke, and John all tried to counter the belief that Jesus was an ordinary magician. At the time many magicians claimed to be a "son" of one of the pantheon of gods. But after Christian writers adopted the idea of a single god they realized that the son of that sole god would assume a unique and powerful position. It was because of this exceptional status that Jesus's power ran to much more than simply exorcising demons— a routine task well within the job description of any "regular" magician. More impressively, Jesus could forgive sins,[8] and he could raise the dead.‡ The gospels were written to convince people that Jesus possessed these, and other divine qualities.

---

*That Joseph was the true father of Moses was explained in chapter 4.

†Morton Smith (1915–1991) was a noted professor of ancient history who taught at Brown and Columbia universities.

‡Most notably the raising of Lazarus from the dead in John 11.

Matthew tells the dramatic story of Jesus's unprecedented encounter with the two most awe-inspiring figures in the people's lives. The three disciples who accompanied him witnessed not only his meeting with Moses but a blessing by God.

At this point Jesus was

> transfigured before them: and his face shone as the sun, and his raiment was white as the light. And behold, there appeared unto them Moses and Elias talking with him. . . . While he yet spake, behold, a bright cloud overshadowed them: and behold a voice out of the cloud, which said, This is my beloved Son, in whom I am well pleased; hear ye him. And when the disciples heard it, they fell on their face, and were sore afraid. And Jesus came and touched them, and said, Arise, and be not afraid. And when they lifted up their eyes, they saw no man, save Jesus only. And as they came down from the mountain, Jesus charged them, saying, Tell the vision to no man, until the Son of man be risen again from the dead.[9]

This image may well be the way Jesus intended to be remembered: talking with Moses while God certified his divinity, guaranteeing his natural right to step into the great man's sandals. What an image to stamp on history! Instead, his most common depiction became that of his brutal crucifixion.

The common picture of the shining face of Jesus mirrors the memorable glowing face of Moses. But unlike Israel's prophet, Jesus never hid behind a mask. Instead, as we will show, he forfeited his life to reveal the truth about the murder of Moses. He found the courage to confront the scribes and priests of Jerusalem who feared the exposure of the dark secret of the murder of the real Moses. As their snare tightened on him he boldly threatened them, "Every secret you've kept will become known. What you have whispered in hidden places will be shouted from the housetops."[10]

Jesus timed his entry into Jerusalem to coincide with the Passover, the sacred day set aside by the Jews to commemorate their history-changing flight from Egypt led by Moses. Reaching the outskirts of the town Jesus asks that two of his disciples, "Go into the village over against you, and straightway ye shall find an ass tied, and a colt with her: loose them, and bring them unto me."[11]

He rides the ass into Jerusalem accompanied by the colt thus fulfilling the prediction of the prophet.[12] Zechariah had prophesised that the Messiah would come "riding upon an ass, and upon a colt the foal of an ass."[13]

As he rode into town, so significantly at the time of the Passover, the people, keen to believe the Messiah had finally arrived, tossed palm leaves across the road before him.[14] The tumultuous gathering soon drew the attention of the "chief priests and scribes" who were not amused by this display of adulation.

On the day that Jesus entered Jerusalem to such acclaim, Rome controlled the known world. Normally, the Romans found it pragmatic to use local princes or kings as proxies to rule on their behalf. But on that fateful day the Roman Procurator Pontius Pilate (ruled 26–36 CE) was in charge. Pilate was one of three key characters who figure in the plot to kill Jesus. The others were Joseph Caiaphas, the Levite high priest of Jerusalem, and Herod Antipas, the "half Jew" ruler of Galilee.[15] Jesus called him "that fox."[16] Antipas (20 BCE to 39 CE) was considered only a "half Jew" because his ancestors were from Edom, the homeland of Reuel.

As we've seen, Moses was murdered by the Edomite Reuel, with the cooperation of the father of the Levites, Levi. Such a conspiracy between Edomite and Levite, we suggest, was also responsible for the crucifixion of Jesus.

But how did they pull off such a public murder?

And how did Jesus discover the truth about the murder of Moses?

THE EDOMITE KING

In 141 BCE, the Romans appointed a Levite high priest to the position of king of the Jews. It was the first time the tribe of Levi had taken on the role of monarch in addition to their priestly duties. But this "Hasmonean dynasty" was soon wracked with internal civil conflicts while externally they pursued territorial expansion, conquering Edom and forcing the Edomites to adopt Judaism. Edom was renamed Idumea and became a Roman province, which attracted high profile Edomites into the new center of power, Jerusalem. They soon became so invaluable to the Romans that they were appointed the de facto administrators of the Roman provinces of Judea, Galilee, and Idumea.

This Edomite elite administered under a weak Levite monarchy appointed by the Romans. All this changed when the Roman Senate, at Mark Anthony's urging, appointed Herod the Great (ruled 39–4 BCE) to become "the king of the Jews."[17] As a result, the Jews came under the direct rule of an Edomite monarchy. It was the first time they'd been controlled by Edomites since Reuel, himself a prince of Edom, ruled as the masked Moses.

Mark Anthony became governor of Syria (37–35 BCE) and Herod showered his benefactor with wealth confiscated from the rich families of Jerusalem. Mark Anthony and Herod remained loyal friends despite the manipulations of that other powerful political figure of the time, Cleopatra. Josephus offers an insight into the intrigues of the Egyptian queen who was Anthony's lover. She was "a slave to her lusts" and Anthony was so "bewitched to do whatsoever she would have him." Josephus wrote,

> Now at this time the affairs of Syria were in confusion by Cleopatra's constant persuasions to Anthony to make an attempt upon everybody's dominions; for she persuaded him to take those dominions away from their several princes, and bestow them upon her; and she had a mighty influence upon him, by reason of his being enslaved to her by his affections. She was also by nature very covetous, and stuck at no wickedness. She had already poisoned her brother, because she knew that he was to be king of Egypt, and this was when he was but fifteen years old; and she got her sister Arsinoe to be slain, by means of Anthony.[18]

Anthony continued to grant more and more territory to Cleopatra but managed to keep any land that fell under Herod's jurisdiction out of her grasp. Inevitably, the Egyptian queen tried to seduce the king of the Jews, but Herod was so mortified by the duplicity of his friend's lover that he decided to take the extreme step of "preventing her intrigues, by putting her to death."[19] He only relented when close friends advised caution. Herod then shifted his energies to the task of raising an army to recapture Petra from the Arabians.

This suited Cleopatra. She had designs on both Judea and Idumea and anticipated a battle between the two nations that would weaken them, leaving them vulnerable to the predations of her Egyptian army. Herod delayed his attack on the Arabians in case Anthony needed his support in the Roman civil war he was waging with Octavius. But Cleopatra's charms were strong enough to persuade Anthony to free Herod's troops to move against the Arabians, taking Egyptian reinforcements with him.

On Anthony's orders Herod's forces overran the Arabians and were about to reclaim Petra for the Jewish kingdom when Cleopatra's troops, who had held back in the fight, now turned against Herod's exhausted forces and defeated them. Herod retreated into the desert mountains with a skeleton army where he "could only act like a private robber, and make excursions upon many parts of Arabia and distress them by sudden incursions, while he encamped among the mountains, and avoided by any means to come to a pitched battle; yet he did greatly harass the enemy."[20]

Eventually Herod's guerrilla forces prevailed—in no small part because of a rousing speech that lifted his men's fighting spirit. Meanwhile Anthony, left without the support of Herod's forces, lost the battle of Actium to Octavius who became the sole emperor of Rome under the title "Caesar Augustus." This was a "Caesar" whom Cleopatra realized she could not sway. So rather than face the humiliation of being paraded through Rome as a captive, she committed suicide.

Herod's victory over the Arabians was now overshadowed by his concern for his own fate under the new Roman emperor. His career depended upon maintaining good relations with the leaders of Rome, so he traveled to Rhodes to meet Caesar Augustus. Herod removed his crown to appear more humble before the emperor then offered the philosophical-minded Caesar Augustus a speech about friendship saying, "for, if a man owns himself to another's friend and knows him to be a benefactor, he is obliged to hazard everything, to use every faculty of his soul, every member of his body, and all the wealth he hath."[21] He explained how he had tried to steer Anthony away from Cleopatra's influence and put the blame for his friend's defeat squarely on the Egyptian queen.

Finally, Herod said that if Caesar would "only examine how I behave myself to my benefactors in general, and what sort of a friend I am, thou wilt find by experience that we shall do and be the same to thyself."[22] His speech so impressed Caesar Augustus that he promptly confirmed Herod as king of the Jews.

The Edomite control of the Jews was secure allowing Herod a free hand in all his territories that lay under Rome's protection. He was able to turn his attention to the needs of his people and began a series of ambitious building projects that culminated in the construction of a magnificent temple in Jerusalem. But the priests of Jerusalem were still skeptical about Herod because he was of Edomite ancestry, which they considered not fully Jewish. So, when he proposed to replace their temple with a much grander edifice, they were distrustful. Once again, Herod used his power with words and promised that he wouldn't demolish the existing temple until all the materials and manpower were ready at hand for the much grander edifice he had designed. Only with this promise did the Jews accept Herod's offer. But there was one more obstacle to their full compliance. They would not tolerate anyone who was not of pure Jewish blood setting foot on the holy ground. To circumvent this problem Herod trained a thousand priests in the necessary skills of masonry and carpentry so that they could build the new temple.[23]

It was complete within eighteen months even though Herod, as an Edomite, was prohibited from entering the building. Outside the holy grounds he continued the vast building project that would ensure Jerusalem's place in the pantheon of great cities.

Beyond Judea, Herod persuaded Caesar Augustus to prohibit the persecution of the Jews throughout the empire so that Herod the Great could claim, "I have advanced the nation of the Jews to a degree of happiness which they never had before."[24]

However, the people didn't agree with his own rosy assessment of the temper of the times. There was a dark side to Herod's reign. He insisted that guards surround him at all times and refused to

> permit the citizens either to meet together, or to walk, or eat together, but watched everything they did and when they were caught, they were severely punished; and many there were who were brought to the citadel Hyrcania, both openly and secretly, and were there put to death; and there were spies set everywhere, both in the city and in the roads, who watched those that met together; nay, it is reported that he did not himself neglect this part of caution, but that he would oftentimes himself take the habit of a private man, and mix among the multitude, in the nighttime, and make trial what opinion they had of his government; and as for those they could no way be reduced to acquiesce under his scheme of government, he persecuted them all manner of ways; but for the rest of the multitude, he required that they should be obliged to take an oath of fidelity to him.[25]

Herod's political successes were founded on the uncompromising powers of a police state. Such a government bred paranoia: a state of mind that had a disastrous impact on Herod's personal life.

THE HERODIANS

Herod chose as his first wife Mariamne, the beautiful daughter of the previous Levite dynasty. This marriage potentially healed the rift between the Edomites and Levites, which had festered for centuries, going back to the time of Moses. They had two sons whom Herod sent to Rome to receive a first-rate education. But soon things began to fall apart. Over the coming years his paranoia drove Herod to murder Mariamne and, when they were grown, their two sons.

In his old age, he murdered yet a third son so that by the time of his death the only heirs who remained were fourth, fifth, and six princes. These messy domestic politics outraged Caesar Augustus who was forced to sort out the provisions of Herod's will. Three princes laid claim to the kingship of the Jews. It didn't help that while they stood before Caesar awaiting his verdict, revolts broke out in Judea among the Jews who wanted no part of an Edomite-dominated monarchy.

Caesar hid his distaste for the chore and directed that the succession be implemented as Herod's last will and testimony had dictated even though there was a real possibility that he was not in his right mind when it was composed. Half of Herod's territory, including Judea and Idumea (Edom), along with the crown, went to Herod's son Archelaus (ruled 4 BCE–6 CE). By the time Jesus came to Jerusalem, King Archelaus had been deposed and the Roman province of Judea, which included Jerusalem, was ruled directly by a Roman prefect, Pontius Pilate.

Caesar Augustus also gave half of Herod's kingdom to two of his other sons, "Philip and to Antipas."[26] Philip was made the *tetrarch* (Latin for ruler of a quarter) for the Roman province of Syria. Antipas was the tetrarch for Galilee.

Antipas, whom Jesus called "that fox," was known both as Herod Antipas, and Herod the tetrarch. In Galilee, where he ruled, the people called him King Herod, after his father. It was he who had imprisoned John the Baptist because of the prophet's objections over his marriage to his brother's wife. And later, Herod delivered John's head on a platter at the request of his dancing stepdaughter. When Herod learned that Jesus was attracting large crowds, just as John the Baptist once did, he was petrified. He came to believe that Jesus was the reincarnation of John the Baptist, which made him a dangerous enemy. This hatred grew as Jesus preached against divorce. Herod

Antipas had divorced his first wife to marry his dead brother's wife.

The elaborate spy network that Herod the Great created was inherited by his son. The Herodians were educated Edomites who brought their own scribes from Edom to Jerusalem. We suggest that some of these "scribes" spied on Jesus and reported directly to Herod Antipas. Because he was a convert to Judaism, Herod Antipas traveled yearly to Jerusalem during Passover and was in the city when Jesus was crucified.

Light was shone on his critical role in the death of Jesus when, in 1886, the lost gospel of Peter was discovered in a monk's cave in Egypt. It implicates Herod Antipas in the crucifixion. Although not officially a part of the New Testament, the first line of surviving text reads, "but of the Jews no one washed his hands, neither did Herod nor any one of his judges."[27] Luke, who is more familiar with the intricacies of the Herod family than any other New Testament writer,[28] reports that Jesus was warned while he was still in Galilee, "Get thee out, and depart hence: for *Herod will kill thee.*"[29] (Italics added)

Jesus replied, "Go ye, and tell that fox, Behold, I cast out devils, and I do cures to day and to morrow, and the third day I shall be perfected. Nevertheless I must walk to day, and to morrow, and the day following: for it cannot be that a prophet perish out of Jerusalem."[30]

Jesus defiantly traveled to Jerusalem where he knew Herod Antipas was planning his death. But Herod Antipas was not alone in his fixation to get rid of the brash figure whom people were calling the Messiah. In addition to his "scribes" there were "priests" who were also determined that Jesus would die. Who were these obsessed men?

THE PRIESTS OF JERUSALEM

In 538 BCE the Persian leader Cyrus the Great conquered Babylon and freed the Jews who had been held there since 587 BCE by the Babylonian emperor, Nebuchadnezzar. A second temple was built in Jerusalem and dedicated during Passover in 516 BCE. By 400 BCE the words of the Torah were finalized, providing the Levite priests with all the laws they anticipated needing. But the people found these rules too restrictive and over time, nobody knows exactly when, two sects of Jews emerged: the Sadducees and the Pharisees.

The Sadducees were composed of the wealthy Jewish families of Jerusalem, including the Levite priests. They believed in a literal interpretation of the Torah, which contained no notion of an afterlife. Their focus was upon ritual sacrifice at the temple. Since the fabulous Temple of Solomon no longer existed, the Sadducees constructed a less grand version that became the center of their religion. This was the temple replaced by Herod a mere generation before Jesus arrived in Jerusalem. During his time, construction continued with numerous baths and other auxiliary buildings associated with the temple. The complex wasn't completed until thirty years after the death of Jesus.

In 70 CE a Jewish revolt ended in the Romans burning down Herod's temple—a decisive blow to the Sadducees. The temple was the source of their living. The numerous sacrifices, baths, and other forms of income that the temple provided the Sadducees were reduced to ashes. The Sadducees never recovered and subsequently disappeared from history.

Opposed to the Sadducees were the Pharisees, small landowners and traders who held progressive ideas and were the spiritual forefathers of modern Judaism.[31] They believed that the written Torah must be supplemented by the "Oral Torah," which had been passed down by word of mouth from the time of Moses.[32] They accepted the idea of an afterlife and believed in individual prayer.

When Jesus was crucified, "The Pharisees stood aloof from the whole affair . . . not a single Pharisee is found to have participated in the trial, much less in the decision to hand over Jesus to the Romans."[33] But eighty years later, when the gospels were composed, Matthew and Mark found themselves engaged in a hostile debate with the Pharisees who had replaced the Sadducees as Judaism's official voice.

The newly empowered Pharisees refused to accept that Jesus had been the Messiah. It was because of this bitter dispute with the Pharisees that the Christian writers of the gospel retrofitted the word *Pharisees* into the story of Jesus. Although it scored cheap points against them it was not historically accurate. In fact, the Pharisees had nothing to do with the death of Jesus. Luke, for instance, replaced references to the scribes with the more specific, *Pharisees*.[34] In *Jesus the Magician,* Morton Smith demonstrates that all the references in the New Testament that make a case against the Pharisees are anachronistic.[35] The gospels give a false impression that they colluded in the crucifixion of Jesus.

Josephus Caiaphas, a Sadducee from the tribe of Levi, was the high priest of Jerusalem from 18–36 CE. Caiaphas was outraged when Jesus raised Lazarus from the dead because the notion of resurrection stood contrary to his belief, taught in the Torah, that the soul perished with the body. Caiaphas demanded the death, not only of Jesus but of Lazarus as well, assuming he must be part of the fraud.[36]

When Jesus overturned the tables of the temple moneylenders he gave Caiaphas an even stronger motive for putting him at the top of his hit list. First, as the high priest of Jerusalem Caiaphas's public image demanded that he assume responsibility for sustaining peace and order during the festival of Passover, which Jesus was disturbing. And secondly, privately and perhaps more importantly to him, greed was a motive. The temple priests demanded a percentage from the moneylenders. A percentage of that coin always found its way into Caiaphas's pocket.

When Jesus was crucified in 33 CE, Joseph Caiaphas and Herod Antipas had plenty of reason to wish him dead. But above Jesus's disturbing and disrupting activities loomed the necessity to protect a dark secret that could only remain hidden if they permanently rid themselves of him. The secret detailed the definitive role that their ancestors had played in the murder of Moses.

But how did Jesus come to be in possession of such explosive knowledge?

JESUS THE MAGICIAN

Although he was raised by a carpenter, Jesus could read.* Like all literate Jews of the time, he studied the Torah with a passion and knew the

---

*Mark 12:24 and John 7:15 claim that Jesus could read but some scholars are skeptical.

story of Moses inside out. But what led him to believe that the prophet had been murdered? And why would he charge the Levites with such an outrageous crime? The answer can be found in the stories told about Jesus by a Roman writer.

In the second century Celsus wrote an invaluable book about Christianity based on a variety of older, now lost, sources. A Christian writer, Origen, (fl. 247 CE) wrote a reply to Celsus's book, quoting from it extensively. Of special interest is the revealing statement that it was poverty that forced Jesus to hire himself out in Egypt where the son of a carpenter might find work. It was there that Jesus learned "certain arts for which the Egyptians are famous. Afterwards, returning from thence, he thought so highly of himself, on account of the possession of these arts, as to proclaim himself to be a God."[37]

Like an Egyptian-trained magician, Jesus became famous for his ability to cast out demons and cure the mentally ill. It's possible that his skill in utilizing the power of suggestion enabling him to perform these exorcisms was, at least in part, derived from the training in the art of hypnotism that he gained from his Egyptian mentors. (Notably, Jesus was unable to perform these miracles in his hometown where the people were not in awe of his reputation. The power of suggestion was voided by familiarity.)

In the same passage in which Celsus informs us that Jesus studied magic in Egypt he provides an early description of Egyptian puppetry. "These magicians also represent animals as moving, which are not in reality animals, but merely appear to the imagination to be such."[38]

Jesus was a literate, Egyptian-trained magician who knew that the skills of puppetry and hypnotism were perfect tools to gain political leverage. He possessed intimate knowledge of two of the most important keys to unlocking the secret story of the murder of Moses. The gospels contain evidence that this ancient secret is precisely what Jesus was referring to in a pivotal chapter in the testament of Matthew.

Matthew quotes Jesus: "The scribes and Pharisees sit in Moses' seat."[39] This is a clue in understanding why he was crucified. When we replace Matthew's words *scribes and Pharisees* with the more historically accurate "Edomites and Levites" then Jesus's provocative sentence, as originally spoken, reads, "The Edomites and Levites sit in Moses' seat."

The accusation that Edomites and Levites had sat in Moses's seat may have been a veiled warning to Herod Antipas and Josephus Caiaphas that Jesus was fully aware of their ancestors' involvement in the murder of Moses. In the same chapter of Matthew, Jesus makes his accusation crystal clear. When we replace (as discussed previously) the words *scribes and Pharisees* with "Edomites and Levites" his damning words read: "Woe unto you, Edomites and Levites, hypocrites! because ye build the tombs of the prophets, and garnish the sepulchres of the righteous, and say, If we had been in the days of our fathers, we would not have been partakers with them in the blood of the prophets. Wherefore ye be witnesses unto yourselves, that ye are the children of them which killed the prophets."[40]

Jesus's unique education allowed him to discern examples of Egyptian magic within the Torah and identify the criminals who had murdered Moses: stories like that of Hur and Aaron using a puppet to help Moses hold his staff, and the fantastic tale of Balaam's talking donkey. He would have been familiar with the critical role played by masks among Egyptian magicians, leading him to suspect that the masked Moses who returned to the tribe was not the same man who climbed the Mountain of God to receive the Ten Commandments. His less sophisticated tribe believed these stories to be true accounts of miracles. But a man trained in the arts of magic would be more discerning. He only needed to pull one or two threads from the fictional garment that covered the Levite story of Moses before the entire legend unraveled. He had identified the flaws in that carefully woven fabric of lies.

Herod Antipas and Joseph Caiaphas couldn't afford to let Jesus expose the dark secret of their ancestors. At the very least they would be deposed if the people believed their ancestors had murdered Moses. It was too dangerous to respond directly to Jesus's explosive accusations and bring attention to the very thing they were trying to hide. But it was even more dangerous to let the rabble-rouser continue to ignite dissent. It was decided. He must be arrested and tried secretly.

The kangaroo court that was held at the palace of Joseph Caiaphas broke three Jewish laws dictating the conduct of trials.[41] First, it took place in a private home rather than a public council chamber. Second, it was held during Passover, which was prohibited. And finally, it took place at night, unlike the normal procedure when judgment was delivered during daylight. Jesus mocked the nighttime raid, likening Caiaphas's men to thieves who hid under cover of "the power of darkness" to conceal their nefarious deeds.[42]

The fact that Joseph Caiaphas would break these judicial rules speaks volumes about the urgency he felt to silence Jesus.

THE CHARGES

Joseph Caiaphas dared not respond directly to the incendiary accusation that his ancestor murdered Moses. Instead, he looked for other reasons to justify an execution. During his trip from Galilee to Jerusalem "scribes and priests" had continuously sought evidence to condemn Jesus. They accused him of disrespecting the Sabbath by gathering corn on the holy day, thereby breaking the fourth commandment.[43] Because of this "crime" the Levites "held council against him, how they might destroy him."[44]

Even as the gospels were being written, Levite priests continued to gather new charges against Jesus of breaking the restrictions of the Holy Day. Egyptian magicians were known to be tattooed. Rabbi Eliezer (fl. 70–100) charged Jesus with cutting tattoos into his flesh on the Sabbath. He wrote that Jesus "brought magic marks from Egypt in the scratches on his flesh."[45]

Jesus was also charged with using Beelzebub, an agent of the Devil, to "cast out devils."[46] This was followed by the accusation that he had failed to honor his mother and father,[47] thereby breaking the fifth commandment. But none of these specific charges were leveled when the bound prisoner stood before Josephus Caiaphas in his palace on that dark night.

At first, Caiaphas "sought false witness against Jesus, to put him to death."[48] One of these false witnesses proclaimed, "This fellow said, I am able to destroy the temple of God, and to build it in three days."[49] This charge was designed to enrage the attending priests but failed to rouse them to action so Caiaphas was forced to take the argument to Jesus personally, demanding that he answer if he was the Son of God?[50]

When Jesus confirmed the claim, Caiaphas did something considered shocking. He tore at his clothes. Since Moses's time, it had been strictly forbidden for a high priest to "rend his clothes." This prohibition followed the incineration of Aaron's two eldest sons when they offered "strange fire" to Yahweh. Moses warned their father that Yahweh would kill him if he tore at his clothes in grief, as was the custom.[51] So, by ripping his clothes in sight of the assembled priests Caiaphas was emphasizing how terrible a crime Jesus was committing by claiming to be the Son of God.

The High Levite Priest of Jerusalem shouted, "now ye have heard his blasphemy. What think ye?"[52] It was a rhetorical question. The priests clamored for a sentence of capital punishment. Joseph Caiaphas had had his way. Jesus would be silenced—ostensibly because of blasphemy.

The next morning, Caiaphas and his priests, "took counsel against Jesus to put him to death."[53] They bound him over to the Roman governor, Pontius Pilate, with a recommendation that the prisoner be executed. But Pilate said, "I find no fault in this man."[54] And when he learned that Jesus was from Galilee immediately took the opportunity to pass the case to Herod Antipas who was in Jerusalem for the Passover.

Jesus remained silent as he stood before Herod Antipas, which unnerved the Edomite who was still recovering from beheading John the Baptist, an act that had brought him great shame. He didn't want to be involved in the death of *another* prophet so, knowing the outcome to be a foregone conclusion, quickly passed the prisoner back to Pilate.

It was at this point that Pilate famously washed his hands of the problem declaring, "I am innocent of the blood of this just person."[55]

To which the priests answered, "We have a law, and by our law he ought to die, because he made himself the Son of God."[56]

Jesus's legend was built on the foundation created by Moses. To be crucified during Passover linked him forever with the immortal liberator of the Jews. Jesus blamed the Edomites and Levites for the death of Moses and knew exactly which buttons to push to incite them to overreact to his taunts and accusations.[57] Knowing the consequences, he was willing to die, taking on the role of the sacrificial son whose death could redeem the murder of the quintessential father figure, Moses.

The crucifixion was carried out by the Romans. But the death of Jesus was a lynching incited by Joseph Caiaphas with the silent approval of the Edomite ruler of Galilee, Herod Antipas. The two men never responded to the sensational charge that Jesus had leveled against them: that the hands of their ancestors dripped with the blood of the prophet Moses. They had silenced the man who was prepared to unveil the secret that would destroy their power and their lives.

GALILEE

Reuel's obsession with his noble bloodline extended far beyond Galilee, the place where he eventually took up permanent residence. After his grandsons reached maturity and produced their own children Reuel turned his attention to another sacred mission—ensuring the dominance of his descendants in every walk of life: religion, politics, and civil society. Once again, the master magician was incredibly successful. Reuel's noble bloodline lives on even now, intact, and is *still influential*. The Tawheed (the Druze) maintain that their ancestry traces directly back to the Master Magician. By prohibiting intermarriage with outsiders they believe that they've safeguarded the integrity of their heritage.

Surely, that extraordinary legacy included the secrets behind Reuel's magic. The craft and talent that he had spun to his will with flair and drama were as critical a birthright as his DNA. Such covert knowledge would have been bestowed only upon those who demonstrated the aptitude so that riches, rights, and respect would remain secured within the clan. And so, through the generations, these priceless arts were perfected and practiced up to, and including, the time of Jesus.

THE BELOVED DISCIPLE

The only biblical mystery that can compare to the Old Testament murder of Moses is the enigma surrounding the identity of Jesus's "Beloved Disciple." This elusive character plays a pivotal role, seen and unseen, during Christ's final days. It was the Beloved Disciple who rests his head against Jesus's shoulder at the Last Supper. He was center stage at this fateful event and the final holy meal was probably served at his table.

Peter was jealous of the favor that Jesus bestowed upon this unnamed disciple.

The rivalry began early, shortly after Peter's brother Andrew (who also became a disciple of Jesus) witnessed the baptism of Jesus by John the Baptist.

The second witness to the baptism was the Beloved Disciple.

Jesus chose Andrew and the Beloved Disciple as his first two disciples. And so, two magicians—masters of the arts of illusion—formed the inner circle of possibly the most exclusive club in history.

Jesus cherished the unnamed disciple who had witnessed his transformation by baptism at the birth of his ministry.

The Beloved Disciple was a young man when he knew Jesus. In his old age, some sixty-five years after the crucifixion, he wrote an account of all that he was willing to reveal. This record formed the foundation of the Fourth Gospel, known as "John." We say *foundation* because the record that has come down to us was *reinterpreted* by another John—a Greek also known as the Elder.

John the Elder disturbed the original account by adding "a streak of antisemitism"[58] into the text. What he deleted is unknown, but the remaining edited account of the Fourth Gospel offers unique insights about Jesus.

The Gospel according to Saint John was an inspiration for Hugh Schonfield (1901–1998). In his controversial book *The Passover Plot,* which is a radical retelling of the story of Jesus, he portrays the prophet as a genius with an agenda, who willingly risked his life, and ultimately lost it, *unexpectedly,* on the cross. In Schonfield's account, the Beloved Disciple is present, and horrified, when a Roman soldier* thrusts his spear† into Jesus's body—dealing him a fatal blow. Jesus, Schonfield suggests, had expected to survive the crucifixion. He had carefully timed his arrest and trial. Critically, he had calculated the hours he would have to endure on the cross before a drug that he'd ingested to simulate death allowed his rescuers to retrieve and resuscitate him, possibly in the privacy of the tomb. The goal, according to Schonfield, was to convince the disciples to believe that Jesus was truly the Messiah predicted by the Old Testament.

It all went wrong when the Roman soldier killed Jesus with a *coup de grace* he had probably dealt countless other crucifixion victims who took too long to die. This gruesome fate was something that Jesus and the Beloved Disciple had failed to consider. It was literally the fatal flaw in their plan.

Because of this tragic turn of events the Beloved Disciple was forced to take things into his own hands to ensure that the Messiah's desired legacy was fulfilled. It's here that the hand of Reuel reaches through the centuries. He had insured that his descendants possessed a secret weapon: Egyptian magic. The power of illusion and the acting ability to pull it off was something that the Beloved Disciple would demonstrate with the same authority as Reuel. And he wielded the same tricks: acts of illusion, quick-change artistry, impersonation, and the use of confederates.

In Schonfield's interpretation Jesus provoked the powers-that-be to arrest and ultimately crucify him. Immediately following his arrest, Jesus is taken to the luxurious Palace of Annas. Annas, now retired, had once been the High Priest of Jerusalem, and was still influential. Incredibly, the Beloved Disciple gains access to the highly secured Palace of Annas and becomes an eyewitness to dramatic events. How did he acquire such a privileged entree?

---

*Later identified as the Christian convert Longinus.
†Later known as the Spear of Destiny.

We suggest that the Beloved Disciple was an Edomite priest and scribe, which made him a distant relative of Reuel. At the time of the crucifixion of Jesus there were both Edomite priests and Levite priests practicing in Jerusalem. The Romans handpicked the Levite priests who would oversee religion. Simultaneously, they chose the Edomite priests and scribes to act as administrators.

The Beloved Disciple's Edomite genealogy explains how, as an administrative priest and scribe he was able to gain access to Annas's Palace. He knew the workings of the minds of those in power in Jerusalem, because he had interacted with them daily. He used this intimate knowledge to scrutinize the key players, winnowing out their weaknesses and passing on their secrets to Jesus.

Schonfield's Jesus "is like a chess player with a master plan, who has anticipated and knows how to counter the moves of his opponents, and indeed to make them serve the ends of his design."[59] This is certainly true, but what Schonfield didn't realize was that Jesus had an "inside man"—the Beloved Disciple—who knew exactly which buttons to push, at each stage, to keep the Passover Plot on track.

After the crucifixion, when Mary Magdala and the other women reach Jesus's tomb they are shocked to find that the stone that had secured its entrance had been rolled away. Inside, they find "a young man sitting on the right side, clothed in a long white garment."[60] We suggest that this was the Beloved Disciple in disguise.

He tells the women:

Ye seek Jesus of Nazareth, which was crucified: he is risen; he is not here: behold the place where they laid him. But go your way, tell his disciples and Peter that he goeth before you into Galilee: there shall ye see him, as he said unto you.[61]

The youth quickly makes his way back to Jerusalem ahead of the women. He changes clothes, becoming once again the Beloved Disciple, and merges, unnoticed, with the rest of the gathering disciples, including Peter.

The women are afraid to tell anyone about the empty tomb. Such news could trigger a deadly manhunt by the Romans. Anyone harboring the fugitive (or even concealing his corpse) would be in jeopardy. Mary Magdala can only safely reveal the dangerous secret of Jesus's resurrection to Peter and the other dedicated disciples.

When they hear her story, both Peter and the Beloved Disciple are eager to confirm the news. They race back to the Tomb.*

It is critical to the Beloved Disciple's plan that he arrive at the tomb before Peter. Why? If we draw back the curtain, we can glimpse what might well have been going on behind the scenes to warrant such urgency.

This dramatic and enigmatic episode comes into focus if the Beloved Disciple and the youth at the tomb are the same person.

As we've seen, playing several characters is an illusion that Reuel mastered repeatedly: having performed as Jethro, Hur, Balaam, and most significantly, as the masked Moses. Impersonation and quick-change artistry were finely tuned skills that he passed on to his successors. They, in turn, trained each new generation in these sacred arts, including, we suggest—the Beloved Disciple.

Another probable identity assumed by the Beloved Disciple was Lazarus, the man that Jesus raised from the dead. Jesus unreservedly trusted "both" Lazarus and the Beloved Disciple. But are these really two separate individuals?

As in the Moses story, in which Reuel and Jethro were the same man using different identities, Lazarus and the Beloved Disciple are the same person.

Schonfield writes that the Lazarus episode was a dry run for the Passover Plot. We agree that is how the crucifixion was supposed to play out: with a glorious resurrection.

But Jesus was dead. His body had to be removed before anyone discovered the truth. This, we suggest, was done by the trusted Beloved Disciple. Having accomplished this delicate task, he then assumed his

---

*The race to the tomb, won by the Beloved Disciple over Peter, is told in John 20:4–5.

disguise as the young man inside the tomb. In their shock at finding the mysterious young stranger in this sacred place, Mary Magdala and the other women remembered only that he was young and wearing a white robe. The Beloved Disciple's disguise, and his acting skill, deceived the women into thinking that he was someone they had never met before. They didn't recognize him as the Beloved Disciple; the youth in the tomb appeared as a stranger.

The panicked run to the tomb was a clever ploy used by the Beloved Disciple. It exhausted Peter, making him suggestable to what happened next. Although he wins the race, the Beloved Disciple lingers at the entrance. If Peter confirms the evidence of the resurrection the Beloved Disciple can evade the great danger of being discovered as the one who had already removed the body of Jesus from the tomb. As predicted, the wonder of finding the tomb empty overwhelms Peter and guarantees that no skepticism was going to be voiced from the "first" man to enter the empty tomb. The "first" to confirm the resurrection.

There is a simple beauty in his plan: Peter becomes the spokesman for the "miracle," rather than the Beloved Disciple, who is envied and distrusted by the others. Everyone trusts Peter. Since he is the messenger and the first to see the evidence of the empty tomb, the rest of the disciples are easily convinced of the "good news" of Jesus's resurrection.

Another pivotal encounter between Peter and the Beloved Disciple occurs while they are waiting for the return of the resurrected Jesus. The disciples go night fishing on the Sea of Galilee. In the morning, a man calls from shore, asking if they've caught any fish. When they confess their bad luck, the stranger suggests that they throw their lines over the right side of the boat. Fish rush into the nets. The bonanza is nothing less than a miracle. The Beloved Disciple stands up, apparently astonished. He points and shouts that the man on the shore is the Master—Jesus!

Peter jumps into the water and swims to shore, eager to be the first to greet the resurrected prophet—again, unwittingly playing his part in establishing the identity of the stranger on the shore. The Beloved Disciple once again uses Peter's compulsion to be first in the eyes of Jesus to persuade the rest of the disciples that the man on the shore is Jesus resurrected.

Why don't the other disciples recognize Jesus even though they have spent countless hours with him? In a trance of wonder over the bonanza of fish, they rely solely upon the word, the conviction, the drama, enacted by the excited Beloved Disciple. Schonfield sums up this important point in the story:

> The essence of the matter is that the disciples who knew Jesus so well entirely failed to recognize him in the man they saw. They were only persuaded by the belief of the Beloved Disciple.[62]

Regarding the miraculous bounty of fish, one doesn't have to have too much imagination to envisage a scenario whereby fish, previously caught and stored alive in traps, were released to coincide with the appearance of "Jesus." All that was required was a confederate operating the fish traps, in a choreographed drama, timed by the Beloved Disciple. Releasing freshly caught fish would have been unthinkable to fishermen like Peter. But it is a tactic we would expect from an experienced, creative magician.

So who was impersonating Jesus as the miracle maker who provided the fish? It had to be someone who could convincingly play him. But who? Andrew is the most likely candidate. He had been with both Jesus and the Beloved Disciple from the start: at Jesus's baptism. Like the Beloved Disciple, we suggest, Andrew was a practiced magician. Here, Andrew has a brief, stand-in role until the Beloved Disciple (the more experienced magician) can assume the role of the resurrected Jesus.

We assert that the Beloved Disciple was an Edomite priest, a rich property owner, a man with the power to open doors that led where others couldn't enter. An "inside man," who knew the politics of Jerusalem intimately and shared that knowledge with Jesus. And the Beloved Disciple possessed the skills of an Egyptian-trained magician, skills passed down to him from his distant ancestor—Reuel. It is significant that the Beloved Disciple was the only disciple present at the crucifixion. Mary, the mother of Jesus, was also present, and after the death of her son, she accompanied the Beloved Disciple to his home.[63]

At this point, we suggest, the Beloved Disciple assumed another one-off identity. Like the white-robed youth at the empty tomb, this character makes a sudden appearance, out of nowhere, before abruptly vanishing. He is *Joseph of Arimathea,* the rich man who receives permission from Pontus Pilate to take charge of the body of Christ.[64] The Beloved Disciple was probably wealthy. He had the means to bribe the Roman guards at the tomb and to arrange for the rolling back of the rock that sealed it. He assumed responsibility for the body. His plan required a quick-change artist who could outdistance people on both legs of the journey, to and from the tomb. The Beloved Disciple was such a man.

He then had to arrange for the resurrection of Jesus, by first deceiving Mary Magdala (and the other women) and giving them the script of the "good news." And then, secondly, by fooling Peter and the other disciples—despite the evidence of their own eyes—into believing that the stranger on the shore was Jesus.

The disciples came to believe in an impostor, just as the children of Israel, reluctantly despite all their "murmurings," believed in the masked Moses. But unlike Reuel's long, tyrannical rule, the Beloved Disciple's command is brief, surviving only long enough to send the disciples, now known as "apostles," out into the world to spread the good news. The ability of the Beloved Disciple to pull off his most audacious plan—the resurrection of Jesus—is reminiscent of the drama that Reuel used to impersonate the murdered Moses.

THE SHROUD OF TURIN

In the 2017 History Channel documentary *The Jesus Strand: A Search for DNA,* Dr. George Busby, an Oxford University specialist in genetics, and Pastor Joe Basile, a biblical scholar, undertook a fresh examination of the Shroud of Turin, the cloth that was believed to have been wrapped around the crucified Jesus. After a long, extensive investigation, they concluded that it was feasible that the blood on the shroud was from Christ.

That blood had a unique DNA signature. It was linked to a specific group of Middle East dwellers, the Druze.

———●———

The Secret Religion

For he hath triumphed gloriously.[1]

MIRIAM

E very year on April 25 the practitioners of a secret faith make a
pilgrimage to a mosquelike shrine near an extinct volcano overlooking the Sea of Galilee in northern Israel. Worldwide there are
about a million followers of the Tawheed faith. They live mostly
in Lebanon and Syria but there are more than 100,000 in northern Israel.* They claim to be descendants of the lost tribes of
Israel and the builders of King Solomon's Temple. Western scholars call them the Druze (after one of their early missionaries). The
Druze believe their religion represents the culmination of Judaism,
Christianity, and Islam.

Mysteriously, they take great pains to keep their doctrine secret. To
be a Druze, you must be born a Druze. They never accept converts.
Even after decades of rigorous apprenticeship each new generation of
potential leaders must prove their worth, both intellectually and ethi-
cally. Only a few members (male and female) will be granted access to
the sacred scrolls. The Druze have been practicing these rituals for a

---

*There are also small communities in Canada and the United States.

thousand years. And their roots, they claim, go back even further—to the time of Moses.

The tomb that remains the purpose for their pilgrimage to the shrine every year rests in a cave protected by a mosquelike, domed hallway. Shoes must be removed and heads covered before entering. Inside, carpets cover not only the floor but the walls and the raised platform that holds the tomb. Any sound is muffled. Silence is essential here.

This is the holy resting place of an esteemed prophet—their ancestor—Reuel.

No such shrine exists for Moses or Aaron in Israel. Yet Reuel, who is thought to be a minor biblical character, has over a million descendants all of whom refuse to marry outside their tribe and who maintain a strict secrecy uncommon to most religions. Their faith is closed to outsiders.

The Tawheed (as the Druze call themselves) honor Reuel as their forefather.* They believe that he was a "hidden prophet" who served as secret mentor to Moses. In this way Reuel has preserved what he believed to be his holy bloodline. Tawheed blood carries the genes of all the key patriarchs: Abraham, Ishmael, Isaac, Esau, Jacob (Israel), Reuel, Levi, Joseph, Moses, and his sons. If the blood from the Shroud of Turin is genuine, we can add Jesus to this illustrious list.

Ultimately, the magician Reuel succeeded in reaching his obsessive goals. At a cost of a life of endless manipulation, political intrigue, and warfare culminating in brutal murder, he used his ample means and opportunity to take the life of Moses and triumphantly assume his identity and rule, as he was convinced was his birthright.

But would the conquest of the Promised Land have happened without Reuel? The original Moses, the son of Joseph's Egyptian widow, was raised as a priest in the temple of Heliopolis where his teachings were influenced by the monotheism of the pharaoh, Akhenaten. This first Moses, whom the Egyptians called "Osarseph" may even have been

---

*"The Druze people, an ethnic group living in Israel, have the tradition that they are descended from Jethro," according to the Tel Shemesh website article, "Jethro the Shaman."

a pacifist like Akhenaten. Osarseph was not suited to the task of conquest. In sharp contrast, Reuel, as the masked Moses, was no pacifist.
As an Edomite, Reuel knew the lay of the land. He created the man-size
puppet of Moses that inspired the Israelites to resist the Amalekites. It
was Reuel, in his disguise as Balaam, who struck fear into the hearts of
the enemies of the Israelites. Without Reuel, the Promised Land would
never have been won.

History was changed because of the masked Moses, the Egyptian-
trained magician who almost got away with the perfect crime.

———•——

Coming upon the Story

W hile researching a project on mythology, I (Rand) came across the terrible biblical story of Aaron's two eldest sons who were burned alive as punishment for daring to approach Yahweh. It seemed to me that the only real crime committed by the two young men was curiosity. Since that has always been the driving force behind my own research—to call this an act of cruelty by the omnipotent Creator of the Universe seemed a major understatement. I was further disturbed by the ruthless reaction of the prophet Moses to the painful death of his nephews. Immediately following this horrific moment, Moses warns Aaron not to mourn for his sons because he might be incinerated since his body was also covered in "the anointing oil of the Lord."[1] This reference to flammable oil raised my suspicions. Were the boys' deaths the result of a supernatural act as depicted? Or was there something more sinister going on here?

I'm aware that anomalies in science often lead to breakthroughs. But I soon discovered that anomalies in the religious record are more often ignored. This was a challenge that I couldn't resist.

Decades of studying world mythology had given me a close familiarity with its various schools of thought. As a result, I'd developed a skepticism of supernatural explanations for historical events. Instead, I took the attitude that "miraculous" stories could usually be explained rationally. I also knew that many cultures have been manipulated by shamans and priests practicing their colorful and mesmerizing arts of illusion in the pursuit of political ends.

On vacation and experiencing a serious shortage of reading material (pre-Kindle days!), I came across Jonathan Kirsch's biography, *Moses: A Life,* in a tiny bookstore otherwise filled with horror and children's books. While reading Kirsch's account I became convinced that there was something not quite right about the traditional depiction of the life of the prophet. The patchwork nature of his family tree seemed contrived. From Kirsch's bibliography, I identified two books that proved to be instrumental: Sigmund Freud's *Moses and Monotheism* and Richard Elliott Friedman's *Who Wrote the Bible?*

Intrigued by the idea that the story of Moses was not all that it appeared to be and determined to trace the various contradictory accounts back to their origins, I copied out the entire story of the Torah from Abraham to the death of Moses. Numerous biblical scholars had concluded—most noteworthy is Julius Wellhausen, the original synthesizer of the documentary hypothesis—that the passages attributed to the Levite scribes (known in the documentary hypothesis as **P**) seemed to be deliberately interfering with, and distorting, the earlier oral accounts. Following this theory, I omitted the **P** passages in my transcription. The story reads very differently without **P**'s contributions. By incorporating two important additional layers of the subterranean story into the research—a study of Jewish folklore and the critical role of illusion in ancient Egypt—I was able to discern what I believe to be the true intent of the original oral stories. After a decade of reading and research I was convinced that Moses had been murdered and replaced by his father-in-law, Reuel, a man who had the motive, means, and opportunity to pull off such a brazen crime without detection.

The more I read, the more I also became convinced that Jesus knew the truth about the murder of Moses and that quite possibly this knowledge contributed to his crucifixion.

I was fascinated to learn that there still exists today a secret religion, based in Israel and Lebanon, that claims that Reuel was a hidden prophet who mentored Moses. This religion admits no outsiders. It is not possible to convert. Only those born into their ranks can read the sacred texts. They claim that their holy bloodline originated with their most important prophet—Reuel.

The more I dug the more I became convinced that Reuel was not the minor character depicted by most biblical scholars but a major force whose obsessions swayed the course of Western Civilization.

APPENDIX 2

———•———

Research Methodology

Today orthodox Jews, as well as millions of Christians, still assume that God divinely inspired every word of the Torah. Yahweh communicated his wishes face-to-face with Moses from atop the sacred mountain and the prophet carefully transcribed every word. Archaeologists, after decades of exploration in Israel and throughout the Middle East, can find no convincing physical evidence for a vast exodus of thousands of people from Egypt as described in the Bible. Within academic circles there is considerable debate about the historical reliability of the books attributed to Moses and doubt as to whether the celebrated prophet even existed. We live in a time when blind faith and deep skepticism reign side by side.

For centuries several Jewish and Catholic scholars found solace in the notion that Moses was God's sole scribe. Then some uncomfortable facts and contradictions began to nudge against the credibility of that view. How, for instance, if Moses was the author of the entire text, could he write an account of his own death? Why did he sometimes refer to himself in the third person? These and other thorny questions began to strain the belief that the prophet from Egypt was the sole author of the first five books of the Bible.

A Spanish rabbi, Isaac ben Jasos of Toledo (982–1057)* focused his

---

*For a history of the textual criticism of the Torah we have used Carpenter, *The Composition of the Hexateuch*; several works by Martin Noth; plus Friedman, *Who Wrote the Bible?*

critical comments on the following verse: "And these are the kings that reigned in the land of Edom, before there reigned any king over the children of Israel."[1]

How could Moses know that the Israelites would someday adopt the institution of monarchy? The text didn't fit with any rational chronology of events. And how did Moses know the names of kings who lived centuries after his death? Of course, to the true believer these questions were irrelevant since God is All Knowing and could easily pass knowledge of the future to Moses. But this response did not entirely satisfy and the suspicion that Moses was not the sole author of the Torah began to take root.

The Rabbi Ibn Ezra (1088–1167) was skeptical about Moses's role but didn't have the courage to declare that the prophet couldn't have been the sole author of the Torah. His fears in proclaiming such a radical theory were obvious when he said, "he who understands will keep silent."

Scholars were worried about questioning the validity of the authorship of God's chosen prophet. Disagreement over theological issues was a serious affair. People could lose their heads or be burnt at the stake for voicing doubts about the content of the Holy Bible. When scholars eventually did summon the courage to point to problems in the text they were always quick to say that some other legitimate prophet, notably Joshua or Ezra, had added phrases that were divinely inspired. No one was ready to consider that ordinary men, with earthly motives, had tampered with the words of a prophet.

If the Torah was considered above reproach, progress in unraveling the hidden elements of the story was impossible. No one doubted that Moses lived a hundred and twenty years and no one questioned why he wore a veil over his face during the last forty years of his life. The Torah was the Work of God and His words were sacrosanct. The idea that there might be more than one author, let alone more than one Moses, was something scholars dared not contemplate.

Things started to change in the sixteenth century as more Christians entered the fray. In 1520, Carlstadt published an essay that argued that the style of writing found in the books immediately following the Torah seemed to be the same voice as that attributed to Moses. This raised the possibility that Moses was not the author and that the true author had lived long after Moses died.

In 1570, Andrew du Maes, a Flemish priest, published a commentary on the book of Joshua, the sixth book of the Old Testament. He noted that Moses mentions cities that had not been founded until after the Israelites conquered Canaan. Since Moses was prohibited from entering the Promised Land, how could he know the names of cities founded after his death? These were troubling questions but du Maes was quick to point out that the unknown "editor" had simply added phrases and altered names to make the Bible more contemporary. Du Maes saw no dark motives in the changes but his book was still considered heretical and was put on the "Catholic Index of Prohibited Books."

Christopher Marlowe was called to answer for his blasphemy after he proclaimed Moses a second-rate illusionist and charged that the stories of the exodus were wildly exaggerated. Marlowe's thoughts were only heard by the Queen's Privy Council. They were never put into print so that scholars might debate them. The next day Marlowe was murdered by one of Queen Elizabeth's secret agents.

By 1651 the cultural atmosphere had settled enough that the British philosopher Thomas Hobbes was able to write that expressions like "to this day" that are found throughout the Torah imply that the writer is describing events long past, casting more doubt upon Moses's authorship.

Twenty years later, in Holland, the philosopher Benedict Spinoza (1632–1677) devoted a great deal of his 1670 book *Theologico-politicus* to exposing numerous chronological embarrassments in the Torah. The work was published anonymously. He became convinced that Ezra, the scribe who brought the Torah out of Babylon and returned it to Jerusalem, was responsible for making changes to the book. Ezra reconstituted the *Pentateuch* from older documents he had in Babylon that have not survived to our times. The whole narrative was, in Spinoza's words, "jumbled together without order . . . [and with] . . . no regard to time."[2] This led him to argue that it is "clearer than the sun at noon that the Pentateuch was not written by Moses, but by someone who lived long after Moses."[3] For his efforts, Catholics and Protestants banned his book and he was excommunicated from Judaism.

In 1682 a French priest, Richard Simon, published a book arguing that later prophets, divinely inspired and aided by *older sources,* had added to Moses's works. His book was supposed to be an attack on Spinoza but that is not how it was received. He was expelled from his order. All but six copies of his book were burned. Father Simon's notion of multiple ancient sources being brought together by prophets after Moses's death laid the foundation for a more critical study. Hobbes and Spinoza had both commented upon the repetitive nature of some of the stories. Modern scholars call these "doublets." For Simon and for the scholars that followed, the doublets constituted evidence of multiple sources. Scholars were finally boldly stating that Moses was not the sole author of the Torah.

In the eighteenth century the task of separating the various sources of the Torah from one another became an obsession for some. Almost simultaneously, several scholars came to the same conclusion: more than one ancient source was used to compile the work attributed to Moses. These authors enthusiastically set about the task of unraveling this ancient mystery.

TAKING THE PEN FROM MOSES

The mystery of who wrote the various parts of the Torah began to unravel in the late eighteenth and early nineteenth centuries. The subterranean story hidden within the book of Exodus was potentially open for all to see.

In 1753, the French author Jean Astruc (1684–1766) published *Conjectures on the Reminiscences Which Moses Appears to Have Used in Composing the Book of Genesis.* It was a landmark in the history of what came to be known as "source criticism"—the theory that the Torah was composed by various authors at different times. Astruc noted that different parts of Genesis referred to the Supreme Deity by different names. One source used the name *Elohim* (God) while the other used *Yahweh* (Lord). The implication was clear and revolutionary: the Torah was *man-made*.

In 1787, Astruc's ideas were taken further by the German professor Johann Gottfried Eichhorn (1752–1827) in his *Introduction to the Old Testament*. He identified different styles of writing in the text, those annoying repetitions that Goethe, Hobbes, and Spinoza had found so tiresome. Eichhorn argued that the doublets were different versions of the stories written by different authors who had lived long after Moses died.

The picture of Moses as author of the Torah was quickly fading.

In 1806, W. M. L. De Wette revealed reasons why the book of Deuteronomy might be considered a forgery. According to the text, the priest Hilkiah claimed to have discovered the book in the Jerusalem temple in 622 BCE. The priest presented his treasure to King Josiah who immediately accepted it as a long-lost book written by Moses. De Wette demonstrated that the contents of the "lost" book faithfully mimicked not so much the teachings of Moses but more the reforms urged by the very priest, Hilkiah, who supposedly unearthed it. De Wette called Deuteronomy a "pious fraud."[4]

In 1865, K. H. Graf made a valiant attempt at dating the various sources. His work, to paraphrase Winston Churchill, was the end of the beginning of what would come to be known as the "documentary hypothesis."

The scholar that brought together all the lines of investigation and created a synthesis that has stood the test of time was Julius Wellhausen (1844–1918). His influential book was published in Germany in 1883. When *Prolegomena to the History of Israel* was released in English it had a profound impact upon the whole issue of Moses's authorship of the Torah.

THE PRIESTLY AGENDA

Wellhausen carefully examined what each source assumed. He was able to tease out the order of the writings and identify their agendas.

The earliest source (**JE**) assumed that worship could be performed in many places. Jerusalem was not a more sacred site in which to worship than any other. Wellhausen wrote "throughout the whole of the earlier period of the history of Israel, the restriction of worship to a single selected place was unknown to any one even as a pious desire."[5]

JE was fond of spontaneous banquets with merrymaking and recognized no priests whatsoever. The mood was natural, free and optimistic. It includes Miriam's joyous dance after her people escaped the Egyptians.

D was a source with a mission to establish one central temple in Jerusalem. Wellhausen wrote: "In that book the unity of the cultus is *commanded;* in the Priestly Code it is *presupposed.*"[6] **D** was much more formal than **JE** and with him we begin to see the makings of the Israeli priesthood. **D** would argue that contemporary events mimicked events in the past and he insisted on this point even when it wasn't true. **D** has a different chronology of events, most notably in Moses's address to Reuben, Levi, and all the elders of the tribe of Israel other than Simeon.

P (the Levite scribes) did not feel the necessity to argue for one temple. They assumed it. The temple in Jerusalem was the sole sanctuary for sacrifice and worship. No debate. No doubt. No questions asked. Wellhausen wrote: "The assumption that worship is restricted to one single centre runs everywhere throughout the entire document. . . . One God one sanctuary, that is the idea."[7]

P was obsessed with rules and regulations and regarded merrymaking as sinful. This was the very thing that the **JE** authors loved so much. The Levites had a deep need to elevate their ancestor to the highest position. Wellhausen notes that **P** was "unable to think of religion without the one sanctuary, and cannot for a moment imagine Israel without it, carrying its actual existence back to the very beginning of the theocracy, and, in accordance with this, completely altering the ancient history."[8]

The Levite scribes *rewrote* much of the Torah to suit their agenda. It was **P** who invented a sacred tent that served as a surrogate temple for Moses: "For the truth is, that the tabernacle is the copy, not the prototype, of the temple at Jerusalem."[9] The Priestly agenda was one that favored the Levites and was hostile to some of the beliefs of the earlier sources.

P assumed that Judaism could not exist without priests, yet it was they who finalized the need for them. **P** inserted all the *begats* into the text. **P** insisted on the vast time between the age of Joseph and the rise of Moses. It was **P** who went on and on about the Egyptian bondage. **P** hated Egyptian magicians. And it was **P** who would clip, edit, and conceal the true genealogy of Moses.

The passages that dealt with Joseph's death were also changed by the Levite scribe. They distorted the text so that they could claim Moses as one of their ancestors. And by denying Moses's true heritage they took a final swipe at the child of Israel that Levi most hated, Joseph.

THE EDOMITE SCRIBE

In 1941, Harvard's Professor Robert H. Pfeiffer (1892–1958) wrote *Introduction to the Old Testament*, in which he suggested the existence of another oral tradition that had made its way into the Torah around 430 BCE inserted by a biblical editor from Reuel's homeland, Edom.* Pfeiffer suggests that many of the stories the Levite scribes wished to suppress were inserted by an Edomite scribe before the text was finally set. It is precisely these **S** stories,† ascribed by Pfeiffer to an Edomite priest, that have allowed us to unravel the role Reuel played in the murder and impersonation of Moses. It is from them, for instance, that we learn that the father-in-law of Moses (Reuel or Jethro) was from Edom, a fact that is central to our attempt to recapture the Moses stories repressed by the scribes.

The **S** stories also include unflattering sections about the Levites

---

*Pfeiffer asserts the possibility that a collection of stories normally attributed to the **J** source were instead the product of an Edomite scribe whom he called **S**.

†**S** stands for "Seir," the original name for Edom before Reuel's father Esau conquered the land and renamed it. Pfeiffer could not use the capital letter *E* because other scholars had already used it to represent a collection of oral stories by Hebrews who called God by the name "Elohim."

such as Simeon and Levi's murder of Shechem, his father, and the males of the village after the "rape"; Reuben's incest; and Reuel's family tree. Without these revelations our story could not have been told.

METHODOLOGY

Our method of dealing with the various sources in the Torah was to create a version of the text that identified each passage by source. We color-coded the text for our purposes and took everything written by the Levite scribes (P) and put it to one side. In the writing of this book we relied primarily upon the epic sources (E, J, JE, and S) augmented by D to correct for P's false timeline. We only relied upon P when the equivalent epic sources were missing.*

The purpose of this appendix is to give a brief description of the documentary hypothesis as it was understood by Wellhausen, Noth, and Friedman. Subsequently, the so-called supplementary hypothesis was developed by John Van Seters (b. 1935). Van Seters's scholarship determined that Deuteronomy was the oldest source of the Torah. Deuteronomy places Joseph and Moses in the same time period and supports what the Romans and Egyptians long asserted: that Moses was the third son of Joseph and Asenath. This in turn, places the "first" Moses inside the Heliopolis Temple where the prophet's father-in-law was High Priest of a secret continuance of the monotheism of Akhenaten. This corrected timeline resolves Freud's dilemma of not being able to place Moses inside the Temple of Heliopolis where mono-theism was born.

---

*Most notably with Israel's last will and testament where he disinherited Reuben, Simeon, and Levi while cursing Benjamin. This is likely a P source. The story of the incineration of Aaron's sons by Yahweh when they offered strange fire is a story told only by P.

Notes

EPIGRAPH

Kennedy, John F. *Listening In,* 14.

CHAPTER 1.
AN UNLAID GHOST

1. Gay, *Freud: A Life for Our Time,* 637.
2. Gay, *Freud: A Life for Our Time,* 621.
3. Bernstein, *Freud and the Legacy of Moses,* 37.
4. Gay, *Freud: A Life for Our Time,* 37.
5. Freud, *Moses and Monotheism,* 69.
6. Gay, *Freud: A Life for Our Time,* 626.
7. Gay, *Freud: A Life for Our Time,* 628.
8. Gay, *Freud: A Life for Our Time,* 629.
9. Freud, *Moses and Monotheism,* 103.
10. Bernstein, *Freud and the Legacy of Moses,* 17.
11. Gay, *Freud: A Life for Our Time,* 637.
12. Gay, *Freud: A Life for Our Time,* 315.
13. Freud, *Moses and Monotheism,* 3.
14. Freud, *Moses and Monotheism,* 5–6.
15. Exodus 2:8.
16. Speiser, "The Legend of Sargon," 119.
17. Freud, *Moses and Monotheism,* 35.
18. Hosea 12:13.

19. Feiler, *America's Prophet*, 21.
20. Feiler, *America's Prophet*, 4.
21. Leviticus 25:10.
22. Trachtenberg, *The Statue of Liberty*, 2.
23. Feiler, *America's Prophet*, 35–36.
24. Feiler, *America's Prophet*, 106.
25. Feiler, *America's Prophet*, 170.
26. Research conducted by Charles Stewart, as cited in Feiler, *America's Prophet*, 171.
27. King, "I've Been to the Mountaintop."
28. Feiler, *America's Prophet*, 6.
29. Hoffman, *The Murder of the Man Who Was Shakespeare*, 66–67.
30. Goethe, "Israel in the Desert."
31. For an example, see Gardner and Anderson, *Criminal Evidence*, 71.
32. Dozeman, "Masking Moses," 29.
33. Nunley and McCarthy, *Masks*, 15.
34. Exodus 3:6.
35. Exodus 33:20.
36. Exodus 34:29–33.
37. Exodus 34:30.

CHAPTER 2.
PRIME SUSPECT

1. *Boyd's Bible Dictionary*, 238.
2. Exodus 21:24.
3. Genesis 25:27–34.
4. Genesis 27:1–5.
5. Genesis 27:6–13.
6. Genesis 27:19–23.
7. Genesis 27:41.
8. *Boyd's Bible Dictionary*, 106, 253.
9. Genesis 20:29.
10. Genesis 29:25.
11. Genesis 29:26.
12. Genesis 31:32.
13. Genesis 31:35.
14. Auerbach, *Moses*, 140.

15. Genesis 32:11.
16. Genesis 32:24–29.
17. Hosea 12:5.
18. Friedman, *The Hidden Face of God,* 214.
19. Friedman, *The Hidden Face of God,* 10.
20. Friedman, *The Hidden Face of God,* 37.
21. Genesis 32:30.
22. Friedman, *Commentary on the Torah,* 230.

CHAPTER 3.
BLUEPRINT FOR MURDER

1. For an in-depth study of Egyptian magicians please see Pinch, *Magic in Ancient Egypt.*
2. Pinch, *Magic in Ancient Egypt,* 112.
3. Pinch, *Magic in Ancient Egypt,* 47.
4. Foucart, "Divination (Egypt)," 793.
5. Foucart, "Divination (Egypt)," 793.
6. Pinch, *Magic in Ancient Egypt,* 76.
7. Pinch, *Magic in Ancient Egypt,* 56. Geraldine Pinch writes, "Very little is known about whether priestesses participated in ritual magic in temples."
8. Hoffmeiler, *Israel in Egypt,* 142.
9. Hoffmeiler, *Israel in Egypt,* 142.
10. Pinch, *Magic in Ancient Egypt,* 18.
11. Pinch, *Magic in Ancient Egypt,* 150.
12. Erman, *The Literature of the Ancient Egyptians,* 38–40.

CHAPTER 4.
DECEIT AND DISGUISE

1. Genesis 34:3.
2. Genesis 34:2.
3. Genesis 34:5.
4. Genesis 34:7.
5. Genesis 34:15.
6. Genesis 34:13.
7. Genesis 34:15.
8. Genesis 34:25–26.
9. Genesis 34:30.

10. Genesis 34:31.

11. See for example, Wellhausen, *Prolegomena to the History of Israel,* 145.

12. Genesis 37:3.

13. Genesis 37:4.

14. Genesis 37:5.

15. Genesis 37:8.

16. Genesis 37:9.

17. Genesis 37:15.

18. Genesis 37:18.

19. Genesis 37:20.

20. Genesis 37:21–22.

21. Genesis 42:21.

22. Genesis 37:28.

23. Genesis 37:30.

24. Genesis 37:32.

25. Genesis 37:33.

26. Genesis 37:35.

27. Rappoport, *Myth and Legend of Ancient Israel,* 2:39–41.

28. Orne, "Hypnosis," 350.

29. Maldonado, "Hypnosis in Psychosomatic Medicine," 266.

30. American Psychiatric Association, "Narcissistic Personality Disorder."

31. Genesis 39:6.

32. Genesis 39:7–8.

33. Genesis 39:19.

34. Genesis 40:14.

35. Genesis 42:2.

36. Boyd's Bible Dictionary, 55.

37. Boyd's Bible Dictionary, 55.

38. Genesis 42:4.

39. Genesis 42:7.

40. Genesis 42:6.

41. Genesis 42:22.

42. Genesis 42:24.

43. Rappoport, *Myth and Legend of Ancient Israel,* 2:10.

44. Genesis 42:36.

45. Genesis 42:37.

46. Genesis 42:38.

47. Genesis 43:10.

48. Genesis 43:8–9.

49. Genesis 43:23.

50. Genesis 43:32–34.

51. Genesis 44:9.

52. Genesis 44:15.

53. Genesis 44:16.

54. Genesis 44:34.

55. Genesis 45:3.

56. Mussies, "The Interpretation of Serapis," 189–214.

57. Justinus, in Duncker, *The History of Antiquity*, 461.

58. Justinus, in Cory, *Ancient Fragments*, 80–81.

59. Justinus, in Duncker, *The History of Antiquity*, 461.

60. Josephus, *Against Apion*, 1.33, in *Josephus: The Complete Works*.

61. Josephus, 1.26, in *Josephus: The Complete Works*. Quote is attributed to Manetho.

62. Freud, *Moses and Monotheism*, 35.

63. Freud, *Moses and Monotheism*, 36.

64. Exodus 1:8.

65. Josephus, *Against Apion*, 1.26, in *Josephus: The Complete Works*. Quote is attributed to Manetho.

66. Josephus, 1.27, in *Josephus: The Complete Works*. Quote is attributed to Manetho.

67. Josephus, 1.27, in *Josephus: The Complete Works*. Quote is attributed to Manetho.

CHAPTER 5.
THE WIDOW'S SON

1. Genesis 45:28.

2. Genesis 48:6.

3. "Goddess Cosmologies," from the series "Deasophy," on the Suppressed History website.

4. Freud, *Moses and Monotheism*, 14.

5. Freud, *Moses and Monotheism*, 35.

6. Genesis 49:3–4.

7. Genesis 35:22.

8. Genesis 49:5–7.

9. Genesis 48:5.

10. Genesis 50:1.

11. Genesis 50:5.

12. Genesis 50:6.

13. Genesis 50:25.

14. Genesis 50:26.

15. Exodus 13:19.

16. Van Seters, *Abraham in History and Tradition, Part Two.*

17. Exodus 1:6.

18. Deuteronomy 33:6.

19. Genesis 49:6.

20. Deuteronomy 33:9.

21. Deuteronomy 33:8.

22. Exodus 29:30.

23. Exodus 17:3.

24. Exodus 17:7.

25. Wellhausen, *Prolegomena to the History of Israel,* 122.

26. Wellhausen, *Prolegomena to the History of Israel,* 145.

27. Cross, *Canaanite Myth and Hebrew Epic,* 206.

28. Genesis 49:6.

29. Genesis 41:45.

30. *Boyd's Bible Dictionary,* 328.

31. Jonas, *Vengeance,* 366.

32. Exodus 15:20.

33. Exodus 15:20.

34. Numbers 12:1.

35. Numbers 12:15.

36. Auerbach, *Moses,* 64.

37. Genesis 50:15.

38. Fox, *Iranian Cinema.*

39. Rappoport, *Myth and Legend of Ancient Israel,* 2:149.

40. Rappoport, *Myth and Legend of Ancient Israel,* 2:150.

41. Rappoport, *Myth and Legend of Ancient Israel,* 2:150.

42. Rappoport, *Myth and Legend of Ancient Israel,* 2:151.

43. Rappoport, *Myth and Legend of Ancient Israel,* 2:153.

CHAPTER 6.
A FAMILY DIVIDED

1. Josephus, *The Antiquities of the Jews,* 2.10, in Whiston, *The Genuine Works of Flavius Josephus, the Jewish Historian.*

2. Rapport, *Myth and Legend of Ancient Israel,* 2:244–45.

3. Kirsch, *Moses: A Life,* 90.

4. Finkelstein and Silberman, *The Bible Unearthed,* 118.

5. Exodus 1:8.

6. Judges 1:16.

7. Budde, *Religion of Israel to the Exile,* 21.

8. Rice, "Africans and the Origin of the Worship of Yahweh," 4.

9. Exodus 18:12.

10. Rappoport, *Myth and Legend of Ancient Israel,* 2:254–56.

11. Rappoport, *Myth and Legend of Ancient Israel,* 2:256.

12. Rappoport, *Myth and Legend of Ancient Israel,* 2:256.

13. Rappoport, *Myth and Legend of Ancient Israel,* 2:256.

14. The Koran, Hud 11:91.

CHAPTER 7.
PSYCHIC DYNAMITE

1. Exodus 4:24–26.

2. Friedman, *Commentary on the Torah,* 184.

3. Noth, *Exodus: A Commentary,* 49–50.

4. Rappoport, *Myth and Legend of Ancient Israel,* 2:275.

5. Josephus, *The Antiquity of the Jews,* 1.18.8 in Whiston, *The Genuine Works of Flavius Josephus, the Jewish Historian.*

6. Genesis 16:5.

7. Genesis 16:1–11.

8. Genesis 21:9–10.

9. Ide, *Moses,* 92.

10. Genesis 17:11–12.

11. Exodus 2:11–15.

12. Auerbach, *Moses,* 19.

13. Noth, *Exodus: A Commentary,* 36.

14. Exodus 1:8.

15. Exodus 2:15–21.

16. Exodus 2:15–21.

17. *Boyd's Bible Dictionary,* 162.

18. Kirsch, *Moses: A Life,* 8–9.

19. Craigie, *Ugarit and the Old Testament,* 72.

20. Bryan, *Religious Aspects of Hypnosis,* 31.

21. Ide, *Moses,* 29–30.
22. Churchill, "Moses," 287.
23. Kirsch, *Moses: A Life,* 101.
24. Exodus 3:1.
25. Exodus 3:2–6.
26. Exodus 3:13–14.
27. Exodus 4:14.
28. Exodus 3:1.
29. Genesis 50:26.
30. Rappoport, *Myth and Legend of Ancient Israel,* 2:186.
31. Rappoport, *Myth and Legend of Ancient Israel,* 1:351.
32. Exodus 4:18–19.

CHAPTER 8.
INTO THE WILDERNESS

1. Rappoport, *Myth and Legend of Ancient Israel,* 2:276.
2. Rappoport, *Myth and Legend of Ancient Israel,* 2:277.
3. Assmann, *Moses the Egyptian,* 3.
4. Wilson, *The Exodus Enigma,* 121.
5. Exodus 10:21–22.
6. Exodus 9:6.
7. Exodus 9:23.
8. Exodus 9:9.
9. Exodus 7:20.
10. Exodus 8:21.
11. Exodus 8:6.
12. Phillips, *Act of God,* 233.
13. Phillips, *Act of God,* 233.
14. Phillips, *Act of God,* 233–34.
15. *The Oxford Illustrated Dictionary,* 392.
16. *The Oxford Illustrated Dictionary,* 547.
17. Douglas, *In the Wilderness,* 32.
18. Noth, *Exodus: A Commentary,* 108.
19. Humphreys, *The Miracles of Exodus,* 174.
20. Humphreys, *The Miracles of Exodus,* 180.
21. Exodus 14:21.
22. Humphreys, *The Miracles of Exodus,* 247.

23. Humphreys, *The Miracles of Exodus,* 247.

24. Humphreys, *The Miracles of Exodus,* 252.

25. Exodus 15:24.

26. Exodus 15:27.

27. Exodus 16:2.

28. Exodus 16:12.

29. Humphreys, *The Miracles of Exodus,* 85.

30. Exodus 17:3.

31. Exodus 17:4.

32. Exodus 17:6.

33. Phillips, *The Moses Legacy,* 200.

34. Numbers 11.

35. Auerbach, *Moses,* 85.

36. Noth, *Exodus: A Commentary,* 156.

37. Cross, *Canaanite Myth and Hebrew Epic,* 167.

38. Cross, *Canaanite Myth and Hebrew Epic,*169.

39. Finkelstein, *The Bible Unearthed,* 62–63.

40. Burckhardt, *Travels in Syria and the Holy Land,* 421.

41. Burckhardt, *Travels in Syria and the Holy Land,* 422–23.

42. Burckhardt, *Travels in Syria and the Holy Land,* 424.

43. Robinson, *The Sarcophagus of an Ancient Civilization,* 3.

44. Robinson, *The Sarcophagus of an Ancient Civilization,* 133.

45. Robinson, *The Sarcophagus of an Ancient Civilization,* 116–18.

46. Exodus 20:26.

47. Robinson, *The Sarcophagus of an Ancient Civilization,* 45.

48. Robinson, *The Sarcophagus of an Ancient Civilization,* 43–44.

49. Robinson, *The Sarcophagus of an Ancient Civilization,* 110.

50. Robinson, *The Sarcophagus of an Ancient Civilization,* 168.

51. Phillips, *The Moses Legacy,* 190.

52. Phillips, *The Moses Legacy,* 214.

53. Exodus 19:12.

CHAPTER 9.
THE MASKED MOSES

1. Connor, *Dumbstruck,* 24.

2. Connor, *Dumbstruck,* 23.

3. Robinson, *The Sarcophagus of an Ancient Civilization,* 43–44.

4. Exodus 20:6.

5. Aldred, *Akhenaten*, 240.

6. Exodus 20:6.

7. Aldred, *Akhenaten*, 245.

8. Genesis 49:27.

9. Deuteronomy 33:12.

10. Exodus 33:8–11.

11. Numbers 20:18.

12. Exodus 18:5–7.

13. Exodus 18:12.

14. Noth, *Exodus: A Commentary*, 148.

15. Noth, *Exodus: A Commentary*, 149–50.

16. Auerbach, *Moses*, 89.

17. Exodus 18:13–18.

18. Friedman, *Commentary on the Torah*, 230.

19. Exodus 18:19–20.

20. Exodus 18:21–22.

21. Exodus 18:23.

22. Exodus 18:24–26.

23. Exodus 18:27.

24. Josephus, *The Antiquity of the Jews*, 3.2.4.

25. Exodus 24:1–2.

26. Exodus 24:12–15.

27. Exodus 24:24.

28. Exodus 32:1–6.

29. Exodus 17:8.

30. Exodus 32:17.

31. Exodus 17:9–10.

32. Exodus 17:11–13.

33. Noth, *A History of Pentateuchal Traditions*, 166.

34. Exodus 15:20–21.

35. Cross, *Canaanite Myth and Hebrew Epic*, 112–44.

36. Exodus 34:29–33.

37. Exodus 32:19–20.

38. Exodus 32:19–20.

39. Exodus 32:21–24.

40. Exodus 32:4.

41. Deuteronomy 9:20.
42. Noth, *Exodus: A Commentary*, 244.
43. Auerbach, *Moses*, 95.
44. Exodus 32:26–28.
45. Exodus 18:24–25.

CHAPTER 10.
SKULL AND BONES

1. Finnestad, *Image of the World*, 88, 93.
2. *Boyd's Bible Dictionary*, 238.
3. Exodus 25:10.
4. Rux, *Architects of the Underworld*, 279.
5. Tompkins, *Secrets of the Great Pyramid*, 278.
6. Mark 6:18.
7. Mark 4:12.
8. Mark 6:22–23.
9. Mark 6:25.
10. Mark 6:25.
11. Mark 6:26–28.
12. Mark 6:16.
13. Laidler, *The Head of God*, 52.
14. Laidler, *The Head of God*, 52.
15. Laidler, *The Head of God*, 71.
16. Laidler, *The Head of God*, 60.
17. Rappoport, *Myth and Legend of Ancient Israel*, 2:301.
18. Exodus 25:11–14.
19. Numbers 7:89.
20. Numbers 10:35.
21. Deuteronomy 10:8.
22. Deuteronomy 9:21.
23. Psalms 104:15.
24. Exodus 40:20–32.
25. See Exodus 26:33 for the sacred tent, and II Chronicles 5:7 for the temple.
26. Josephus, *The Antiquity of the Jews*, 3.7.4.
27. Leviticus 10:1–2.
28. Leviticus 10:6–7.
29. Pinch, *Magic in Ancient Egypt*, 24.

30. Auerbach, *Moses,* 139, on calling Moses's veil a "mask."
31. Joshua 6.
32. I Samuel 4:5.
33. I Samuel 4:11.
34. I Samuel 5:2.
35. I Samuel 5:2.
36. Josephus. *The Antiquity of the Jews,* 6.1n.
37. As cited in Knight and Lomas, *The Hiram Key,* 37.
38. Laidler, *The Head of God,* 178.
39. Laidler, *The Head of God,* 179.
40. Laidler, *The Head of God,* 180–81.
41. See Knight and Lomas, *The Hiram Key.*

CHAPTER 11.
THE SPY AND THE LEPER

1. Auerbach, *Moses,* 98.
2. Noth, *Numbers: A Commentary,* 125.
3. Josephus, *The Antiquity of the Jews,* 4.2.4.
4. Numbers 16:1–3.
5. Rappoport, *Myth and Legend of Ancient Israel,* 2:319–20.
6. Numbers 16:12–15.
7. Wellhausen, *Prolegomena to the History of Israel,* 35n.
8. Numbers 16:21.
9. Numbers 16:28–30.
10. Numbers 16:31–34.
11. Rappoport, *Myth and Legend of Ancient Israel,* 2:323.
12. Numbers 12:1.
13. *Boyd's Bible Dictionary,* 196.
14. Numbers 12:2.
15. Numbers 12:4–10.
16. Numbers 12:11–15.
17. Noth, *Numbers: A Commentary,* 97.
18. Noth, *Numbers: A Commentary,* 97.
19. Auerbach, *Moses,* 95.
20. Friedman, *Commentary on the Torah,* 468.
21. Friedman, *Commentary on the Torah,* 468–69.
22. Numbers 12:12.

23. Numbers 20:1.

24. Noth, *Numbers: A Commentary*, 93.

25. Friedman, *Commentary on the Torah*, 465.

26. Noth, *A History of Pentateuchal Traditions*, 127.

27. Noth, *Numbers: A Commentary*, 94.

28. Cross, *Canaanite Myth and Hebrew Epic*, 204.

29. Exodus 18:2.

CHAPTER 12.
BALAAM AND THE WAR
AGAINST THE MIDIANITES

1. Numbers 20:1.

2. Numbers 20:17–21.

3. Noth, *Numbers: A Commentary*, 150.

4. Numbers 13:17–26.

5. Numbers 13:25.

6. Josephus, *The Antiquity of the Jews*, 4.4.7.

7. Phillips, *The Moses Legacy*, 201.

8. Noth, *A History of Pentateuchal Traditions*, 178.

9. Numbers 20:23–29.

10. Numbers 22:6.

11. Numbers 22:13–14.

12. Numbers 22:21–25.

13. As first discovered by Connor, *Dumbstruck*, 146.

14. Numbers 22:26–28.

15. Numbers 22:29–31.

16. Numbers 22:32–35.

17. Numbers 24:4.

18. Numbers 24:10.

19. Numbers 25:1–5.

20. Numbers 25:7–8.

21. Numbers 25:12–13.

22. Numbers 31:7–8.

23. Numbers 31:17.

24. Numbers 31:18.

25. Deuteronomy 34:4–6.

26. Josephus, *The Antiquity of the Jews*, 4.8.48.

CHAPTER 13.
THE DEADLY SECRET

1. Powelson and Reigert, *The Lost Gospel Q,* 79.

2. Freud, *Moses and Monotheism,* 174.

3. Freud, *Moses and Monotheism,* 42.

4. John 6:46.

5. See for example, Green, *Jesus and Moses.*

6. Smith, *Jesus the Magician,* 64.

7. Smith, *Jesus the Magician,* 69.

8. Mark 2:7.

9. Matthew 17:2–9.

10. Powelson and Reigert, *The Lost Gospel Q,* 79.

11. Matthew 21:2.

12. Matthew 21:4.

13. Zechariah 9:9.

14. John 12:13; Matthew 21:8.

15. Josephus, *The Antiquity of the Jews,* 14:15.2.

16. Luke 13:32.

17. Josephus, *The War of the Jews,* 1:14:4, in Whiston, *The Genuine Works of Flavius Josephus, the Jewish Historian.*

18. Josephus, *The Antiquity of the Jews,* 15:4:1.

19. Josephus, *The Antiquity of the Jews,* 15:4:2.

20. Josephus, *The Antiquity of the Jews,* 15:5:1.

21. Josephus, *The Antiquity of the Jews,* 15:5:6.

22. Josephus, *The Antiquity of the Jews,* 15:5:6.

23. Josephus, *The Antiquity of the Jews,* 15:11:2.

24. Josephus, *The Antiquity of the Jews,* 15:11:1.

25. Josephus, *The Antiquity of the Jews,* 15:10:4.

26. Josephus, *The Antiquity of the Jews,* 17:11:4.

27. Gospel of Peter.

28. Bruce, "Herod Antipas, Tetrarch of Galilee and Petraea," 14.

29. Luke 13:31.

30. Luke 13:33.

31. Sadducees & Pharisees, from the *Jewish Virtual Library* website.

32. Sadducees & Pharisees, from the *Jewish Virtual Library* website.

33. Epstein, *Judaism,* 107.

34. Smith, *Jesus the Magician*, 30.

35. Smith, *Jesus the Magician*, 157.

36. John 12:10.

37. Origen, *The Arguments of Celsus*, 5.

38. Origen *The Arguments of Celsus*, 7.

39. Matthew 23:2.

40. Matthew 23:29–31.

41. BBC, "The Passion."

42. Luke 22:52–53.

43. Matthew 12.

44. Matthew 12:14.

45. Smith, *Jesus the Magician*, 47.

46. Matthew 12:24.

47. Matthew 15:3–4.

48. Matthew 26:59.

49. Matthew 26:61.

50. Matthew 26:63; Mark 14:61.

51. Leviticus 10:6.

52. Matthew 26:65–66.

53. Matthew 27:1.

54. Luke 23:4.

55. Matthew 27:24.

56. John 19:7.

57. See Schonfield, *The Passover Plot*.

58. Schonfield, *The Passover Plot*, 99.

59. Schonfield, *The Passover Plot*, 65.

60. Mark 16:5.

61. Mark 16:6–7.

62. Schonfield, *The Passover Plot*, 16–17.

63. John 19:27.

64. John 19:38.

EPILOGUE: THE SECRET RELIGION

1. Exodus 15:21.

APPENDIX 1: COMING UPON THE STORY

1. Exodus 30:25.

APPENDIX 2. RESEARCH METHODOLOGY

1. Genesis 36:31.

2. Carpenter, *The Composition of the Hexateuch,* 41.

3. Friedman, *Who Wrote the Bible?,* 21, quoting Benedict Spinoza.

4. Friedman, *Who Wrote the Bible?,* 102.

5. Wellhausen, *Prolegomena to the History of Israel,* 22.

6. Wellhausen, *Prolegomena to the History of Israel,* 35.

7. Wellhausen, *Prolegomena to the History of Israel,* 34.

8. Wellhausen, *Prolegomena to the History of Israel,* 36.

9. Wellhausen, *Prolegomena to the History of Israel,* 37.

Bibliography

Aldred, Cyril. *Akhenaten: King of Egypt*. London: Thames & Hudson, 1988.

American Psychiatric Association. "Narcissistic Personality Disorder." In *Diagnostic and Statistical Manual of Mental Disorders*. 4th ed. Arlington, Va.: American Psychiatric Association, 2000.

Assmann, Jan. *Moses the Egyptian: The Memory of Egypt in Western Monotheism*. Cambridge, Mass.: Harvard University Press, 1997.

Auerbach, Elias. *Moses*. Translated by Robert A. Barclay and Israel O. Lehman. Detroit: Wayne State University Press, 1975.

BBC. "The Passion." (website).

Bernstein, Richard. *Freud and the Legacy of Moses*. Cambridge: Cambridge University Press, 1998.

Boyd, James P. *Boyd's Bible Dictionary*. Nashville, Tenn.: Holman Bible Publishers, n.d.

Bruce, F. F. "Herod Antipas, Tetrarch of Galilee and Petraea." *The Annual of Leeds University Oriental Society* 5 (1963/65): 6–23.

Bryan, William J. *Religious Aspects of Hypnosis*. Springfield, Ill.: Charles C. Thomas Publisher, 1962.

Budde, Karl. *Religion of Israel to the Exile*. New York: G.P. Putnam's Sons, 1899.

Burckhardt, John Lewis. *Travels in Syria and the Holy Land; by the late John Lewis Burckhardt*. London: John Murray, 1822.

Carpenter, J. Estlin. *The Composition of the Hexateuch*. London: Longmans, Green and Co., 1902.

Churchill, Winston S. "Moses." In *Amid These Storms: Thoughts and Adventures*. New York: Charles Scribner's Sons, 1932.

Connor, Steven. *Dumbstruck: A Cultural History of Ventriloquism*. New York: Oxford University Press, 2000.

Cory, I. P. *Ancient Fragments*. Rev. ed. London: Reeves and Turner, 1876.

Craigie, Peter C. *Ugarit and the Old Testament*. Grand Rapids, Mich.: William B. Eerdmans Publishing, 1983.

Cross, Frank Moore. *Canaanite Myth and Hebrew Epic*. Cambridge, Mass.: Harvard University Press, 1973.

Douglas, Mary. *In the Wilderness: The Doctrine of Defilement in the Book of Numbers*. Sheffield, U.K.: Sheffield Academic Press, 1993.

Dozeman, Thomas B. "Masking Moses and Mosaic Authority in Torah." *Journal of Biblical Literature* 119, no. 1 (2000): 21–45.

Duncker, Max. *The History of Antiquity*. London: Richard Bentley and Sons, 1877.

Epstein, Isidore. *Judaism*. London: Penguin Books, 1959.

Erman, Adolf. *The Literature of the Ancient Egyptians*. London: Methuen, 1927.

Feiler, Bruce. *America's Prophet: Moses and the American Story*. New York: William Morrow, 2009.

Finkelstein, Israel, and Neil Asher Silberman. *The Bible Unearthed: Archaeology's New Vision of Ancient Israel and the Origins of Its Sacred Texts*. New York: Free Press, 2001.

Finnestad, Ragnhild Bjerre. *Image of the World and Symbol of the Creator*. Wiesbaden, Germany: Otto Harrassowitz, 1985.

Foucart, George. "Divination (Egypt)." In James Hastings, *Encyclopedia of Religions and Ethics*, Vol. 4. Edinburgh: T.T. Clark/New York: Charles Scribner's Sons, 1908.

Fox, Megan. "Iranian Cinema—the Censorship Issue." The Real Megan Fox (Wordpress blog), March 19, 2012.

Freud, Sigmund. *Moses and Monotheism*. New York: Vintage Books, 1939.

Friedman, Richard Elliott. *Commentary on the Torah*. New York: HarperSanFrancisco, 2001.

———. *The Hidden Face of God*. New York: HarperSanFrancisco, 1995.

———. *Who Wrote the Bible?* New York: HarperSanFrancisco, 1987.

Gardner, Thomas J., and Terry M. Anderson. *Criminal Evidence: Principles and Cases*. Belmont, Calif.: Wadsworth, 2010.

Gay, Peter. *Freud: A Life for Our Time*. New York: Doubleday, 1988.

Goethe, Johann von. "Israel in the Desert." In *West-East Divan*, 244–56. Translated by Martin Bidney. Albany: State University of New York Press, 2010.

Gospel of Peter. Available online at Early Christian Writings (website).

Green, Joey, ed. *Jesus and Moses: The Parallel Sayings.* With a Foreword by Rabbi Stewart Vogel. Berkeley, Calif.: Seastone, 2002.

Hammer, Jill, and Shoshana Jedwab. "Jethro the Shaman." Tel Shemesh (website).

Hoffman, Calvin. *The Murder of the Man Who Was Shakespeare.* New York: Grosset & Dunlap, 1955.

Hoffmeiler, James K. *Israel in Egypt: The Evidence for the Authenticity of the Exodus Tradition.* New York: Oxford University Press, 1996.

The Holy Bible. (King James Version).

Humphreys, Colin J. *The Miracles of Exodus: A Scientist's Discovery of the Extraordinary Natural Causes of the Biblical Stories.* New York: HarperSanFrancisco, 2003.

Ide, Arthur Frederick. *Moses: Making of Myth & Law; the Influence of Egyptian Sex, Religion and Law on the Writing of the Torah.* Las Colinas, Tex.: Monument Press, 1992.

The Jewish Encyclopedia (1906), s.v. "Moses."

Jewish Virtual Library. "Ancient Jewish History: Pharisees, Sadducees, and Essenes." (website).

Jonas, George. *Vengeance.* Toronto: HarperCollins Publishers, 1984.

Josephus, Flavius. *The Genuine Works of Flavius Josephus, the Jewish Historian.* Translated by William Whiston. London: W. Bowyer for the Author, 1737.

Kennedy, John F. *Listening In: The Secret White House Recordings of John F. Kennedy.* Selected and introduced by Ted Widmer with a foreword by Caroline Kennedy. New York: Hyperion, 2012.

King, Martin Luther, Jr. "I've Been to the Mountaintop." Speech delivered at the Mason Temple, Memphis, Tenn., April 3, 1968, available at the American Rhetoric website, last updated February 7, 2017.

Kirsch, Jonathan. *Moses: A Life.* New York: Ballantine Books, 1998.

Knight, Christopher, and Robert Lomas. *The Hiram Key.* London: Arrow, 1996.

The Koran. Translated by N. J. Dawood. London: Penguin Books, 1956.

Laidler, Keith. *The Head of God: The Lost Treasure of the Templars.* London: Weidenfeld & Nicolson, 1998.

Maldonado, Jose R. "Hypnosis in Psychosomatic Medicine." In *Psychiatric Care of the Medical Patient,* edited by Barry S. Fogel and Donna B. Greenberg, 266–304. Oxford: Oxford University Press, 2015.

Mussies, Gerald. "The Interpretation of Serapis." In *Studies of Hellenistic*

Religions, edited by Maaten Josef Vermaseren. Leiden, Netherlands: E. J. Brill, 1979.

Noth, Martin. *Exodus: A Commentary.* Translated by J. S. Bowden. Philadelphia: Westminster Press, 1962. First published 1959, in German.

———. *A History of Pentateuchal Traditions.* Translated by Bernhard W. Anderson. Englewood Cliffs, N.J.: Prentice-Hall, 1972. First published 1948, in German.

———. *Numbers: A Commentary.* Translated by James D. Martin. Gottingen, Germany: Vandenhoeck & Ruprecht, 1966.

Nunley, John W., and Cara McCarthy. *Masks: Faces of Culture.* St. Louis, Mo.: Harry N. Abraham, 1999.

Origen. *The Arguments of Celsus against the Christians.* Translated by Thomas Taylor. 1830. Reproduced by Project Gutenberg (website).

Orne, Martin T. "Hypnosis." *Academic American Encyclopaedia.* Danbury, Conn.: Academic American Encyclopaedia, 1998.

The Oxford Illustrated Dictionary. London: Book Club Associates, 1981.

Pfeiffer, Robert H. *Introduction to the Old Testament.* New York: Harper & Brothers, 1941.

Phillips, Graham. *Act of God: Moses, Tutankhamen and the Myth of Atlantis.* London: Sidgwick & Jackson, 1998.

———. *The Moses Legacy: The Evidence of History.* London: Sidgwick & Jackson, 2002.

Pinch, Geraldine. *Magic in Ancient Egypt.* Austen: University of Texas Press, 1994.

Powelson, Mark, and Ray Riegert, trans. and eds. *The Lost Gospel Q: The Original Sayings of Jesus.* Berkeley, Calif.: Ulysses Press, 1996.

Rappoport, Angelo S. *Myth and Legend of Ancient Israel.* 3 vols. London: Gresham Publishing, 1928.

Rice, Gene. "Africans and the Origin of the Worship of Yahweh." *Journal of Religious Thought* 50, nos. 1–2 (1993–1994): 27–44.

Robinson, George Livingston. *The Sarcophagus of an Ancient Civilization: Petra, Edom and the Edomites.* New York: MacMillan Company, 1930.

Rux, Bruce. *Architects of the Underworld.* Berkeley, Calif.: Frog, 1996.

Schonfield, Hugh J. *The Passover Plot: New Light on the History of Jesus.* London: Hutchinson, 1965.

Smith, Morton. *Jesus the Magician.* New York: Barnes & Noble, 1978.

Speiser, E. A., trans. "The Legend of Sargon." In *Ancient Near Eastern Texts*

Relating to the Old Testament, edited by James B. Pritchard. Princeton, N.J.: Princeton University Press, 1901.

Tompkins, Peter. *Secrets of the Great Pyramid.* New York: Harper & Row Publishers, 1971.

Trachtenberg, Marvin. *The Statue of Liberty.* New York: Penguin Books, 1986.

Van Seters, John. *Abraham in History and Tradition,* New Haven: Yale University Press, 1975.

Wellhausen, Julius. *Prolegomena to the History of Israel.* With a foreword by Douglas A. Knight and preface by W. Robertson Smith. 1885. Reprint, Atlanta, Ga.: Scholars Press, 1994.

Wilson, Ian. *The Exodus Enigma.* London: Weidenfeld and Nicolson, 1985.

Index